This book examines the changing role of the governor in our federal system, giving particular attention to recent developments. The expansion of gubernatorial responsibilities into managerial, executive, and intergovernmental positions has taken place at the same time that the governor's role as leader of his political party has declined. In discussing the contemporary role of governors, the editors provide a view of how the office functions on a day-to-day basis.

The editors base their data on personal experience; interviews with governors, former governors, and staff; on-site visits; and responses to a series of nineteen surveys of governors and their staff conducted between 1976 and 1981. The research was undertaken by the Center for Policy Research of the National Governors' Association.

Being Governor
The View from the Office

Edited by
Thad L. Beyle *and*
Lynn R. Muchmore

Duke Press Policy Studies
Durham, N.C.   1983

Printed in the United States of America on acid-free paper

Library of Congress Cataloging in Publication Data
Main entry under title:

Being governor.

(Duke Press policy studies)
Bibliography: p.
Includes index.
1. Governors – United States – Addresses, essays,
lectures.   I. Beyle, Thad L., 1934–   .   II. Muchmore,
Lynn R. (Lynn Roy), 1943–   .   III. Series.
JK2447.B42 1983   353.9′131   82–24234
ISBN 0–8223–0506–2

Contents

VI. The Structural Role

Tables

Preface

This book attempts to explain how the American governorship currently operates in our federal system of government. From its very weak beginnings in the Revolutionary colonies, the American governorship has grown over the years. Reacting to the experiences with the colonial governors, states generally placed the executive under the tight reign of the legislature. Since then there has been a gradual but certain growth in the governorship, away from earlier legislative domination and toward the governor's holding increasing power and responsibility.

None of this growth and change has been greater than in the last two decades when governors not only gained more power and responsibilities within their own states but gegan to play more significant roles at the national level. At the same time, the state governments over which they presided were modernized. Some of the results of these changes have transformed the governorship. For example, the governor's political party role has declined significantly, while the governor's managerial, executive, and intergovernmental roles have expanded.

Our perspective is biased by our backgrounds and sources of our inormation. Both editors have had considerable experience in state governments and in working with governors. The main sources of data on which we rely in this book are surveys of governors, former governors, and their staffs conducted in 1976–81. We also rely heavily on fifteen lengthy interviews of governors conducted in 1978 and 1979. All of these were conducted under the auspices of the Center for Policy Research of the National Governors' Association. The works of several other authors who have used these materials as their base in analyzing particular aspects of governorship are also included.

We should thank many people and institutions for their assistance.Grants from the U.S. Civil Service Commission, National Science Foundation, Earhart Foundation, and the University of North Carolina Faculty Research Council allowed us both to obtain the information and help to work with the information. The data were originally obtained for the National Governors' Association; we thank them and especially Stephen Farber, Jack Brizius, and Daniel Garry for allowing us to reuse these data. Several graduate students and other assistants provided long hours in working with some of these materials: Phillip Lyons, Stephen Bernheim, Charles Williams, Robert Dalton, Don Haynes, and Jeffery Beyle. We also thank them for their help. Finally, we must thank those who really made this possible with their translation skills: Debralee Poe, Betty Taylor, and Stella Jones.

We absolve all these people and organizations for our errors in judgment and analysis.

Thad L. Beyle

July 1982

Lynn R. Muchmore

Being Governor

Introduction

During the mid-twentieth century, the American governorship has grown in importance not only within the states themselves, but also within the context of our federal system of government. Part of this growth has stemmed from events within the states themselves as state governments have been overhauled and brought up to date with an eye toward making the governor the state's chief executive in fact. Part of the growth has been imposed from outside state government as national level priorities and policies have increasingly been placed on governors and states, and as local pressures have called on states and their governors to act. And part of the growth has been evident in the caliber of people seeking the office and serving as governors—they are no longer perceived as "good-time Charlies."[1]

Personifying the state to many, the governor is a politically powerful personality in almost all states. The imprint of the governor is seen on much of what the state legislature considers as it meets, the agendas of the various state bureaucracies, the focus of the state-level media, the context of the state political situation, and many of the policies in which the state is involved.

This book attempts to present the governorship as it has evolved, utilizing the perspectives of governors and their immediate staffs. While there has been a growing literature on the states—their politics, governments, policies and principal actors—too little of this literature has been based on the practitioner's viewpoint. We hope the addition of this book will enhance both the existing literature and our understanding of what being governor is all about.

The book is divided into six sections: The Setting; Being Governor; The Political Role; The Managerial Role; The Legislative Role; The Structural Role. In order to provide the reader with a guide to these sections, we present the following outline of the contents of each.

The Setting

Chapter 1 describes developments in the states which led to a growth in gubernatorial ability and responsibility. Examined first are changes in the overall structure of state governments, followed by those changes and reforms which focus specifically on the governor. The chapter closes by analyzing the developments in three roles governors perform: the political role, the intergovernmental role, and the managerial role.

Being Governor

Much of the writing on the governorship omits a most important perspective—the governor's. Too few of our many gubernatorial administrations are ever fully chronicled: only a few former governors have written their own stories;

some states present the documents and events of a governor's tenure without prejudice; a few governors' tenures have been subject to scholarly and journalistic study. Comparative analyses of gubernatorial performance of various activities and roles do exist. Social scientists often attempt to place numerical values on such aspects of the governorship as their powers, their success with legislation, and their political careers in order to conduct comparative statistical analyses of the governorship and governors.

The two chapters in this section present governors' perspectives on their tenure in office. Chapter 2 summarizes the results of surveys of former governors (pre–1976) as to their experiences as governor. Some of what they say we already knew or guessed; but some we have overlooked. There is no surprise as to how much time is spent being governor, or that managing state government and working with the legislature are time and energy demanding for the governor. Careful observers have noted also the increasing impact of intergovernmental relations on the governorship. What we do so often forget, though, is the personal side of the governorship—the loss of personal privacy and the loss of family time.

Chapter 3 was developed as part of a handbook for newly elected governors who were to attend a seminar expressly conducted for them two weeks after their election. The faculty were incumbent governors who were trying to prepare these newly elected governors for the responsibilities and problems they would soon face. Of the prepared materials for the seminars, this case study of a "typical day" was given the highest marks as a helping device by faculty who wished they had read it prior to their inaugurations. It may seem breathless and overdone to some, but to those who have experienced the office it is accurate.

Not all governorships or governors operate in this frenetic a fashion. Some have more staff and processes to protect them, others fewer problems or demands. And whether the legislature is in town or not can make the difference between a virtually intolerable schedule and situation for a governor and a more realistic job to fulfill.

The Political Role

This section explores some of the politics governors face while in office. We know quite a bit about the politics of becoming governors—campaigning, polling, coalition building, the primaries, general elections. But we often overlook the essentially political nature of the governorship itself, and that being a governor is only a variation on the politics of becoming a governor. Several governors of recent vintage have attempted to divorce themselves from the crass politics that got them into office, to devote their time and energies to the administration of government. The result in some cases was their being called former governors before they wished that title as the voters turned them out of office.

The chapters in this section focus on three aspects of the governor's political role or side. Chapter 4 looks specifically at his political role and how that role is viewed by former governors. Of major importance in campaigning for the governorship, it declines in significance to the governor once in office. Once the singular goal of winning an election is achieved, the multi-purposes and goals of being the state's chief executive reduce the points upon which the political party can be relied.

Yet, the same need to relate to the public is there, and governors must seek other avenues and vehicles than the party to do this. Chapter 5 explores the governor's public role and focuses in on another major actor in any state's political system—the state level media. On the gubernatorial side, it is not only the various approaches and techniques utilized to get the word out, keep the public informed, and allowing access to the governor; it is also the work and style of one of a governor's key assistants, the press secretary, that often determines just how a governor and his administration is viewed. And the media link between the governor and governed is of significance as the people only learn or understand through what they view on television, hear on radio or read in the paper. When this media link is weak, it directly affects both the governor and the governed.

Chapter 6 speaks to an aspect of gubernatorial politics all too familiar to us today—ethics. As the chapter points out, several recent postgubernatorial careers have been spent in court and ultimately in jail for official misconduct. As part of the politics of being governor and getting things done, ethical standards are often put to a strain with the attendant consequences when such misdeeds or mistakes are discovered. In other cases self-aggrandizement or greed overwhelm the public trust placed in the office. The views of former governors indicate just how murky and uncharted an area is ethics in government.

The Managerial Role

It would seem to be clear to everyone that governors are elected to "run state government." And since to most people this means running or directing the various departments and agencies of the executive branch, the title of chief executive officer fits neatly as a gubernatorial role. However, of what this role consists has not always been clear. In this section, one of the current definitions or "state of the art" concepts of the chief executive role is explored — the governor as manager.

Chapters 7 and 8 set out some basic definitions of just what the governor as manager means, and what approaches and tools are available to carry out this role. Difficulties in carrying out the role are also delimited, especially in the second chapter which points out the political implications of really fulfilling the role. Chapter 9 brings the idiosyncratic views of former governors to bear on the role indicating, in sum, that there is great diversity in how each governor views the role, the problems faced, and the tactics used. Again it is instructive to note that politics is never far from the activities in which governors are involved, and that governors are advised to keep their attention on the politics or the possible political impact of a particular role.

Chapters 10 and 11 explore a major gubernatorial power used to control both the executive branch and policy implementation: the appointment power. Long known as the power of patronage, the rise of merit-civil service systems and just current usage have turned a power which previously suffered from a bad image to a positive power. Specific attention is paid to the most recent state government reforms and their impact on this power, and on how the power differs among various parts of the state executive branch. The question is raised as to whether too much of this power is good for a governor.

The Legislative Role

A governor's relationship and success in dealing with the legislature often determines the success of his administration. While the governor takes the lead, it is still the legislature which must adopt the state budget, set or agree to basic policy directions, and in many cases confirm major gubernatorial appointments. A governor and legislature at loggerheads over a tax proposal, a budget, a policy direction, or a major department head's confirmation can bring part or nearly all of state government to a halt. Added to the constitutional separation of powers are the political facts of life in so many states where the governor is of one party and one or both of the legislative houses are controlled by another party.

Of importance here is to note the different perspectives the members of each of these two major branches bring to state government. In terms of constituency the governor represents the whole state; the legislature is a congery of individuals representing much smaller parts of the state. The governorship is a full-time job with complete responsibility placed on the shoulders of one man; the legislature is not a full-time job, although the time involved varies by the state, and responsibility is diffused widely among a number of leaders and many members. The governor's chair sits atop the states' political ambition ladder; legislative seats are among some of the rungs available to climb the political ladder.

Chapters 12, 13, and 14 focus on this gubernatorial-legislative relationship from different viewpoints. First, the views of former governors are presented to provide a broader perspective on their experience in working with the legislature. What emerges from their comments is less a sense of continual conflict than a conscious effort on both sides to develop a consensus. There is a hint of uneasiness among the governors as they have witnessed the increasing reach of legislative oversight efforts into executive branch activities.

Chapter 13 takes an intensive look at how governors go about fulfilling their legislative role. Special attention is paid to how the governor's office is organized and staffed to aid the governor, how the governor and staff work with legislators, and how the veto is used. We find the governors use a subtle interplay of both their formal and informal powers to achieve the goals they want.

Finally, we look at an anomalous office in the states — the lieutenant governor. Established to accede to the governorship in case of death, infirmity or other cause for vacancy, the office in many states is given substantial legislative powers, and few executive branch powers. Unlike the vice-presidency in many ways, states are often confronted with power struggles between a governor and lieutenant governor which can debilitate the functioning of state government. And it is the legislative power base provided some lieutenant governors, in addition to their own electoral power base, that gives them the foundation from which to act as a counter force to the governor.

The Structural Role

Obviously, a governor does not operate alone in carrying out his various roles. He needs the organization of assistants, staff functions and organizational processes that surround him and provide the necessary assistance and oversight of governmental and political activities in state government. Here we use the notion of the governor's extended office which includes not just those physically located in the immediate office but those individuals and functions working primarily to assist the governor no matter where they are located in the state government's organization chart.

Over the past few decades, governors' office budget and staff sizes have increased greatly, as have their responsibilities. While not on a par with the White House and the Office of the President, there are nevertheless intriguing commonalities on how these state and national level offices have developed and performed. Chapter 15 explores this office, paying special attention to the types and degree of effectiveness of gubernatorial advisory systems. The views of former governors seem to indicate they prefer advisory systems in which people to whom they are close personally are active participants—sometimes to the detriment of a really structured organization chart.

Chapter 16 explores the relationship of the governor to two of the most important parts of his extended office: budget and planning/policy offices. In a careful, comparative analysis we see that these offices are involved in a gubernatorial administration on a great variety of issues.

We then turn to one of the problems facing policymakers at all levels of government—how to bring scientific knowledge and advice into the policy process. Many governors have been faced with a problem or policy decision that requires more than the ordinary sources and types of advice including environmental problems such as hazardous waste spills; infestations of pests threatening prime agricultural crops; natural disasters such as storms, droughts, and floods; and scientific breakthroughs whose direct and side effects can cause severe problems. In searching for solutions for such problems, governors cannot turn to their tried and true advisory network if it does not contain the needed information or assistance. Where does a governor turn for scientific advice and how does he do so? Chapter 16 explores this growing problem area, and presents some initial insights on how to integrate scientific advice into the gubernatorial advisory system.

The world that a governor must address is not constrained by the boundaries of his state. Out-of-state efforts were previously limited to occasional trips to attract industry, attend the more socially oriented governors conferences, and to participate in the presidential conventions every four years. However, in recent decades the states and the governors have become impressed by the need to focus on the issues, problems, and governmental activities that are part of the larger intergovernmental system in which individual states are lodged. Some of these larger questions concern several states at once such as a common river pollution problem. Others are regional in scope such as higher education in the South following World War II. Still others like general revenue sharing are national in scope, finding all states with a common interest focusing on our nation's capital—the Congress and national executive branch.

Governors had been slow to move in these circles. They tightly circumscribed their concern and interests to their own states and left national government concerns to the state's congressional delegation. But in the past twenty years governors and states have been forced to develop their intergovernmental relations roles at varying levels of government—national, regional, substate, and local. This development has generally coincided with the geometric growth in national programs since the 1960s under the Kennedy-Johnson presidential administrations, and it is also tied to the increasing articulated demands of the state's citizens for the government to do more about a wider range of concerns.

Chapter 18 looks at how governors have viewed this tremendous change in roles and activities, and how they have attempted to fulfill their intergovernmental role. One step was the establishment of a joint gubernatorial presence in Washington in the form of the National Governors' Association and the Hall of the States. Another was the increasing tendency for governors to open a Washington, D.C. office in order not only to have a particular state's presence to lobby the bureaucracy and the Congress on behalf of the state, but also to work with and educate the state's own congressional delegation to the state's and state governments' interests. Other steps were taken within the governor's own office to provide him with the assistance and guidance needed in working on intergovernmental affairs.

The direction of gubernatorial involvement in intergovernmental relations at the national and regional levels can only be seen as leading to more intensive interaction. But the other side of intergovernmental relations for the governors cannot be overlooked either. As the budget squeezes and taxation needs escalate at the local levels, governors are finding themselves immersed in difficult situations all across their states.

Although the main focus of the book is on the American governorship, the reader will note variation in the chapter by chapter presentations. Part of this is due to different authorship, part to the type of data available for presentation, and part to the different goals of the individual chapters. For example, some chapters are presentational in nature, describing the state of the art in a particular area (e.g., being governor, public contacts, legislative relations); others explore a particular question or questions to obtain a better view of how the governorship operates (e.g., a day in the life of the governor, relationships with lieutenant governors); and still other chapters are more thought pieces focusing on certain aspects of the governorship (e.g., ethics, science advice). We hope in total the reader will come away with a sense of what being a governor, or working with or for a governor, is like.

Not covered in this volume is the relationship of the governors to the politics by which they became governors. The omission is intentional; the book describes what being a governor is about and not how to become a governor. In part this bias is tied to our background and the sources of our information—especially the National Governors' Association which does not enter the gubernatorial picture until after a person is elected governor. It is also tied to our desire to focus attention on the functions, responsibilities, and activities associated with the governorship itself from the perspective of those who serve or have served in the office.

Part I. The Setting

1. Governors in the American Federal System

Thad L. Beyle and Lynn R. Muchmore

The center of the state system, and its chief proponent in the eyes of the people, is the governor. The governor's prestige and his power to move people and ideas within his state are the strongest weapon s in each state's arsenal. The future of the American system could well be determined by his performance.[1]

This was the agenda and the challenge Terry Sanford issued to governors and states in 1967. Sanford cited ten principles that should by followed in revitalizing the states and their governorships: make governors the chief executives in fact; revise state constitutions; reduce constraints on gubernatorial tenure; provide governors more budgetary power; allow governors to become chief planners; grant governors greater reorganization authority; reduce separately elected executive officials and eliminate independent boards and commissions; reduce the stultifying effects of some aspects of the state personnel systems; provide more adequate staff for governors; and open governors' offices to new ideas and to the experiences of other states and governors.[2]

By the late 1970s political scientist Larry Sabato was able to report: "Within the last fifteen years, there has been a virtual reform in state government. In most of the states as a result, the governor is now truly the master of his own house, not just the father figure."[3]

Many of the efforts at reform were based on the view that the state government performance is critical to an effective federal government system. Further, like Sanford, most contend the governorship is the focal point and the leader of each state. While these were not predominant views prior to the 1960s, the activities and accomplishments of the last two decades have brought more support to them.

Recent Changes and Reforms in States

The changes that have occurred in the states are significant and varied. They range from structural, to fiscal, to programmatic, to managerial, to intergovernmental. Several of these aspects have direct relevance to the governorship: constitutional revision, reorganization, cabinet systems, functional reorganizations.

Constitutional Revision. Beginning in 1959 with the creation of the new states of Alaska and Hawaii, and continuing with the legislative reapportionment cases of the sixties, a surge of constitutional revision has occurred. Excluding those two new states, "between 1965 and 1976, new constitutions became effective in nine states: Connecticut, Florida, Illinois, Montana, North Carolina, Pennsylvania, Virginia, Louisiana, and Georgia. Since then, no state has adopted a new constitution although numerous states have amended their constitutions or plan to hold constitutional conventions".[4] Several other states have had revisions proposals defeated at the polls. As political scientist Mavis Mann Reeves has noted, however, "diligence was frequently rewarded . . . as portions of the rejected documents were submitted piecemeal by the legislature and adopted. These frequently revised entire articles and contained major reforms."[5] The reforms have generally aimed at modernizing these basic documents, removing outmoded constraints on governors and legislatures and providing a more flexible framework for state government.

Reorganization. Between 1965 and 1977, twenty-one states engaged in comprehensive reorganization, and nearly every state participated in partial reform.[6] As the Advisory Commission on Intergovernmental Relations (ACIR) noted:

> no other period in history has witnessed such intense activity. The reorganization activity that began during the 1960's resulted from pressures on the states to establish the policy, organization and fiscal machinery to enable them to meet the demands made by an increasingly urban population. They also sought to rationalize functional responsibilities, to create clearer lines of authority, and to increase accountability.[7]

Nine of the states moved toward the *traditional model* "in which the reduction of the number of agencies is accomplished to some degree within the existing pattern of agencies headed by elected officers and boards and commissions"; four states moved toward the *cabinet model,* "whereby heads of reorganized departments are all appointed by and responsible to the Governor"; three states moved toward the *secretary-coordinator model,* "in which the structure and authority of agencies is unchanged and the Secretaries (appointed by the Governor) have primarily a coordinating function"; and, the five other reorganizing states' adopted combinations of these models.[8] In every case, the executive branch was consolidated to a certain degree as was the power of the governor.

Cabinet System. There has been an increase in the number of states using a cabinet system over the last decade from 26 in 1969 to 40 as of 1982. These cabinets generally are coordinating bodies organized either in whole, or as subcabinets with specific functional responsibilities. However, while few states have provided these cabinets with policy-making authority, they do often serve as "an effective problem-solving group involved both in identifying priority issues and areas, and in developing new ideas and approaches to executive branch operations . . . [especially] for issues that cut across departmental lines." Most importantly it does afford "the governor the opportunity to interact directly with key executive branch officials."[9]

Functional Reorganization. The "copy-cat" concept or "decision by emula-tion" is a well recognized phenomenon in the states. Jack Walker calls this "a national system of emulation and competition" among the states, which often has a regional base. "The rule of thumb [state decision makers] employ might be formally stated as follows: look for an analogy between the situation you are dealing with and some other situation, perhaps in some other state, where the problem has been successfully resolved."[10]

For example, since 1959, thirty-eight states have created state Departments of Transportation (DOT), emulating Hawaii (1959) and California (1960) and the creation of a federal DOT (1966). These departments normally contain highways and transit with aeronautics, waterways, regulation, railroads, high-way patrol, motor vehicles, and tolls being added, depending on the state and the concept of the DOT in that state.[11]

In the area of environment, beginning with Minnesota and Wisconsin (1967) and the creation of the federal Environmental Protection Agency (1970), thirty-two states had reorganized their environmental activities into several distinct models by 1974.[12] And since 1975, ten states have created Departments of Energy.[13]

One of the more recent trends in functional consolidation is in human services where states have increasingly attempted to consolidate such related activities "as public assistance and social services, health, mental health, mental retarda-tion, corrections, youth institutions, vocational rehabilitation, and employment security." There are now twenty-five states with some variant of a comprehen-sive human services agency or department, but in this area the main problem concerns which activities should be included in a comprehensive agency.[14]

The goal in functional reorganization is to bring as many functionally related agencies into one organization as is feasible. This will reduce interdepartmental frictions and hassles, allow for more coherent planning, coordination and imple-mentation of effort.

All in all, these structural changes add up to more modern structures of government over which the governor is to perform his or her roles.

Changes in the Governorship

Sabato's recent review of the American governorship begins with this assess-ment of the office:

Once parochial officers whose concerns rarely extended beyond the bounda-ries of their home states and whose responsibilities were often slight within the states, governors have gained major new powers that have increased their influence in national as well as state councils. Once maligned foes of the national and local governments, governors have become skilled negotiators and, importantly, often crucial coordinators at both levels. Once ill prepared to govern and less prepared to lead, governors have welcomed a new breed of vigorous, incisive, and thoroughly trained leaders into their ranks. The implications of all changes for the federal system, its constituent parts, and the nation as a whole are not insignificant.[15]

Sabato talked about the personal qualities of the governors also. They "are much younger, better educated than ever, and more thoroughly trained for the specific responsibilities of the governorship."[16] And he indicated that with the changes already noted in the structure and processes of state governments, "the new governors are in a position to use their appreciable talents and to work relatively unhindered."[17]

As far as the governorships themselves, there have been significant changes in their powers over the past few years:

Length of Terms. Between 1955 and 1980, the number of governors running for and serving four year terms rose from twenty-nine to forty-six. Only Arkansas, New Hampshire, Rhode Island, and Vermont retain two-year terms.[18] This allows governors to spend less time on reelection politics and more on policy and administration.

Number of Terms Possible. Over the twenty-five year period the number of governors precluded from succeeding themselves in a second term dropped from seventeen to four, while the number who could serve two consecutive terms increased from six to twenty-three.[19] The number of states allowing unlimited terms is now twenty-two.[20] This allows for greater continuity from program and policy initiation to implementation.

Budgetary Power. The number of states giving the governor sole budget-making power rose from forty-two to forty-seven between 1955 and 1980.[21] Further, as Kenneth Howard has observed:

Governors are being consulted and given more information about federal grants, their approval may be necessary before an agency may apply for a grant, and their approval is increasingly being required for some other program matters; consolidation among federal categorical grants is taking place so that supported agencies can less readily obtain money independently of the governor; additional responsibilities and authority for meeting pressing domestic problems are devolving upon the states; budgetary innovations are being initiated that can strengthen a governor's participation in these matters.[22]

This allows governors more control over the basic policy document of state government, the state budget, and the process by which it is developed.

Appointment Power. There is a mixed picture on what has occurred vis-à-vis the power of the governors to appoint "their" people to positions in state government. At one level, this ability has been enhanced by the series of reorganizations discussed earlier. There are fewer Boards and Commissions and other state officials appointing administrators and other personnel in those states with reorganized structures. However, the continuing impact of civil service, merit or other personnel systems has been to reduce the ability of governors to impact on the bureaucracy. In a series of interviews with outgoing governors in the late 1970s, most governors cited this as a nuisance they faced during their tenure.[23] As the civil service-professionalism drive (often encouraged under federal grant-in-aid programs) pushes upwards into the realm of policy, the governors find their abilities constricted and must take steps to overcome this.

Separately Elected Offices. The trend over the past decade has been to reduce the number of separately elected state officials who can and often do compete with governors in their policy domains. This is usually, although not necessarily, an outcome of a major state reorganization. Despite the general trend, the long ballot is still alive and healthy as evidenced by the number of states still electing secretaries of state (36), treasurers (38), attorneys general (43), auditors (25), and secretaries of agriculture (13), insurance (9) and labor (5).[24] Beginning with New York in 1953, the number of states which have the governor and lieutenant governor running as a team has grown to 21 at the latest count. In each case where a separately elected office is eliminated, and appointment by the governor substituted, a separate political constituency is removed and the governor gains more appointive and thereby more administrative and policy power. Again all these changes are in the direction of providing governors and their staffs with greater capacity and flexibility. In conjunction with the structural changes in state government noted earlier, the changes provide most governors with more adequate structures and tools with which to work in fulfilling their roles.

Changing Roles for Governors

However, the greater changes in the decade may be in the very definition of gubernatorial roles which governors are expected to perform. The old litany of roles had the governor as ceremonial head of state, chief legislator, chief administrator, head of the party and chief legal officer. These traditional roles still hold to a certain degree although some have become even more significant (chief legislator) and others less (head of party). Of greater importance is the focusing of additional roles and responsibilities on the governorship in the context of state government's position in the federal system.

While the changes in structures and tools allowed governors to be better equipped for office responsibilities, it is the increase in office responsibilities which appear to be most important and indeed may have been critical to the arguments for the structural changes. Further, turning Sabato's assessment on its head, it may be that the increased responsibilities of the American governorship attracted, possibly even necessitated, the "new breed of vigorous, incisive, and thoroughly trained" governors that he found in his survey.

When one compares the gubernatorial roles most typical of the 1950s with the profiles that emerged during the 1960s and matured during the following decade, three themes become significant.

The first theme is the difference in the political environment in which the governors function. The influence of the traditional political party apparatus is no longer perceived as significant. Governors no longer take themselves seriously as "titular head of the party" in their state. Credentials established through party affiliation and leadership are insufficient as a basis for seeking office. Successful candidacy depends upon the ability to forge alliances among interest groups whose membership rarely respects party lines and on the complicated process of creating the proper image of leadership through the media directly to the voters. Thus, the parties are no longer a required vehicle for transportation into office.

Some consequences:

1. Loss of the party as an instrument of governance and discipline; particularly important in dealings with the legislature;

2. The withering of patronage at the sub-policy level; replaced by a more complex patronage requirement at the policy level (needed to maintain the support of special interest alliances);

3. Greater consciousness of *issues,* because the interest groups are generally formed around specific issues;

4. Concentration on media related activities and approaches;

5. Somewhat less stability in the political support base;

6. Less time spent on traditional party activities; and

7. Loss of the party framework as a mode within which to deal with the Congress and the President.

The second theme is the appearance and growth of the governor as a principal in the arena of federal-state relations. The stream of grants-in-aid created a new arena of conflict and cooperation that involves the federal executive branch and the state executive branch, with the Congress and the state legislatures as bystanders. In this arena, the old notion that states are represented at the federal level by senators and congressmen is inadequate. Major policy decisions embedded within the regulations and guidelines issued by federal mission agencies have been virtually impervious to congressional oversight, and the politics of policy played out within the executive branch.

This created a new role for the governor as chief executive, one in which he appeared as the chief lobbyist for his own state government. As the state governments were being used by the federal government as a delivery system for programs whose goals were nationally derived, the governors began to assert a much more strident opinion on the wisdom of particular federal policies and administrative practices especially when national goals and state goals were not parallel.

Some consequences:

1. Creation of Washington offices for governors and states;
2. Enhancing the lobbying capacity of the National Governors' Association in Washington;
3. Establishment of regional coalitions of governors to focus on policy issues;
4. Creation of "federal-state coordinators" and similar staffing positions in the governor's offices;
5. Rise in tension between program officials (specialists) and elected officials (generalists);
6. Federal pressure to improve "management capacity" in the states and their local governments;
7. Creation of A-95 and other related federal project review procedures;
8. Increase in responsibilities for administrating federal programs unfettered by the desires of the state legislature; and
9. Increase in the availability of significant program resources over which the governor could exert unilateral influence.

The third and final theme is the emergence of the governorship as a management position. The 1960s and 1970s were decades in which the legacy of the Little Hoover commissions finally began to take on some meaning. Executive reorganization was precipitated by the sheer growth in the size of the state government, and was encouraged by the penetration of the state bureaucracy through federal grants-in-aid. Each grant-in-aid program carried with it some "standards" presumed to insure that administration was carried out rationally and effectively. These forces were aided by political reaction against big government, sentiment capitalized upon by reformers who suggested that reorganization was a measure to control the bureaucracy.

Virtually every reorganization strengthened the governorship, not only by creating new gubernatorial authority where none existed before, but by consolidating a large collection of small agencies into a manageable number of departments. Reorganization was often marketed as a means to make the bureaucracy more accountable, and one consequence was to force the governors to take a greater interest in the operations of line agencies.

This resulted in the creation and enhancement of gubernatorial management support staffs under the traditional labels of planning, budgeting, personnel, and general services, who served to reinforce the gubernatorial management role. The goal has been something called policy management, an elusive yet compelling concept within the federal system.[25] One only needs to peruse the National Governors' Association Handbook for New Governors, *Governing the American States,* to see just how prominent a role management at the gubernatorial level has become.[26]

Some consequences:

1. Greater capacity to implement specific programs;
2. Growth of governor's office as a bureaucratic organization;
3. Change in the mix of skills that governors were expected to possess;

4. Ability to lead state government through policy formulation;

5. Identification of the governor with the failures and successes of line agencies, and

6. Ascendency over the legislature as a source of innovation and change.

In the last two decades, the states and the governorships have been transformed by a series of reforms and awakenings. Reasons given for the transformation vary. For some, it was the jolt of the U.S. Supreme Court decisions in the 1960s on reapportionment which forcibly brought new blood into the legislative halls; for others, it was the push of the wide-ranging programs undertaken in the Kennedy-Johnson-Nixon years which forced the states to take action; and for still others it was a response to citizen pressure for state governments to fulfill an agenda of long overdue responsibilities. Regardless of the reasons, today's federal system and state governments operate differently than they did in the past. And the governors, with their heightened powers and responsibilities, are pivotal in this.

Part II. Being Governor

2. Governors' Views on Being Governor

Thad L. Beyle

The study of the American governor has relied on the concepts of role and function to describe and explain gubernatorial activity. Coleman Ransone, in his study of the then-forty-eight governors of the U.S., indicated there was "a hard core of gubernatorial powers and duties which are sufficiently similar in all states to warrant the formulation of what may be called 'the executive function' at the state level."[1] Nearly thirty years later in another intensive review of the modern governorship, Larry Sabato suggested: "Governors must possess many skills to be successful. They are expected to be adroit administrators, dexterous executives, expert judges of people, combative yet sensitive and inspiring politicians, decorous chiefs of state, shrewd party tacticians, and polished public relations managers."[2]

The governors' own organization, the National Governors' Association (NGA), in developing a handbook for newly elected governors, led off its presentation by stating that "in his capacity as head of the state government he has a number of different roles, including head of the executive branch . . . , legislative leader . . . , head of party . . . , national figure . . . , family member . . . , and, ceremonial chief."[3] There are other roles which have been suggested by other observers such as the governors' intergovernmental role,[4] a policy management role,[5] and now even an international role is being sketched out but as yet is not fully described in the literature.[6]

There seems to be no lack of roles, and like agencies in state government and federal programs, they continue to proliferate. This chapter will explore how governors themselves view their roles, using as a starting point Sabato's view that no governor can "fulfill fully and balance well all of these conflicting roles simultaneously, or even singly."[7] The analysis is based on the proposition that there is something akin to a continuum underlying the various governors' roles which runs from the personalized governorship to the institutionalized governorship. In the personalized governorship, there are relatively smaller staffs in the office of the governor, with each staff member usually serving several roles. The governor is involved in the various operations and processes of the office to a greater extent than his or her counterparts in the more institutionalized offices. These latter offices have considerably larger and more diversified staffs, and are able to institutionalize some of the roles and functions in the office, thereby relieving the governor of some of the burdens that still lie heavily on the governors at the more personalized end of the spectrum.

This chapter is based on the responses to two 1976 surveys: sixteen incumbent governors as of 1976 and fifty-eight former governors who had served and left office by 1976. While the response rates are not high (16 of 50 and 58 of approximately 185—about 32 percent each), they do provide the views and opinions of seventy-four individuals who have held the governorship in all but eight of the states during the 1960s and 1970s. In analyzing the data from the responses, several variables were used:

Size of State.   States were ordered from largest to smallest by their 1975 U.S. Bureau of the Census population estimates and divided into thirds.

Power of the Governor.   Power of the governor was based on an updated (1975) version of Joseph. A. Schlesinger's index of formal gubernatorial powers, including appointment power, budget power, tenure, and veto. Using his scale which runs from a low of 7 to a maximum of 20, the categories used were high (20–18), moderate (17–14), and low (13–7). This variable is highly related to the size of state variable.[8]

Governor's Party.   The two major parties, Democratic and Republican, were used here and those few independents who responded were excluded.

Time of Service.   A cutoff date of 1970 was arbitrarily selected to roughly coincide with the advent and impact of several systemic changes, i.e., upgrading of state governmental capacity and the shift in federal government activities under the Nixon administration to provide broader grants-in-aid and decentralize the federal system.

Length of Service.   More or less than five years service was used to separate governors who served more than one term in office.

One major and frustrating caveat must be stated at the outset: under the ground rules established for obtaining the data, no individual state or governor can be identified in any report or presentation of the data. Therefore, we must talk in terms of categories of governors: big state/small state; party identification; power; and length and time of service.

The discussion that follows will be based on separate groupings of gubernatorial responses: 1976 incumbent governors (16), former governors (58), and these two samples combined (74 governors). Not all former-governor responses could be used in the following analysis as some were received in letter form or in telephone discussion with the author. Wherever possible, these responses were placed into the survey format, but too often without much success.

Difficult Aspects of Being Governor

If there is a variation from a personal to an institutionalized governorship across the American states, it should be reflected in the difficulties that governors have faced while serving. The hypothesis is that the greater the institution-alization of the office, the fewer the difficulties encountered.

Former governors were asked which aspects of the job of being governor they found to be the most difficult and demanding, and which were the easiest. The questionnaires provided eleven specific areas for the governors to check off the most difficult and demanding tasks, and asked them to provide indications of any other areas which were difficult and demanding for them but not included in the list provided. The eleven areas were not repeated for their answers to the easiest aspects of the job, but due to the proximity of the first question there was no variation in those indicated difficult by some and easy by others. No direc-tions were provided as to how many aspects to indicate, and there was an average of 3.4 indications of difficult aspects per respondent.

The former governors' responses are presented in Table 2.1. Overall, they felt that interference with their family life was the most difficult aspect of serving as governor (49 percent). Further, 29 percent also indicated that invasion of their own privacy was a particular difficulty they faced. These problems for the family and the individual were more pronounced in the very largest and smallest states (although in varying degrees) and among governors who served longer terms. Republican former governors were more likely to cite these intrusions than their Democratic counterparts. Significantly, we see the beginnings of a pattern—those governors with moderate powers find these difficulties most burdensome. Therefore, while these private life aspects are not considered part of the formal roles of the governorship, the data indicates that the interaction of the public and the private roles while serving as governor does pose serious personal difficulties.

Of the more standard roles performed, the former governors clearly found their legislative role and performing the wide variety of ceremonial activities demanded of them to be most difficult of all.

The importance of the governors' legislative role has been attested to by many observers.[9] That it poses difficulties should also be easily understood considering the inherent problems in the concept of separation of powers and that party control of the legislature and the governorship has been split so often.[10] Of particular interest is the indication that working with the legislature was more burdensome again for governors with moderate powers and governors who had served since 1970. The latter point can be attributed to the significant increase of legislative activities over the decade 1966 to 1976. For example, while only eleven states had annual sessions in 1966, by 1976, forty-three states were holding annual sessions under either formal or informal arrangements. Further, the sheer volume of legislation introduced into all state legislatures escalated dramatically between the 1966–67 biennium and the 1975–76 bien-nium, from approximately 134,000 bills to 198,000 bills—nearly 50 percent.[11] These changes greatly increased the demands on time and energies, as indicated in the data.

The responses from the former governors on their ceremonial role present an

Table 2.1. Former governors' views of most difficult aspects of the job, by size of state, power of the governor, governor's party, time of service, and length of service

Aspect	Overall		Size of state[a]						Power of governor[b]						Governor's party				Time of service				Length of service			
			Large		Med.		Small		High		Mod.		Low		Dem.		Rep.		Pre '70		Post '70		Under 5 years		Over 5 years	
	No.	%	No.	%	No.	%	No.	%	No.	%	No.	%	No.	%	No.	%	No.	%	No.	%	No.	%	No.	%	No.	%
Interference with family life	25	49	8	57	9	39	8	53	7	47	10	53	8	47	11	39	14	61	15	47	10	53	10	37	15	63
Working with the legislature	22	43	6	43	10	44	6	40	5	33	10	53	7	41	13	46	9	39	11	34	11	58	12	44	10	42
Ceremonial duties	21	41	4	29	10	44	7	47	3	20	11	58	7	41	8	29	13	57	13	41	8	42	9	33	12	50
The hours	18	35	3	21	11	48	4	27	5	33	9	47	4	24	8	29	10	43	9	28	9	47	7	26	11	46
Tough decisions	16	31	5	36	9	39	2	13	6	40	8	42	2	12	6	21	10	43	8	25	8	42	7	26	9	38
Invasion of privacy	15	29	2	14	9	39	4	27	2	13	9	47	4	24	5	18	10	43	8	25	7	37	6	22	9	38
Intermural govt. squabbles	14	27	2	14	9	39	3	20	2	13	8	42	4	24	8	29	6	26	6	19	8	42	7	26	7	29
Working with the federal govt.	12	24	5	36	5	22	2	13	4	27	5	26	3	18	7	25	5	22	5	16	7	37	4	14	8	33
Building and keeping staff	10	20	5	36	5	22	0	0	4	27	3	16	3	18	6	21	4	17	5	16	5	26	6	22	4	17
Working with the press	10	20	1	7	6	26	3	20	2	13	4	21	4	24	5	18	5	22	7	22	3	16	5	19	5	21
Management of state govt.	9	18	1	7	6	26	2	13	4	27	3	16	2	12	5	18	4	17	5	16	4	21	4	14	5	21
Number of resp.	51		14		23		15		15		19		17		28		23		32		19		27		24	
Total mentions	172		42		89		41		44		80		48		82		90		92		80		77		95	
Average	3.4		3.0		3.9		2.7		2.9		4.2		2.8		2.9		3.9		2.9		4.2		2.9		4.0	

a. Size based on 1975 population estimates, divided into thirds.

b. Power of the governor was based on an updated version of Joseph A. Schlesinger's index of formal gubernatorial powers, including appointment power, budget power, tenure, and veto. See Schlesinger, "The Politics of the Executive" in Herbert Jacob and Kenneth N. Vines, eds., Politics in the American States (Boston, Ma.: Little, Brown and Company, 1971), p. 232. Using Schlesinger's scale, which runs from a low of 7 to a maximum of 20, the categories are high (20–18), moderate (17–14), and low (13–7).

interesting contrast in views. For over two out of five of them, the ceremonial role was most demanding—nearly equal to those citing the legislature as demanding. Part of the reason for this lies in the variety of activities the role can encompass. "They may include such diverse functions as receiving foreign dignitaries, receiving petitions, announcing national dill pickle week, crowning the queen of the gooseberry festival, shooting film extolling the virtues of his state or its products, presiding over the opening of the state fair or the graduation of the state police academy, and having his picture taken with the state's oldest veteran."[12] Obviously, the ceremonial role is time consuming and not an altogether focused effort—except to keep the governor before the public's eye, to satisfy certain special interests, and to perform certain necessary and symbolic activities. Too often it must be perceived by governors as diverting them from the more substantive activities and responsibilities of the office. Again, we see the pattern of governors from states with moderate power citing ceremonial activities as a difficulty more than their counterparts do, especially those from the states with higher gubernatorial powers.

But there is a most interesting contrast here, as sixteen former governors (31.3 percent) indicated that their ceremonial activities were among their easiest duties to perform. There was no pattern to these responses as there was to those who cited it as difficult. Alan Wyner suggested after a mid-1960s survey of governors that the many restrictions and constraints on governors performing their other major roles may lead them to take "the line of least resistance" and move into the role of industrial promoter and other activities "in which the governor can almost do as he pleases, and at the same time gain considerable and usually favorable publicity."[13] The ceremonial role is obviously a bittersweet role which is easy for some governors to perform and difficult for others.

A second grouping of aspects which governors found most difficult during their tenure consisted of the long hours the job took to perform, the difficult decisions they had to make, the squabbles among governmental officials and agencies that they were too often called in to settle or mediate, and working with the federal government. This is a list which could be predicted as providing difficulty for governors as each involves direct gubernatorial involvement of time and effort. Again the pattern, as those governors in medium-sized states and states with moderate levels of formal powers felt these difficulties more than others. The latter finding indicates that the larger and more complex governmental activities in our federal system have an impact on governors and state government.

Finally, there are several roles and functions which do not seem to pose great difficulties for governors, such as building and keeping staff, working with the press, and the day-to-day management of state government. This holds no matter what type of state, governmental structure, or governor is involved. Thus, some of the traditional bread-and-butter roles of the governorship pose the governors with the least problems as they are well covered by staff and become fairly routinized.

There are several general points that should be made concerning the data.

Former governors from medium-sized states were more likely to nominate difficulties (average 3.9 per respondent) than were their counterparts in the larger (3.0) or smaller states (2.7). This tendency was also true for governors who had served in states with moderate formal powers (4.2 per respondent) as opposed to those from states with high formal powers (2.9) or low formal powers (2.8).

Since it is clear that size of state and size of the governor's office staff are directly related,[14] those former governors from larger states, with their larger staffs, were able both to buffer themselves from some of these difficult problems by using their staff, and had more staff to institutionalize or routinize some functions. While former governors from smaller states with smaller staffs had considerably less flexibility in doing either, they still did not perceive as many difficulties in carrying out their more personalized governorship. It is in the mid-range states—in both population and gubernatorial powers—that the former governors reported more difficulties. Undoubtedly, they had many of the larger state problems without the requisite staff or institutionalized processes to reduce the burden on them.

Also, governors who served in the 1970s or served longer terms indicated more difficulties in their tenure. While they varied as to which aspects were more difficult, there is another bittersweet relationship—an attractive and ever more significant job, which has a heavy price tag, both personal and public, attached to it. Sabato's "Say Goodbye to Goodtime Charlie" thesis is not without its drawbacks to governors.

It is clear that Republican former governors indicate considerably more difficulties overall in being governor than do their brother Democrats—especially on the personal level (family life and invasion of privacy), the time involved (ceremonial functions and hours spent), and in making tough decisions. Why this should be so is not clear, but Sabato may have provided a clue in his analysis of gubernatorial backgrounds:

> Republican governors (1950–1975) tend to come from the legislature or are elected without an office background more frequently than Democrats. On the other hand, more Democratic governors come from law enforcement, statewide, administrative and local elective offices.[15]

The proposition here would be that previous experience in elective executive positions, and service in state-level administrative positions more adequately prepared Democrats for the job of being governor than did the previous experiences of Republican governors.

Gubernatorial Advice to New Governors

While not a direct measure of gubernatorial roles and their fulfillment, certain insights can be obtained by reviewing the advice incumbent and former governors provided newly elected governors. First, without any more specific directions, the former governors were asked: "If you had to provide only three pieces of advice to a new governor, what would they be?" While there were many separate and distinct pieces of general advice, there were several consistent suggestions made:[16]

1. Appoint and keep good people in key positions.
2. Avoid crisis mentality and don't panic.
3. Be yourself, be in command, make your own decisions.
4. Highlight the importance of image and press relations.
5. Watch carefully your own work schedule and level of work effort.
6. Some general management approaches (set up a small cabinet or advisor system, select a few priorities, develop a management system to fit your objectives, delegate to departments, etc.).
7. Various defensive strategies and warnings.
8. Avoid isolation.

By and large, the overall theme these former governors were stressing was for the new governors to be themselves, be a governor, and surround themselves with personnel, processes, and approaches which allowed them to fulfill the governorship as they felt it should be done.

In a considerably more structured approach, a series of specific items with fixed responses was provided to all governors—both incumbent and former—as examples of advice people often give to newly elected governors (see Table 2.2). While not providing as rich or diverse a range of comments or advice, it does provide the advantage of comparison in levels of importance or agreement, and by which type of state or governor.

As can be readily seen, there are some items of advice on which there is almost total basic agreement—keeping an open door for legislators and serving the first six months in office without any thought of a long vacation. Only some governors from states with higher formal gubernatorial powers were likely to demur a bit from this nearly unanimous view on vacations. One only has to recall the negative publicity received by Governor James Thompson of Illinois in winter 1978 when he took his family on a long scheduled Florida vacation while his state and Chicago were involved in a major blizzard to see how vacations can backfire politically.

At a second level, we find between two-thirds and three-fourths of all the governors agreeing that a systematic process of working with the public is desirable, as is hiring a good speech writer, holding regular staff and department head meetings, and keeping a separation between their personal and official lives. Also included at this level is the advice not to hire staff from the campaign staff.

Differences between incumbent and former governors on the first two levels of responses were not great enough to be really significant, except for the item regarding moving campaign staff onto the governor's office staff, where not one incumbent governor advised doing so.

The third level contains those items for which there is no agreement, and a

Table 2.2. Incumbent and former governors' responses to standard advice given to new governors[a]

Items	Number responding	Percent agree	Percent disagree
Keep an open door policy for legislators	68	97.1	1.5
Be prepared not to take a week or more vacation in the first six months	65	90.8	6.2
Develop a well-advertised and well-managed process of meeting with citizens	66	74.2	7.6
Hire a good speechwriter	67	73.1	14.9
Hold meetings of immediate staff on a regularly scheduled basis	66	72.7	15.1
Hold meetings with department heads on a regularly scheduled basis	66	66.7	15.2
Rely primarily on campaign staff to staff governor's office	66	18.2	63.7
Separate personal social life from official contacts	66	63.6	19.7
Do not schedule press conferences on a regular basis	68	47.1	51.4
Use memos and letters rather than meetings where possible	65	46.2	38.5
Do not attempt to keep an open door policy for press	52[b]	42.3	48.1
Make sure press secretary has been in statehouse press corps	64	20.3	29.7

a. These responses are based on answers to the following questions: "Below are some samples of advice given to new Governors. Please indicate whether you agree with this advice." The twelve items listed above were provided and respondents had five possible responses: Agree Strongly, Agree, Indifferent or No Opinion, Disagree, Disagree Strongly. For purposes of this analysis the two agree and two disagree categories were collapsed into a single category each.

b. Due to the review process prior to the sending of each survey, incumbent governors were not provided with this item.

fairly even split as to whether the governors agree or disagree. These primarily concern the press: scheduling a regular press conference, keeping an open door for the press, and selecting a press secretary from the capital press corps. Of special interest here is the data indicating governors of large states are more likely to suggest holding regular press conferences, and governors of medium-sized states are more likely to agree not to have an open door policy for the press—again, supporting the impact of the institutionalization hypothesis. This symbiotic relationship between the governor and the press, while mutually advantageous, certainly leaves the governor's side of the relationship with a bittersweet taste, not unlike that noted earlier in the governor's ceremonial role, of which these items are in part indicative.

There are two fairly clear clusters of attitudes found in these items which further relate to the institutionalization of the governorship:

Management Style. Regular meetings with staff and department heads and the use of memos and letters rather than meetings form this grouping in which the former governors tend to lean toward meetings as a mode of managing, while incumbent governors are split on each of the items. There is thus a hint here that as state government has become more complex and managerial demands greater in the 1970s, the ability to maintain the more personalized management style is declining. This supports the institutionalization hypothesis that as government and its management become more complex, the governorship itself tends to become more institutionalized—at least in the views of the governors. This is in contrast to the observation of one perceptive observer of governors: "Governors tend to rely on verbal rather than written communications, to place more credence upon the advice of personal acquaintances than upon 'experts' that they do not know socially, and to rely upon intuition rather than written or formal criteria as a basis for decisions."[17]

Staffing. What type of staff and where they are sought forms another cluster—a speech writer, the press secretary, and general staff. In this cluster there is a tendency for the recent governors—incumbents and those who have served since 1970, and those serving for longer terms—to be less likely to make the "political" decision on the choice of staff than were their earlier counterparts. This probably reflects a heightened awareness of the importance of staff and their abilities, plus a wider range of individuals with varying abilities from which to choose staff. Sabato has further suggested "that the more recent, capable chief executives—and the more substantial and powerful gubernatorial office—have attracted better individuals to want to serve as staffers in the governor's office. So it is not just a matter of governors exercising greater wisdom in staff selection."[18]

Institutionalization of the Governorship

The data and opinions from governors lead to several general observations about the governorship in the American states. First and foremost is the conflicting relationship of the governor as a person and as a public figure. Throughout their responses to various questions, the governors reflected the strains they felt between these two roles. From their basic advice to new governors that they be themselves and watch their own work schedules, to indicating that intrusions into their privacy and family life were the most difficult aspects of being governor, the theme is clear that the tensions between their private and public roles are significant, and are greater with longer and more recent service. It seems for those governors in the larger states and those with more power that some of these public pressures on their private lives are reduced because of their larger staffs and institutionalized offices.

Second, the data appears to uphold the hypothesis of a continuum underlying governors' offices and styles running from the personal to the institutional. The larger states with their larger staff resources provide the governor with considerably more support to fulfill his or her roles than do the smaller states with their lesser resources.

The responses also suggest that it is those states in the middle of this continuum, the mid-sized states and those governorships with moderate powers, which appear to be in transition between the personalized and the institution-alized governorship. These states have many of the problems and demands on the governor that larger states do, but have not yet provided the governor with sufficient staff and institutionalized processes to perform the roles with as much ease as in the larger states. Therefore, in these states a considerable burden still rests on the governor as a person.

This is not an argument for or against either the personalized or the institu-tionalized governorship. The reforms of the past decade, the increasing burdens on the states and their governors, the increasing caliber of the individuals serving in the governorship, and the reform agenda still afoot in the states all aim toward a more institutionalized and less personal governorship.

3. A Day in the Life of a Governor[1]

Center for Policy Research, NGA

It is difficult to convey to a new governor the importance of maintaining control over his time. One approach is to present a typical day of a governor who has been in office for some time and is no longer concerned with transition problems. This chapter hypothetically portrays such a day—assuming that there is anything like a typical day (which there isn't) of a typical governor (which there isn't). It is presented here to point out the importance of managing time well, and of developing time-management ideas during the transition period.

The Governor's Typical Day

8:00-9:00 a.m.

Scheduled office time; no staff or calls allowed. The governor instituted this practice after realizing that if he wanted to work alone for as much as an hour, he would have to demand it.

Reads newspaper stories on state government; dictates short congratulatory notes to juvenile delinquency director for fine press coverage on opening of new facility, and to editorial staff of major newspaper for editorial commending his support of the facility. Writes note to mental health director on press story about beating of retarded child in state facility.

Notes local controversy about highway location in southern part of state; makes mental note to discuss it with highway commissioner. Notes editorial and news comment that next legislative session is likely to be a rough one. Notes speculation that he is about to appoint Jones as new bank commissioner; tells his press secretary to get speculation killed; he hasn't decided, but knows it won't be Jones.

Starts working on screened morning mail (a small part of mail actually received). Mayor of large city wants to be moved up on sewer project priority list; refers mayor's letter to the department. Official of smaller city complains that mass transportation money is unfairly going to larger cities; refers letter to department. National party chairman requests governor's cooperation in upcoming congressional campaign financing; governor writes a reminder to discuss with political advisor. Major contributor comments that branch banking law changes being considered by the staff would seriously threaten savings and loan institutions; governor dictates letter indicating he is aware of problems and is concerned.

Reviews telegrams from environmental groups requesting that he reverse his decision to support Corps of Engineers water supply project; other telegrams from local mayor and county leaders and builders ask him to reaffirm support of project. Decides to stay with earlier decision.

9:00 a.m.

Receives delegation of legislators and mayor of suburban community seeking superhighway. Highway department briefing materials say that the road shouldn't be built at all; and if it is, it couldn't be started for years, unless, of course, the governor wants to propose new gasoline taxes to fund commitments in other areas. Governor tells delegation he is working on the problem and is sympathetic, but has other pressures for use of funds.

Asks friendly legislator to stay after the meeting, and finds out that the county chairman is wavering from support of his candidate for state senate and is unhappy with the way state party headquarters is run.

10:00 a.m.

Kicks off National Cancer Week campaign with pictures and awards plus handshaking with county chairmen. One person catches him at end of meeting and asks that he solve problem of son who is in trouble with the Army. Governor pleads inability to handle problem, but offers to try. Calls federal relations aide aside to explain, and asks if aide can work something out to get friendly congressman to check on the case.

10:30 a.m.

Checks secretary for phone calls: has calls from two cabinet officers, one board chairman, his wife, two legislators, one local business leader, plus three aides who "must" see him.

Starts to return phone calls, but gets interrupted by press secretary who says major local issue is developing over announced layoff of twenty employees in state TB hospital; department says it's true; press secretary recommends saying governor is looking into it and to tell the department to hold off. Governor tells press secretary to hold off comment until he has talked to department.

Now makes call, postponing 11 a.m. meeting with transportation secretary and budget director on additional matching money for highway construction until 11:30 a.m., and 11:30 meeting with insurance commissioner until noon.

Mental health director advises that he is having some success with local mental health directors in meetings governor had asked him to hold. Notes in passing (obviously real reason for call) that he is having some trouble with governor's political advisor on staffing the department and is convinced that the professionalism of the department must remain inviolate.

Arts board chairman says he's getting lots of pressure from legislators for local interest arts projects and has decided to emphasize these projects almost solely in this year's fund allocation. Reports considerable sentiment in the business community that adminstration spending is getting out of hand and warns against proposing any tax increases.

Wife reminds him to do something about getting some state agency to support a statewide program to put art and music in state institutions for mentally retarded. Governor calls budget director and asks for prospects of doing it. Budget director believes the art board has no new statewide projects this year—concentrating on local concerns instead. Does governor want it changed? Governor is not sure, and budget director offers a memo later in the week explaining the choices; governor decides to wait for the memo.

Expecting the first of the legislators on the telephone, governor gets his legislative aide instead—his secretary explaining that he had asked that Governor talk to him before the legislator. Legislative aide says legislator is extremely upset because governor's budget bureau and perhaps higher education coordinating council are apparently not going to approve a community college for which locals have already raised money. Legislative aide feels it is absolutely essential that the project be approved before the fall election and asks the governor to pry the issue out of whatever agency it is in.

Legislator says just what legislative aide said he would. Governor agrees to look into it and call him back.

The other legislator whose call governor returns is concerned about a rumor that governor is firing employees in TB hospital and planning to close it; says he understands problem but hopes that governor will understand his, and that he'll have to issue a press release this afternoon criticizing lack of concern with TB patients and local community if governor goes through with it. The local business leader is also concerned about the TB issue.

12:00 noon

Secretary says transportation secretary, budget director, and transportation aide are waiting; also insurance commissioner. Meeting at 12:15 p.m. with major newspaper reporter pending, and more phone calls.

Governor has brief meeting on transportation funding. Budget director argues for passing up federal money for new highway construction on grounds of governor's austerity program. Transportation secretary notes that funds are 80 percent federal and argues for a go-ahead. Governor says he'll read both memoranda and decide after checking with executive assistant.

Governor is scheduled to leave at 1 p.m. for a ribbon-cutting highway opening about an hour away. Asks secretary to see if he can scrub highway opening and to hold calls, and says he will see the reporter after press secretary has a minute to brief him. Press secretary says press is all over him on TB thing—what has the governor decided? Governor asks secretary to get health director on phone, finds he is addressing public health association lunch right now—does the governor want to interrupt? No, have him call just as soon as he is through speaking.

Reporter comes in to begin interview on whether governor is taking position in key party leadership fight over mayoral nomination in eastern part of the state; governor sets ground rules as background and begins to expound on his preferences.

Secretary buzzes on intercom and reports that top aides (all of whom are now waiting to see him) advise OK to cancel highway opening, highway commissioner will handle but governor should call mayor and apologize because there may be a big crowd which the mayor gathered. Governor tells her to call the mayor on his behalf and explain situation, and that he will call the mayor himself later in the day.

Interview concluded, secretary brings in lunch that he was originally scheduled to have during trip to ribbon cutting.

1:15 p.m.

Health director on the phone reminds governor that there are no more TB patients to be cared for, that most of the people in TB sanatorium are alcoholics who can be readily cared for elsewhere, that firings are part of his budget plan, and that he has no funds to continue employees. Governor finds employees were offered job elsewhere, but many of them don't want to leave the community. Director says he can keep the facility open as long as the governor provides the money. Governor asks press secretary to tell press of meeting on subject at 2 p.m.

Asks secretary to tell legislator to please hold off the press conference criticizing the TB closing for another day. She says she has had three calls from union leaders and a couple of legislative calls protesting the closing and that his political advisor wants to talk about them as well as other things. Governor sets up meeting for 2 p.m. with health director, budget director, press secretary and political advisor.

Secretary provides messages from other calls: Three different people with candidates other than Jones called to express hope that the press story on Jones was not true. One wanted to talk to governor before an appointment is made so he could tell him some confidential information about Jones—Jones called, said he didn't know he was being considered, but would be happy to talk about the job—Chairman of the commission on higher education said please make no commitment on the community college matter without talking to him. Budget director called with the same message—Federal relations aide called, wants a decision this afternoon on what to ask Senator Smith to do on strip-mine control amendments affecting state regulation. Senate votes tomorrow, and the senator wants to go with governor's position. Memo in in-box (which has been resting untouched on desk since 10 a.m.).

1:45 p.m.

Governor tries to call federal relations aide while reading memorandum. Can't reach, he is on the way back from Washington. Governor asks secretary to find out whether he has talked to head of state environmental protection agency on subject—no one knows, he'll call in about an hour.

Governor tells secretary to tell insurance commissioner he is sorry to keep him waiting and for him to get lunch and check back about 3 p.m. Secretary says aides are still waiting, some of their business is pretty urgent, plus remember the 4 p.m. meeting on office space, and that he has an engagement this evening.

2:12 p.m.

Meeting with health director and others (now including legislative personnel and legal advisors) on TB matter. Political and legislative advisors say they don't care how we got where we are, it is imperative that the state not be laying off employees right before election, and with key labor negotiations going on in other departments. Personnel advisor tends to agree, but notes that employees had some prior knowledge of likely layoffs. Budget director and health director are adamant on merits of closing the facility; health director says he will keep it open if budget is increased; budget director says no chance, the legislature cut the overall health budget last year. Legal advisor proposes compromise to keep the facility open until after election, funds to come from health budget, but administration would have to seek some supplemental appropriation to reimburse health budget. Health director is dubious, budget director opposed, personnel advisor says that where he comes from, if you are going to bite a bullet you do it all at once, not in stages. Meeting drags on. Obvious that these layoffs are just the beginning if governor stays with health director's plan.

Meeting continues while governor takes call from federal relations aide. Yes, he has talked to the environmental protection agency, and the position he recommends on strip mining is concurred in by them. Governor returns to TB meeting. Finds potential solution is to have mental health department take over part of facility instead of closing it. Unknown if mental health director will agree; health director is on phone to him now.

Governor leaves TB meeting with legal advisor to discuss status of suit by welfare rights organization to require higher welfare payments.

3:20 p.m.

Returns to TB meeting, which now includes mental health director. Mental health director says he can't make a final decision now, needs to review the facility and prospects for transferring some patients and doctors from another of his facilities. Press secretary proposes to tell media the administration is looking into new possibility and layoffs are deferred. All agree, except budget director, who argues for closing, and political advisor, who urges a solution that will hold for a few months, not a few weeks. Governor accepts the solution anyhow. Instructs press secretary to inform media and legislative advisor to inform local legislators.

3:35 p.m.

Secretary advises that insurance commissioner is back, other advisors are waiting, and governor hasn't done anything about in-box. Plus more messages: Neighboring governor called and wants to discuss developing a common regional position on safety rules for zinc mining. Governor has secretary call federal relations aide to get in touch with neighboring governor's staff to see what can be worked out—Press secretary calls with information that p.m. papers are breaking a story that a legislative leader of the governor's party is suspected of selling real estate to the highway department, using inside information on new highway location—Highway commissioner is back from ribbon cutting and needs to talk. President of largest state university would like to chat briefly about prospects of a new law school—Speaker of the house wants to talk, important and personal—Secretary has arranged the scheduling meeting at 5 p.m., after the office space meeting.

Insurance commissioner is still waiting, has staff with him and two hours worth of visual aids. Governor calls the commissioner in alone—commissioner is prepared to talk about the new insurance consumer protection program he was asked to prepare; meeting was rescheduled twice already. Governor tells him he's sorry about the scheduling problem, asks him to leave the written material and promises to try to read it tonight and to make apologies to his staff.

Calls political advisor in. Asks about speaker's call; finds that speaker wants to be reassured that governor would not back rival for speakership even if party wins handily in fall election. Political advisor says leave him hanging for awhile; call tomorrow and say that governor doesn't control the membership but appreciates his support in the past, etc.

Political advisor discusses bank commissioner appointment and recommends someone other than Jones; governor agrees and asks him to prepare press release. Political advisor stops at door to remind him that he had agreed to spend more time away from the office and with the people; says he must schedule more local events like the ribbon cutting today and then keep to the schedule; asks if mayor who arranged it has been called yet.

4:30 p.m.

Governor calls the mayor and has a fifteen-minute conversation in which the mayor says pretty much what the political advisor did. Agrees to check a bridge situation within city limits and instructs secretary to check the point with the highway commissioner.

4:45 p.m.

Governor begins the 4 p.m. office space meeting, knowing he still has the scheduling meeting and a couple of calls to go and that he should be receiving guests at the mansion at 6:30. The meeting requires his presence because the public works department, which allocates office space, is at loggerheads with the agencies. The agencies want more space—whether they have to lease it, get private companies to build it, or whatever—while public works wants to hold them off and build a new office building which would require the governor's approval. The meeting is incredibly dull, with charts and graphs about office space, so at 5 p.m., the governor leaves, indicating he has another meeting and leaving two or three agency heads, budget director and one aide with instructions to work out a recommendation for him that they can agree on.

5:00 p.m.

Handles more messages. Has secretary get the facts on the law school from budget bureau and commissioner of higher education before calling president of university back tomorrow. Reminds secretary to call the speaker tomorrow. Calls the highway commissioner to find out what the mayor has already told him.

Has secretary tell aide who is waiting to talk about a project for cooperation between university students and law enforcement department to wait until tomorrow. Has consumer protection advisor do likewise.

Reviews brief remarks prepared for dinner session with group of business leaders. Remembers that one of the leaders is board chairman of the community college that all the fuss was about earlier in the day. Asks an aide to quickly collect the views of the higher education commissioner and the budget director and give him a briefing before he leaves the office.

5:30 p.m.

Governor enters scheduling meeting. His secretary asks if he wants the aide left in the office space meeting or brought into the meeting; he answers "both." The scheduling meeting is no different from the last one, not likely to be different from the next.

The political advisor wants governor to make fund-raising appearance at five geographically diverse places in the next week, appear at supermarkets with two legislative candidates, and attend two rallies for legislative candidates. In addition, advisor suggests strongly that governor drop in at the Chinese-American society dinner next Saturday night and appear at a teacher's convention the following day.

Secretary says wife wants to hold Saturday all day at home and prefers to spend that evening with friends. Wife does not want to travel on Sunday, secretary says, reminding governor that one of his children is making his debut as a high school football player on Friday. Governor's scheduler ticks off the remaining demands for time the following week:

1. One state trade association meeting (already accepted) and two more which request his presence and will schedule for a major address if he can make it;

2. One statewide labor meeting;

3. Three requests for local political functions beyond the ones the political advisor knows the governor had;

4. A request from the federal relations aide to visit the congressional delegation in Washington next week and deliver testimony for the National Governors' Association before a Senate subcommittee;

5. A request from two key agency directors to accompany them to Washington to resolve problems with federal agencies;

6. A request from the press aide for a news conference announcing the new bank commissioner, a backgrounder with a representative of a national magazine, and at least one additional general-purpose news conference during the week;

7. Six cabinet officers and three board or commission chairmen want to discuss one subject or another; and

8. Three county chairmen, four legislators, five major contributors, six local delegations seeking highways or other state construction, and the usual flow of private citizens wanting to see their governor.

In addition, the schedulers report back on various events the governor requests be scheduled, which have not been scheduled yet, including a visit to a mental hospital for inspection and employee relations, a meeting with educational advisors on potential for improving the state aid formula, a meeting with the planning director and several cabinet officers on land-use planning, and the remainder of the meetings on the consumer protection program similar to that with the insurance commissioner today.

Secretary reports governor should take one complete day off just to concentrate on the paperwork in the in-box.

The scheduling meeting goes to 6 p.m., at which time the governor expresses preferences, delegates the exact schedule to the group, and receives a delegation from the office space meeting seeking to resolve a couple of questions. Indicating that he has to shower and change to be ready at the mansion by 6:30, governor asks them either to write it up or talk to him in the morning (not remembering that tomorrow's schedule is worse than today's).

His secretary shouts out a couple of other phone calls; he says "tomorrow" and leaves office accompanied by aide trying to brief him on the community college situation, matching him pace for pace as he walks out. The community college situation is complicated indeed, so governor decides not to decide yet and to finesse the situation if it comes up in the evening.

After a quick shower and change accompanied by as much recitation of family affairs as time permits, governor finds himself in the receiving line not quite promptly at 6:40, facing the ordeal of trying to remember 40 people whom he knows he should know. Cocktail conversation centers on bank regulation issues, exhortations to avoid tax increases, discussion of the business climate, costs of workers' compensation, and some general discussion of national politics. After dinner governor talks briefly about some of his major programs and the need for good business climate in the state and retires to family quarters about 9:45 p.m.

In these moments of potential relaxation, governor retrieves in-box correspondence from his brief-case. First, the "information only" items consisting of magazine articles, FYI memos from staff, and the like; these he scans briefly, primarily to see if there is any action he need take. A memo from the welfare secretary which indicates negotiations may break down with hospitals over Medicaid reimbursement rates is sent to his political advisor with a question, "Can we handle this if negotiations fail?"

Now the "action" items. Some 20 letters to sign prepared by staff; 16 are OK, two require rewrite instructions to someone, and two more the governor rewrites himself. Now it is 10:15 p.m., his definite cutoff time for relaxation and talking to his family, even though he has five or six complicated problems, including the community college issue, left hanging.

This example is obviously atypical for some, while typical for other governors, only because it happens to cover a quiet time without a major crisis (prison riot, natural disaster), or having the legislature in session. It suggests a governor's constant need to make choices in the use of his own time and, more important, to avoid becoming a captive of the pressures on him. In a day such as the one described, it is hard to imagine the governor contemplating, much less doing much about, his broad strategies for government leadership and party affairs.

When the moment of reflection does come, a governor may find that his campaign did not result in his capturing the office, but in the office capturing him. He will see that many aspects of his predecessor's style that he wanted to change are things he is unable to change.

There is no obvious solution to these problems. There are ways to make them manageable only if a governor designs his administration's priorities during the transition—and avoids being totally "captured."

What Goes On around the Governor

While the governor goes through these frenetic paces, his staff attempts to stay one step behind—or at least only a few steps behind—anticipating his needs and following up commitments made on this typical day. Since a governor is often judged by the quality and thoroughness of his staff's work, it is worth considering who did what around the governor in connection with just a part of this "typical" day. Consider for example, the 15 minutes at midday encompassing the highway-funding meeting and a few of the staff involved:

The Scheduler. Three weeks previously, the governor's scheduler had addressed some hard decisions. Should the governor attend the highway ribbon cutting, or should he turn it down and send a representative? How many people would be annoyed or slighted? As the "typical" day approached, the scheduler had perhaps 20 or so similar decisions to make before making final the public portion of the governor's day. And, even then, the schedule was changed.

The Executive Assistant. Sitting with the governor and the suburban legislators early in the day, the executive assistant to the governor worried about his phone messages, large numbers of which mounted up in little pink piles on his desk. He usually kept two secretaries busy sorting correspondence, responding to requests, and placing calls. The suburban group's request for a new superhighway reminded him that the governor was going to meet later in the morning with the budget director and transportation secretary on highway funding in general. The two men disagree and each will come well prepared with opposing arguments; he knows the governor will ask him to help resolve the problem, but when will he have time to study it?

As the governor's day unfolded, he reminded himself that his symbol of power—the office next door to the governor's—was also a millstone around his neck. Much of his life, he realized, was taken up in "hand holding" and being a "sounding board." If only he could get caught up, he thought, he would be able to work on that new tax-reform initiative which the revenue department had failed to deliver in adequate form. But Senator Brown had called, and he had to get back to him before noon because the governor might run into him at the ribbon cutting that afternoon. Perhaps this evening he could stop to think about the governor's tax program.

The Budget Director. "Why is the executive assistant allowing the transportation meeting to be delayed?" the budget director wondered at five minutes until noon as he waited to see the governor. After all, the budget office's work on this issue had been going on, in fits and spurts, for six months. In fact, last night he and his unit chiefs were up until 3 a.m. completing the memorandum which would be devastating to the department of transportation's case for more highway construction. But if the governor ran out of time this morning, the decision could be delayed again. The budget director had called the executive assistant to urge him to hurry the governor along, but his call was somewhere at the bottom of the pink pile in the inner office.

The Secretary of Transportation. The secretary of transportation didn't enjoy the budget director's dry personality, so he had passed the time waiting for the governor's meeting by drifting across the hall to chat with the governor's personal secretary. Besides the fact that he was a gregarious soul, he knew that staying on the good side of the governor's secretary never hurt. Sometimes he absolutely had to talk to the governor, and she would always put him through.

He was nervous about the governor's reaction to his request for more highway money, in light of the governor's austerity campaign. Just for insurance, he had let the governor's political advisor know that many of the campaign pledges made in the politically critical rural areas of the state could not be met without the road funds. And then, of course, there were seventy-five campaign workers from key areas of the state whom he had hired at the political advisor's request—they might have to be laid off if the new money was not found in the budget somewhere. He hoped that the advisor had mentioned these problems to the governor. If it seemed that the decision was not going his way, he planned to ask for more study—a delaying tactic to ensure that the governor would make the final decision only after being apprised of all the financial and political ramifications of the decision.

The Planning Director. The planning director sat in his office working on the "Rural Development Plan" which the Governor had promised during the campaign, and which was now six months and scores of public hearings in the making. He was worried because he feared that the governor's meeting on road money was going to preempt consideration of the section on farm-to-market road repair, a centerpiece in the rural development program he was about to unveil. If the road funds were put into the budget, he might still have time to influence the pattern of expenditures. "If we don't rebuild the small bridges on our rural roads," he thought, "five years from now the farm economy will be in deep trouble." He knew that the budget director had been working on a memorandum to convince the governor that the department of transportation's spending plan was premature, but the planner was unsure of the outcome. Until the issue was clearly resolved, he could not move forward on his development plans.

Others worked, watched and waited on the outcome of the short meeting with the governor.

The press secretary was concerned; the Washington office director wanted to be able to credit her office with getting the federal dollars; the environmental protection liaison was quietly lobbying against more highways.

In this "typical" day, these developments were only a small sample of the detailed staff work and intra-staff competition that are inevitable in the governor's office.

Part III. The Political Role

4. The Governor as Party Leader

Lynn R. Muchmore and Thad L. Beyle

The governorship is sometimes modeled as a collection of obligatory roles produced by law or tradition. As a leading American government textbook of the 1960s indicated:

> The governorship is many things, . . . and the governor must play many social roles and must learn to help the public keep their individuality identifiable. The governor is chief of state, the voice of the people, chief executive, commander-in-chief of the state's armed forces, chief legislator, and chief of his party.[1]

Thus, each governor is expected to ride in a reasonable number of parades and cut an appropriate number of ribbons in his role as ceremonial head of state. Every governor inherits a military role—as commander-in-chief of his state's National Guard. Obviously, individual governors will emphasize certain roles and downplay others according to his or her personal preferences, but the boundaries of choice are imposed by a predetermined role structure. Therefore, according to this view, governors have limited control over their own course of official conduct since much of their time is taken up by such role-playing and only the residual is available for use in ways that the governor desires. Unless roles are carefully managed, that residual can dwindle to insignificance, and the governor can become a captive of the office.

One of the principal roles addressed in the literature of the governorships is the party leadership role. Governors are frequently referred to as the "titular head of the party" in their state, suggesting a continuing interest in the party during their tenure of office and a preeminent status in party deliberations. According to the governors' own *Handbook:*

> The Governor is the leader of his state political party. He is expected to play a role in determining who fills party leadership positions, raising funds, formulating and articulating positions, selecting candidates, and participating in national party affairs.[2]

Terry Sanford simply indicated "the governor is the most potent political power in his state."[3]

In the following discussion, recent evidence is examined that illuminates the party leadership role. A somewhat different attitude than might be expected is uncovered, and reasons are presented to explain why the party leadership role of governors is changing so rapidly. The chapter concludes with a brief caveat about the uncritical use of the role model as an approach to understanding the governorship.

Gubernatorial Views on the Party Role

During 1978 and 1979, interviews were conducted with fifteen former governors who had left office since 1976 to secure a current sample of attitudes about the development of federalism.[4] Among questions asked of each governor were several dealing with partisan political matters, including questions about the governor's influence over the party and vice versa, the impact of party ideology and the governor's use of the party as a source of information and advice, and the effect of partisanship on specific processes like personnel selection. The answers given reveal a surprising consistency among individual experiences and attitudes.

It is useful to distinguish several of the relationships between the political parties and the governorship that would appear significant, based upon popular and traditional notions about the political system. First, one might expect to find in any governor's party affiliation some basic ideological mold, a loose system of values and beliefs about the public interest held in common with others of the same party and active as a reference for the broad-scale decisions that governors must make. Second, because the party organizations serve as a framework within which coalitions can be formed, positions articulated, and pressures for various kinds of action developed, one might expect that governors accept, either willingly or unwillingly, the urgings of the party on specific issues or problems facing the state. Third, the election of governors on partisan ballots in every state should force governors into some type of working relationship with their party as a prerequisite for election. Finally, since political parties cannot survive without serving the self-interest of their members, governors might be expected to play an important role by distributing the spoils of the political battle—perhaps as patronage jobs, as new priorities for highway construction, or as appointments to boards or commissions with policymaking responsibilities.

In each of these activities the interaction is bidirectional. While a governor might be faithful to his party's ideology, he is in a position to alter the party's ideological profile; while the governor may find himself facing strong party positions on a particular issue, he might also use the party organization to mobilize support for his own approach; and while patronage is sometimes viewed as a concession of power from the governor to the party, it may also be that the governor relies upon partisan intelligence for judgements about hundreds of potential appointees whose credentials he cannot check personally. This is a useful way to organize the analysis of gubernatorial attitudes toward the party leadership role and toward the effect of partisan association upon gubernatorial behavior.

The Party as an Ideology

If governors in the sample were judged by the importance they attach to partisan ideology, most would score low. Some, as Governor Pryor, observed that the balance of power is so one-sided in their states that any ideological distinctions between Democrats and Republicans is irrelevant: "So far as . . . putting ideology of the Democratic party above that of the Republican party, to be very honest I did not find that a necessity."[5] Even among those states where intense political scraps reflect a more balanced party membership, the ideological dimensions of the battle seem remote. Thus, Governor Shapp responded that party ideology "had very little to do" with his decisions.[6]

This is not to say that all governors consider themselves free of ideological identity. Governor Dukakis described himself as a liberal who shares the "traditional philosophy of the Democratic party";[7] Governor Apodaca claimed that his program decisions were superseded by his philosophy;[8] Governor Bennett saw a "backdrop of philosophy" that affected his approach to issues.[9] Even in these instances, however, it is clear that the governors perceive ideology as a passive and insubstantial explanation for their official behavior. Further, Governors Dukakis and Evans indicated that intraparty fractionalization over ideological issues in their states left their party without any clear ideological basis.[10]

Several governors argued that the duties and responsibilities of their governorship did not permit ideological considerations. Thus, Governor Walker commented that "most of the issues in state government don't cut that way."[11] Hence, ideology is displaced by a common sense approach that translates into a loose pragmatism. It may be argued, of course, that common sense is itself some unnamed ideology. But the significant point is that governors believe that traditional party ideology has little or nothing to do with their conduct while in office.

It is not clear whether governors now regard parties as devoid of ideological content but consider it irrelevant to the governorship. There may be some connection between the indifference toward ideology and the widely held view that the governor should devote his major energies to management. Governor Edwards, for example, while unmistakably a conservative, reflected upon the high points of his administration in terms of the cold statistics of motor pool management, personnel and payroll systems, and data processing.[12] His record as governor can be explained in some ways as an attempt to apply business administration to state government operations. But there is little that the traditional partisan ideologies have to offer on such questions as the techniques for minimizing the cost of the state's automobile fleet.

As attention is focused upon the scientific and objective aspects of management, the importance of Democratic or Republican party principles recedes, and ideology becomes a conversation piece rather than a guide to priorities and action.

The Party as a Source of Policy

If ideology is so vague that governors find it irrelevant to their official duties, what dialogue does occur between the governor and the party on important state issues that can be specifically defined? The party platform is the formal record of party positions, and in some states the construction of the platform is a sophisticated exercise involving public hearings and lengthy debate. Beyond the periodic platforms, party officials are available on a continuing basis to represent the will of the party membership. However, the governors interviewed largely dismissed the party platform as meaningless, and few would admit consultation with party officals on matters of state policy. Governor Wollman's comment on the party platform is typical:

> There are some positions of the . . . party so traditional that you can predict that they're going to crop up in the platform—sort of a "party line"—but nobody is serious about it. . . . There is a lot of hypocrisy in all of this. You say a lot of good things because they are traditional.

Governor Holshouser said that he paid almost no attention to platform planks: "If one of them said something I disagreed with, I just ignored it."[14] Ironically, one governor did regard the platform as a serious matter because he felt an obligation to publicly disavow those parts with which he disagreed.

Sentiments of party officials are not routinely ignored, but as a source of policy input they seem to play a marginal role. Governor Schreiber, who concluded that "party politics is at a low ebb," volunteered that "a state party chairman coming in here advising me 'for the good of the party' really wouldn't carry much water."[15] Governor Lee indicated, "The political party was almost totally useless [as a source of advice], I would say. It just isn't in that line of work."[16]

The image of governors consulting with powerful party bosses and accepting their advice despite the contrary counsel of experts is an outdated caricature. A more accurate perception is probably the remark by Governor Bennett: "But as far as specific decisions—the party hasn't played that much of a part in the specific decisions of this administration nor has it attempted to."[17]

Even the governors who have actively urged their parties to get more involved in the formation of the public agenda and the resolution of complex issues have found the party a difficult partner. Governor Evans argued that the parties in his state are "nowhere near as strong as they ought to be," but confessed that despite his prodding and encouragement, the party was never really able to "respond to issues and seriously develop solutions."[18]

The Problem of Party Maintenance

Because of his executive power, the governor is in a likely position to reward the politically active for their interest and support, as well as punish his partisan enemies, more so than any other statewide elected official. The spoils of office have historically been the glue that binds the self-interested into a political organization. To say that patronage is completely dead among the states would be an exaggeration, but after years of assault from reformers and new legal challenges based upon constitutional guarantees, even those governors who view patronage as a legitimate means of selecting personnel can deliver jobs only sparingly.

Most of these governors viewed patronage as an inappropriate criteria for hiring decisions. They would prefer to make appointments from their own party. Governor Exon indicated, "If I came down to two individuals that I thought were the best two, and I couldn't see a difference between those two, I would lean to the Democrat."[19] However, they cite "qualifications" and "competence" as the overriding considerations in selecting personnel, and they take some pride in appointing persons from the opposite party, or persons whose party affiliation is unknown.

Patronage is in part the victim of the managerial image and the emerging conviction among governors that the business of state government is beyond politics. Governor Evans makes the point:

> You have to realize that during that period of years [1964-76] we were rapidly getting to a point where effective management of state agencies was easily as important as the political orientation. I could provide political direction and orientation as long as I had really good top managers in the agencies who could carry out those functions. In the latter half of my administration I hired many directors of state agencies, and I can't tell you to this day what their party orientation is.[20]

Governors are remarkably consistent in their view that the protection afforded state employees through the civil service systems has become unreasonable. But their motivation seems to lie not in the desire to make more patronage appointments, but in the difficulty they face when trying to discharge an employee they consider incompetent.

Why Be Concerned with the Party?

If the party is only marginally involved with personnel selection, is ideologically irrelevant, and has no influence upon the course of policy development, why should a governor commit energy to the maintenance of the party organization? If, as many observers suggest, parties at the state level have weakened perceptibly and are, therefore, not as useful to governors as they once were, why should a governor attend to his party role?[21] Three reasons are suggested in this series of interviews.

First, governors have to cope with the fact that most legislatures are organized along party lines. Legislators who are members of the governor's own party give him the deference he often needs to push programs through the legislative body, while those of the opposite party are likely to be far more skeptical, if not contrary.[22] The purely partisan nature of legislative wrangling is probably over-emphasized by the popular press, as the great bulk of the legislative business is nonpartisan. But several governors questioned about the importance of partisan politics cited the importance of a legislative majority:

> The state party was important to me because I was dealing with the legislature. (Shapp)
> The parties were very important in terms of their legislative representation. (Evans)
> Then, the second role I felt I had as Governor was to broaden [the party's] influence so that it wasn't just a party concerned about the election of the Governor, but a party concerned about the election of all its candidates—particularly its legislative candidates. (Bennett).[23]

These comments bear out the view that there are several parties in a state: the state apparatus, the county-by-county organization, and the legislative party. It is the latter which is of importance to governors in their policy and programmatic endeavors.

A second reason for party involvement is the effect that governors feel through the intergovernmental system. When the president is of the same party as the governor, avenues of cooperation and communication are likely to be far more effective than when the president and the governor are of opposite parties. The effect of federal program decisions on the operations of state government are extremely important, not only because a large share of state services is funded in part by the federal government but because federal regulatory activities determine what states or their political subdivisions may or may not do in such important areas as energy, transportation, environmental affairs, and education.

Political compatibility does not eliminate the problems that arise out of intergovernmental conflict, but it often means that a particular state's problems will be reviewed more quickly and more sympathetically by federal officials. A comment by Governor Askew about the difference between the responsiveness of two different national administrations makes this point:

> I learned quickly the difference when you are of the same party as the president—that's critically important. . . . That is why governors who sit on the sidelines and say that selection of the president doesn't make any difference are misleading themselves. I have found that it makes a lot of difference.[24]

Third, although governors find reason for partisanship in both the legislative process and federal-state relations, the "bottom line" for each governor is the practical necessity of party nomination as a prerequisite for election or reelection. While the interviews contain some statements that would tend to contradict this hypothesis, the general thrust of the gubernatorial attitudes seems to be that obtaining the party nomination is only a procedural hoop one must jump through. It is not, as one might imagine, the beginning of a long and productive association in which the governor provides leadership to the party and the party responds with continued support as the governor tackles the problems of his state. Rather ironically, it is a point at which the governor begins to leave the party behind. Governor Edwards stated that:

> The party is a mechanism—there's really no other way to get the nomination. But very few people get elected because of the activities of the party . . . for the most part—with today's electronic media—it's the individual who gets elected; it's not the party.[25]

Governor Lee expanded on this by noting that "Once the election is over, they tend to forget that partisan aspect rather thoroughly."[26]

Thus, for many governors, the motivation to play a strong and active leadership role is weak. Some, as Governor Rampton, said that the party role was not really comfortable for them. Others, like Governor Schreiber, observed that the party "really doesn't have much to offer in terms of money or in terms of organizational strength and support," so that it isn't worth the commitment of time and energy required. As one former governor's aide asserted, "The Party can't deliver."[27]

While governors seem to acknowledge the growing remoteness of the party as a factor in the governorship, not all are willing to accept that as a healthy trend. Governors Bennett and Evans, as well as other governors, continue to believe that the party can make a positive contribution to state government. An obvious conflict is that these same governors emphasized the managerial/professional aspects of executive responsibility, which diminishes patronage and politically based influence that parties need to maintain credibility within their membership. One who regretted his lack of attention to the party was Governor Dukakis of Massachusetts—not apparently because he failed to take advantage of any substantial contribution that the party could have made to his governorship, but because he attributed his reelection defeat, in part, to an alienated party.

Conclusion

The evidence contained in this sample of interviews sheds light upon the political role of governors as seen by the governors themselves. It is significant that none of these 15 former governors views party leadership as an important duty. What is more significant is that governors do not perceive politics and party affairs as an obligatory role. Governors may be escaping the confines of the traditional role structure in general, but at least in the important area of partisan politics they seem to have ascended above the parties to a position where they feel free to shape their party involvement in whatever way fits their own concept of the governorship.

For most, the governorship seems to have developed in such a way that the party is no longer the most important instrument of political action. Further, when the political party is of use, it is now one among several potentially useful instruments available to the governor. When the emerging single-issue politics, the media, intergovernmental officials, and bureaucracies are factored into the equation, a sandlot analogy might be apropos: The governor is an individual politician always having to create new and unstable alliances—a kind of sandlot politics, playing with and against pickup teams as they are created.[28]

5. The Governor and the Public

Thad L. Beyle and Lynn R. Muchmore

Relating the governorship—both the person and the office—to the public is one of the more time-consuming and continuous roles which governors must perform. It is through this public role that a governor builds and maintains past, present, and future constituencies, and commands attention as the chief executive and chief legislator in his or her state. Terry Sanford called the governorship the "center of the state system" for "the governor sets the agenda for public debate; frames the issues; decides the timing; and can blanket the state with good ideas by using access to the mass media."[1] The role is thus important in achieving the goals of a governor's administration.

However, creating and maintaining this role is not easy and requires careful attention from the governor's point of view. It means relating directly to the public through public appearances, visits to the office, phone calls, and correspondence; and indirectly through press conferences, background interviews, and normal press coverage of gubernatorial activities.

Not all efforts at relating to the public are successful—witness the assertion of a recent southern governor that unless the press asked him positive questions about the accomplishments of his administration, he would no longer answer any negative questions. This points up the comments of a former governor who felt that "image, which is filtered through or created by the media, is all-important—not only in reelection but in the ability to govern."[2]

This chapter views the governor's public role from the perspective of the governors' office. Surveys of the governor's press secretaries in 1976 and 1979, and of governors and former governors provide the basis for this presentation.[3]

Relating to the Public

It is clear from various accounts of how governors spend their time and energies that their public role is of significance to them. In the 1976 surveys, those who were responsible for scheduling gubernatorial working days were asked to estimate the amount of time governors spent by category of activity (see Table 5.1, Column A). While managing state government and working with the state legislature were each more time consuming, the three categories of meeting the general public, ceremonial functions, and working with the press and media totaled to a greater time commitment than the former two. Further, some governors were reported to have spent over 50 percent of their time in these public-relating activities. The governors themselves, in estimating their

Table 5.1. The governor's time schedule[a]

Activity	Column A[b] (in percent)	Column B[c] (in percent)
Managing state government	29	27
Working with the legislature	16	18
Meeting the general public	14 ⎫	— ⎫
Ceremonial functions	14 ⎬ 37	13 ⎬ 20
Working with the press and media	9 ⎭	7 ⎭
Working with federal government	7	7
Working with local governments	7	7
Political activities	6	8
Recruiting and appointing	6	8
Miscellaneous activities (staff, interstate, reading, phoning)	16	9

a. Sums do not total 100 percent, but are averages of the respondents' estimates of the time devoted to the particular activity by the governor.
b. Percentages based on responses from those scheduling gubernatorial time from forty states.
c. Percentages based on responses from governors of sixteen states.

own time commitments, did not indicate as great an amount of time spent in these activities but, nevertheless, a considerable portion of their time was spent in the public role (see Table 5.1, Column B).

While this role is time consuming and all-important for governors, the responses of fifty-five former governors as to which aspects of the job of being governor they found most difficult and demanding showed "ceremonial functions" (twenty-one former governors) ranking third and "working with the press" (ten former governors) tenth.[4] It is obvious that the role is not that demanding except for the time spent. It may also be, as Alan Wyner suggested, "the line of least resistance" which governors can follow when faced with administrative, legislative or intergovernmental restrictions in attempting to build their image.[5]

Part of the time and energy involved can be illustrated by some representative numbers indicative of the "volume" of activity as of 1976:

1. Twenty-five of forty-six gubernatorial press secretaries responding indicated their governors held regularly scheduled news conferences; eighteen of these were held at least once a week, sometimes more. Thirty-six percent of those without regularly scheduled press conferences held at least three or four a month. These gubernatorial press conferences averaged 37 minutes in length, with a range from less than 15 minutes in length to more than an hour.

2. All press secretaries indicated that their governors granted interviews to individual reporters outside a regular news conference, with six always granting an interview request and forty others usually doing so while trying to direct the query elsewhere or into the regular press conference.

3. Twelve of thirty states reporting estimated over 500 visitors in the governor's office during a month.

4. Sixteen of twenty-nine states reporting estimated over 2,000 phone calls to the governor's office in an average month.

5. Fourteen of 36 states reporting estimated over 3,600 cards and letters received by governors' offices per month. The average across all governors' offices reporting was nearly 200 letters and cards every working day—and nearly as many phone calls.

To place this in a more political perspective:

[when a governor handles] 200 pieces of mail a day and meets 20 individuals outside of normal state government day-to-day contacts, he will have made over 300,000 contacts in a four-year term. Even assuming that 100,000 of these are duplicates, the impact is significant, particularly when it is recognized that Johnny's letter from the Governor will probably affect his parents, grandparents and neighbors—a surprisingly large number of people. If 200,000 unduplicated contacts each affects five people, the Governor would, in four years, have reached personally a million people. In many cases, these will be individuals for whom personal contact may be more real than party loyalties or responses to campaign issues.[6]

Obviously some of these illustrative numbers, such as the number of letters received, are directly related to the size of the state involved. However, the volume of contacts between the governor or the governor's staff and the public, either directly or indirectly, is very high and points out the magnitude of the governor's public role.

Gubernatorial Style

Governors approach their public role with differing perspectives. Some fulfill the role as one of many and carry it out to the best of their ability. They do not seek to expand the role or encourage contacts but are responsive to constituents and the media. This is often a most necessary view of the role due to the sheer volume of public activity facing the governor. Other governors undertake a more aggressive and activist role, seeking out and stimulating public contacts.

In the 1976 survey, twenty-eight governors of thirty-eight states responding were reported as taking such an activist approach to their public role. There were interesting relationships between the size of the state, the formal powers of the governor, and whether they took an activist role.[7] Governors from the fifteen largest states responding were distributed almost equally between being activist or merely responsive, while those from the twenty-three smaller states responding were, with but three exceptions, activist in approach. Whether an activist approach is a luxury which the governors of smaller states can undertake but which the governors of larger states cannot afford due to sheer size, or whether governors of smaller states need to take on such a role to maintain their visibility and their constituencies cannot be ascertained from the data. The finding is clear, however, that an activist approach to relations with the public is part and parcel of the governorship in the moderate- and smaller-sized states.

While not quite as striking a relationship, those governors with moderate or weak formal powers were considerably more likely to take an activist stance. This suggests that governors with lesser power use their public role to overcome the lack of other more formal powers at their command.

. There were several methods mentioned by which the public's involvement was to be increased. In answer to the query as to whether "the governor made a conscious effort to encourage mail, telephone calls and/or personal visits from the general public to the governor's office?" the following methods were reported:

1. Sixteen states—governor's visits to industrial plants, shopping centers, etc., to hear complaints.

2. Fourteen states—the establishment of an ombudsman in the governor's office.

3. Thirteen states—a toll-free telephone line for public calls.

4. Seven states—a governor's open day or the equivalent when anyone can come and talk to the governor on any problem.

5. Six states—the governor encouraged citizens to write and comment.

6. Five states—a publicized "write the governor" campaign.

7. Three states—town hall meetings throughout the state.

Again there are variations among the states according to the size of the state or the power which the governor has in his or her state. Governors from large states and stronger in power were considerably more likely to reach outside the governor's office to hear citizen complaints than were their counterparts from smaller states and with less power. Similarly, governors of larger states were most likely to encourage citizens to write them and comment about various issues. They obviously have the larger office staffs and manpower to handle a greater volume of mail.[8]

At the other end, the smaller states were considerably more likely to establish an ombudsman in the governor's office than were larger states, and thereby create a focal point for citizen contact with the office.

Governors do vary in their approaches to carrying out their public role. Part of the variation is tied to their own personal view and desired style, and part to the state and office in which they serve.

Responding to Citizen Contacts

No area is more sensitive to maintenance of good public relations for a governor and conversely to creating unneeded ill will than the responses made to written and telephonic communications addressed to the chief executive's office. A non-answered letter or a rude telephone response will probably never be forgotten. On the other hand, positive impressions can be made and even a sense of personal involvement can be created by the governor by an effective office system which stresses, on the part of the entire staff, timely and sensitive answers to responsible inquiries.[9]

Table 5.2. Response time to mail received

Mail received	Average days to respond	Maximum time needed by some states to respond
1. School children request governor's picture	4.9	20
2. Request governor issue a proclamation	6.1	30
3. Request for a meeting	6.2	25
4. Substantive letter urging passage of particular legislation	7.2	30
5. Request for employment	7.6	30
6. Request governor appear or speak at a specific function	8.0	25
7. Mail from local elected officials regarding local/state problems	8.2	70
8. Letter from federal cabinet officer	8.5	30
9. Person claiming eligibility for welfare benefits or unemployment compensation	8.9	30
10. Mail from prison inmates	9.8	75
11. Mental health patient complaining about conditions	10.1	30

The former governor providing this comment spoke to a serious problem which most governors' offices must face or lose their constituency: guaranteeing that the governor's public role is fulfilled efficiently and effectively.

Each governor's office establishes procedures whereby mail and phone contacts are processed. In some offices these procedures are similar (eighteen of thirty-five responding); in others there are separate procedures for phone and mail contacts (seventeen of thirty-five responding). These procedures did not vary by size of state or the governor's power and, therefore, were idiosyncratic to the governor's management style for the office. Another major variation in these procedures is whether public contacts are routed directly to a governor's special assistant who is then responsible for responding or answering them (seventeen states), or whether they are routed to departments and agencies and the responses and answers are only monitored by the governor's office staff in some manner (eighteen states). Here, governors' offices in larger states are more likely to keep such contacts within the office and have special assistants respond to them, while smaller states are more likely to ask for help from outside the office while monitoring such responses. Again, size of office staff is the obvious factor involved.

Table 5.2 presents some of the types of mail requests a governors' office receives, and indicates the average and maximum times needed to respond to the correspondence. Clearly, the more perfunctory requests (1–3) can be answered quickly as they usually need no more than routine or "canned," yet personalized, responses. As the content of the correspondence becomes more complex or sensitive, i.e., policy issues and specific requests of the governor (4–9), the response time is greater as more bases must be touched, positions and schedules checked, and an individualized response developed. However, it is mail from people under direct control of the state, i.e., prison inmates or mental health patients (10 and 11) which needs the longest time in terms of receiving a response. Here, investigative activities must either be taken or stimulated by office staff before a carefully, legally sound response can be made to the query or allegation. The amount of time involved is related to a continuum, running from ceremonial, to policy/political, to legal. This did not vary by size of state or power of the governor.

The unanswered questions here are just how well the contacts are handled, and how satisfied the citizen is with the handling of his or her request and the answer provided.

The Press Secretary

The key person in any governor's office for public and especially media relations is the press secretary. When the governor is not on the firing line, it is the press secretary who must handle the day-to-day contacts with the media, and attempt to answer questions and present the governor's position as best as possible. And the press secretary must work very closely with the governor as indicated by the fact that nearly all press secretaries said they reported directly to the governor; 79 percent (thirty-four of forty-three responding) indicated that other members of the governor's staff routinely cleared with the press secretary before responding to media questions presented directly to them; and approximately 84 percent (thirty-two of thirty-eight responding) reported that they normally sat in on meetings where policy or programs decisions were being considered. By all measures, the press secretary is an important person in a governor's office and his or her work places the press secretary directly in the activities of the office.

In 1976, the governors' press secretaries were predominantly male (forty-two of forty-six) and tended to be in their mid-thirties (average age was thirty-five). Since some of the functions that the press secretary performs bear a striking resemblance to those occurring in a gubernatorial campaign, it is no surprise that 39 percent (eighteen of forty-six) of the press secretaries had been members of the governor's campaign staff. This particular background factor is of interest in the face of many governors' advice to new governors not to seek office staff from their campaign organizations. The similarity of the press function in the political campaign and the governor's office and the dissimilarities of the other roles being performed in the campaign and the office suggest that such advice may not apply to the press secretary as much as to other campaign personnel.[10]

Their career backgrounds indicated a marked tendency for the press secretary to come out of the print media as opposed to electronic media, public relations, teaching, or other professions. This tendency was most striking in the moderate and smaller-sized states, and in those states where governors had moderate to weak formal powers. Conversely, it was in the largest states, and the states with higher gubernatorial power, where press secretaries had the more diverse backgrounds such as the electronic media, public relations, or teaching.

Governor's offices also varied as to the size of the press office, ranging from one half-time person to fifteen full-time personnel. Those less than full-time press secretaries also served as administrative assistants, legislative liaisons, or handled special events or assignments. Once more, there is a direct relationship between the size of a state and the size of the press office, with the largest states having four or more on the staff and the smaller states having one person serving the role, either full time or part time.

Role of the Press Secretary

At the outset, however, it must be understood that there are limits to what a press secretary can achieve. A press secretary and a governor cannot create an image of an honest administration when high officials in the administration are not honest. They cannot create the image of an administration that is quick to identify and solve problems if the problems persist. The press secretary cannot be expected to convince the press to write about the openness of an administration that is not open, the responsiveness of an administration that does not respond, and the management skills of a Governor who does not manage well.[11]

The press secretary does fulfill a diverse set of functions in the governor's office. Of course, not all governors and press secretaries operate in a similar manner, so there are variations across the states in the configuration of the actual functions performed. As can be seen from Table 5.3, there are several fairly distinct clusters of activity into which these functions can be grouped. First, nearly all press secretaries perform routine media-governor's office relationship activities such as preparing and issuing news releases, setting up press conferences, and serving as the media contact point (1–3).

The second cluster (4–7), with slightly fewer press secretaries performing these functions, involves the press secretary in more of a review and advisory role. These include such activities as advising on potential media reaction to policies (more likely in larger states); providing background discussions with the press (considerably more likely in moderate or weak governor states); reviewing prospective gubernatorial speeches and messages; and providing the governor with news summaries (slightly more likely in the larger states).

In the third cluster (8–12), the press secretaries become considerably more divided as to whether they perform the functions or not. While some of the activities here might be considered as "busy work," such as preparing proclamations (slightly more likely in some larger states and in moderate and low gubernatorial power states), the general thrust seems to place the press secretary in the midst of gubernatorial and gubernatorial staff functions. These include being contact point for the media-staff relationships (more likely in the smaller and moderate

Table 5.3. Functions of the governor's press secretary[a]

Functions	Normally do (in percent)	Occasionally do (in percent)	Seldom, if ever, do (in percent)
1. Prepare news releases (45)	98	2	—
2. Arrange news conferences (45)	98	—	2
3. Serve as point of contact for media personnel seeking to arrange time with governor (45)	93	7	—
4. Advise governor or top staff on potential media reaction to proposed policies (45)	84	13	2
5. Discuss the administration's point of view with members of the working press (45)	73	20	7
6. Review speeches and messages proposed for the governor's use by someone else(45)	71	24	4
7. Prepare news summaries or clippings for the governor (45)	71	20	9
8. Serve as point of contact for media personnel seeking to arrange interviews with the governor's staff (44)	57	39	5
9. Travel with governor in state or out of state (42)	52	40	7
10. Prepare proclamations (e.g., National Pickle Week) (44)	52	14	34
11. Prepare first drafts of speeches and messages (45)	44	44	11
12. Recommend media events (e.g., ribbon cuttings, ground breakings) to the governor or the person charged with scheduling (45)	42	47	11
13. Serve as a spokesman for the administration, issuing statements in own name rather than that of the governor (45)	33	42	24
14. Review proposed news releases and major speeches from departments and agencies of state government (44)	20	60	20
15. Prepare documentaries, promotional material for state or governor (44)	16	23	61
16. Make arrangements for groups of citizens seeking to see the governor (44)	9	50	41

Others mentioned: Scheduling and nonroutine activities—six states
Committee and agency liaison—five states
Ceremonial; public relations activities
and political advising—three states

a. Totals may not add up to 100 percent due to rounding. Percentages are based on between forty-two and forty-five press secretaries' responses to each item. The actual number responding is contained in the parentheses following each item.

gubernatorial power states); traveling with the governor (considerably more likely in larger states); preparing first drafts of gubernatorial speeches or messages (more prevalent in smaller states and moderate and low gubernatorial power states); and recommending media events (more likely in larger states). In sum, the press secretaries of the larger states seem to get more directly involved with the governor by traveling with him or her and seeking to create media events. In the smaller states with weaker governorships, the press secretary seems to become even a greater focal point in the office by serving as the media contact/clearance person for staff as well as the governor, and by writing basic drafts of gubernatorial copy.

The fourth cluster (13–16) contains activities which suggest an even more powerful and important role for the press secretary. Here, he or she becomes spokesman for the administration by issuing statements in his or her own name (extremely more likely in larger states and, to a certain extent, in the more powerful governors' offices), by reviewing departmental and agency media releases, and by preparing promotional materials. While there are several other volunteered activities, they did not seem to fall into any pattern.

Obviously, the data suggests that certain patterns were discernible in the functions which the governors' press secretaries performed. However, these are only tendencies and there are certainly exceptions to each which reflect the idiosyncratic relationship between particular governors and their press secretaries. Overall, the press secretaries performed certain base-line functions for governors, but their extent of involvement in other activities within the governors' offices and in state government varied. Even in performing these base-line functions, there were different approaches used by the governor and the press secretary. One approach could certainly be categorized as responsive to outside queries and requests from within the office, but in general to take a low-key view of the role. Conversely, others took a more aggressive view and sought to stimulate or create media opportunities for the governor and coordinate "an overall approach to communications including both activities normally performed by press secretaries and activities, such as mail and public contacts, that are not normally performed by press secretaries."[12] This responsive-aggressive dichotomy is not as stark or mutually exclusive across the states as the definitions would imply, but does capture a basic difference in philosophy that governors and their press secretaries can and do have in approaching their jobs.

Another distinctive dichotomy that seems to flow from the data and observers' views of the press secretaries' functions concerns the image held by others of the press secretary. One pattern places the press secretary very close to the governor, involved in and helping out with basic gubernatorial activities—but all in the governor's name. In contrast, some press secretaries moved into a broader role in which they surfaced as personalities in their own right, with functions reaching outside the governor's office and into politics, policy, and administration in state government.

One observer has indicated further that "the key to professionalizing press relations is to hire a press officer who is capable of providing policy advice and to involve him directly in the decision-making process."[13] As an example of what the lack of such an involvement can mean, witness the following on Governor Carey's press relations:

> During Mr. Laird's regime [the former press secretary], reporters complained that he was not part of Mr. Carey's inner circle of advisers and therefore did

not sit in on many of the policy-making sessions that resulted in news. When reporters would call Mr. Laird later for details, he was not able to give them the kind of interpretation of Mr. Carey's thinking that they needed to know.[14]

In any or all of these interpretations of the press secretary's role, he or she clearly plays an important part of any gubernatorial administration. And critical to the performance of this role is the relationship between the governor and the press secretary. As one press secretary stated it:

> It is important for the governor to understand and appreciate that good press relations can make or break an administration. It is imperative that the press secretary and the governor have a good rapport and that the press secretary be assured of ready access to the governor and to policy decisions and other activities within the administration.[15]

But this only highlights the ambivalence that attends the press secretaries' role, an ambivalence based on his or her two constituencies: the governor and the media. There is a built-in conflict in trying to serve these two constituencies which can only be exacerbated when the governor's "man" has been a peer in the capitol house press corps. Another press secretary offered this suggestion on the dilemma:

> The best advice I would offer is that the press secretary be an effective advocate of his two constituencies . . . to represent the media's attitude before the governor and to argue the governor's point of view effectively to the news media.[16]

However there is a larger point to address here, the press secretary's ethical standards. Such standards are based on his "assumed obligations to the public . . . [as he] personifies the politician's obligation to keep the public informed." This aspect of the press secretary's role runs into the public's basic skepticism of government and politics, and the governor's own view that this person is *his* press secretary.[17]

The cross pressures on the press secretary are significant not only to the performance of that particular function, but to the governor's office and its ability to perform. Much of the press and public views of the governor and his performance flow from this office. As one former governor indicated—"Image, which is filtered through or created by the media, is all important—not only in reelection but in ability to govern."[18]

Governors and Their Public Role

Up to this point, the chapter has focused on how governors perform their public role—by the amount of time spent on it; how arduous it is to them; how they approach the role; how they structure their offices to help fulfill the role; and their choice of press secretary and his or her role. Here we want to explore

Table 5.4. Incumbent and former governors' advice to new governors[a]

Advice	Agree (in percent)	Indifferent, no opinion (in percent)	Disagree (in percent)
1. Develop a well-advertised and managed process of meeting with citizens (63)	75	17	8
2. Hire a good speechwriter (63)	73	11	16
3. Separate personal social life from official contacts (62)	61	15	24
4. Do not schedule press conferences on a regular basis (65)	49	2	49
5. Do not attempt to keep an open door policy for the press (50)	44	10	46
6. Make sure press secretary has been in statehouse press corps (63)	21	49	30
7. Rely primarily on campaign staff to staff governor's office (64)	17	19	64

a. Sums may not total 100 percent due to rounding. Percentages are based on between fifty-two and sixty-eight former governors' responses to each item. The actual number responding is contained in the parentheses following each item.

more directly how the governors themselves view this role by examining the advice they would give newly elected governors based on their own experience as governors.

In the course of the 1976 surveys, all incumbent and former governors were provided a list of items which represented various suggestions often provided to newly elected governors. Not all items were presented to both groups but there was sufficient overlap to obtain some understanding of their viewpoint (see Table 5.4).

The governors clearly agree that they should develop a well-advertised and managed process of citizen contacts and hire a good speechwriter (1–2). There was also solid agreement that office and home activities must be separated (3). So, the governors seem to be saying that the public role is most necessary yet certain safeguards and strategies must be undertaken—organize it, get professional help and do not let it interfere with your personal life.

Such consensus disappears once advice about press relations is involved, i.e., holding regularly scheduled press conferences and having an open door to the press. Here the governors are split in their views, with governors who have served since 1970 being more likely to suggest holding regular press conferences and to have an open door policy for the press. The more recent the tenure in office, the more ready for a regularized and open working relationship with the press.

Finally, when searching for governor's office staff, the governors' advice is split on whether or not to look to the statehouse press corps for a press secretary, but most governors are strongly against using campaign personnel in staffing the office. Again, the most significant differences are tied to their tenure; governors who have served since 1970 are considerably more likely to suggest moving outside the campaign organization for staffing and away from the statehouse press corps for a press secretary. This reflects a broadening view on the governors' part of who might be called on to serve them and possibly to a larger market of individuals who are potentially interested in working with governors than had been true prior to the 1970s.

All in all, governors are highly cognizant of their public role, feel rather strongly about seeking the best assistance to aid them in fulfilling the role, and are ambivalent on how best to work with the press.

At a broader level, the governors and former governors saw the media as an important factor in their own success. On the plus side several offered strategic advice to new governors:[19]

1. Build a solid relationship with the press corps so your objectives and policies can be brought before the people of the state. In addition use the media on special occasions for carrying messages to the people of the state.

2. The press, as I viewed it, was one of my strongest allies in informing the people about important issues. The press aided me greatly in getting my views accepted by the people and others in government.

3. [A governor] should not rush to the press to explain every error—if a dangerous felon escapes, let the prison director answer. If a school bond fails, let the school people alibi. The governor should put himself on the side of the people, not the bureaucracy.

There were also several warnings offered by the governors:

1. Do not play games with the media, notwithstanding some very successful operations to the contrary.

2. A governor who is overly apprehensive or arrogant about what he sees as a hostile press and who largely ignores the press' legitimate news gathering needs until the governor's hour of need does so at his own peril.

3. (Be) honest and truthful at all times. Do not cover up material that the public is entitled to know.

4. Don't underestimate the constituency.

State-Level Media

The other side of this equation, the nature of state-level media—print, radio, and television—should also be explored to understand better the constraints on the governor in fulfilling this public role. We do not know too much about the state-level media, but that which we do know suggests some problems.

In the 1960s, former North Carolina Governor Terry Sanford reported that "many papers rely heavily on the wire services for state government coverage, but the wires, like the papers, are not able, or are not disposed, to staff their state capital bureaus with enough people to cover adequately what goes on."[20] Littlewood found state capital wire service bureaus "disgracefully understaffed," and Herzberg felt they "barely scratch the surface." However, soon to be governor Richard Lamm of Colorado felt the wires "report the ordinary well, but they have little nose or capacity for the extraordinary."[21]

Sanford further argued that this lack of staff to cover state government plus the normal space problems a newspaper faces lead to negative reporting—the newspaper fulfilling its primary function of "public watchdog."[22] Twelve years later former Pennsylvania Governor Milton Shapp echoed this point indicating a serious consequence: "I think our press today is so negative, only looking for the negative things, that they are undermining the confidence of the American people with our government itself."[23] The slide from watch dog to perpetual cynic thus has greater impact on basic support people provide government.

Of course many argue that the greatest problem lies in the location of state capitals themselves. Delmer Dunn, after studying the press in Madison, Wisconsin, argued "there are more desirable beats, other places where young people want to go. The young people who were good wanted to get out as soon as they could." Donald Herzberg, a long time political participant-observer was more pointed, "My impression is that Trenton is just a way station for ambitious young journalists and a resting place for tired old ones."[24]

This is obviously true for many states where the state capitals are not lodged in the major state city, e.g., Albany, New York; Springfield, Illinois; Sacramento, California; Olympia, Washington. But there is another group of states where the capital and major city coincide, e.g., Denver, Colorado; Atlanta, Georgia; Boston, Massachusetts. Witness this comment by former Governor Michael Dukakis: "That is not the case in Massachusetts. To begin with, the capital city is the major city. The major media sources are in Boston—television channels, major newspapers, the alternative press, the whole business. There is very heavy coverage of what goes on at the state level."[25] Thus as the old bromide has it, this problem varies from state to state—but nonetheless geographic impacts on the media-governor relationship do exist.

Governor Dukakis' comment about very heavy coverage of state government activities by the media is a fairly recent concern. In part it flows from the rise of investigative journalism à la Woodward and Bernstein where possible and actual governmental wrongdoing is pursued tenaciously. It also flows from the fact that government in general and state government in particular are now more involved in our lives and are more newsworthy than in the past. Former Florida Governor Askew points out the problem that journalistic preoccupation with government can bring: "I really do believe that almost everything we do in government is overreported. . . . Daily, the media demand answers of government, when government was never equipped to furnish the answers to every problem facing mankind."[26] In effect with more coverage, more is sought and demanded and with heightened expectations, lesser achievement is found; another story.

A sidelight on this increasing coverage in some state capitals is the phenomenon observed in the Washington, D.C. capital press: "pack journalism." Former Governor Dan Walker observed: "The reason pack journalism prevails is that some guy who, for some reason or another, the reporters think is knowledgeable says, 'that's what's happening'; and then that's it. It becomes a self-fulfilling prophecy. You throw up your hands; there is nothing you can do about it."[27]

Table 5.5. Media coverage of state government

	During legislative sessions (average number covering)	Between legislative sessions (average number covering)	Ratio of during to between
Newspapers	14.6	8.7	1.69
Radio	6.3	4.4	1.43
Wire service	4.9	3.6	1.36
Television	4.8	3.9	1.23

Source: National Governors' Association unpublished survey, August 1979. Twenty-eight states responded to the survey. Due to the promises of confidentiality no state can be identified as a respondent.

Thus, the argument goes, new competition or a goodly number of reporters covering the state beat does not necessarily ensure better coverage, especially if they all adopt the same line of argument and file variations on the same theme.

There also seems to be a misperception in the media as to what state government is about. What Gormley argues is "a rather bizarre view of the governmental process" is the tendency of the media to provide greater coverage during legislative sessions and to staff down or disappear when the legislature is not in session. This would imply "that only the legislative branch makes decisions important enough to warrant coverage" in the view of some segments of the media.[28]

A 1979 NGA survey of the governors' press secretaries of twenty-eight states documents this drop off in coverage potential. (See Table 5.5). For these states newspapers clearly provide more coverage than do the other media—yet they also provide the greatest dropoff in coverage when the legislature is not in session. The other forms of providing media coverage also do so to a lesser extent when the legislature is not in town. Regardless of the numbers, Gormley finds poor news coverage by television and little better by newspapers in his study of forty-four newspapers and television stations in ten cities in seven different states.[29]

A variation on this media misperception of what state government is about was argued by Morgan in his intensive study of the New York State capitol press corps: "State news is too often presented as somehow filling out local political news, not as emanating from a vitally important, legitimate, *other* level of government."[30] This places state level news and analysis at the bottom of the governmental coverage list, and as an adjunct to the local news. Further much of this coverage is parochial in nature i.e. how state government activity or policy will effect this particular community.

Conclusion

This chapter has presented data on the governor's public role from the perspective of the governor's office. This is a major role for the governor and his staff to perform, for its potential for both success and failure (even outright disaster) is great. This role is one of the tools available in the governor's arsenal as he or she seeks to carry out the duties of the governorship and to enhance his or her personal ambitions.

But we would be remiss to suggest this is just a one way street, from the governor to the press and the public. Gubernatorial concerns over "pack journalism," negative reporting and inadequate media staffing do indicate the press impacts on the governors directly. Even more important are those studies, albeit few in number at present, which find the role of the media significant in agenda setting—i.e. bringing to the fore the issues with which policy makers must come to grips.[31]

At the state level Gormley found that the mass media and state political elites i.e. legislators, have at least the same general political agenda though specifics may vary,[32] and newspapers may actually set two agendas, one by the editorial page and another by the front page.[33] How a governor interacts with those setting these agendas may have much to do with the favorable coverage and image the governor and his press secretary seek for the administration.

6. Governors and Ethics

Robert Dalton

In 1973, Otto Kerner, U.S. circuit court judge and former two-term governor of Illinois, was convicted and imprisoned on charges of mail fraud and tax evasion committed while governor; Vice-President Spiro T. Agnew resigned his office after pleading *nolo contendere* to a charge of tax evasion arising from accusations of participating in conspiracy, extortion and bribery during his tenure as governor of Maryland. Four years later, in 1977, former Oklahoma Gov. David Hall entered prison after conviction of offering a bribe to a state official; Marvin Mandel of Maryland became the first sitting governor since 1924 to be convicted of criminal charges (mail fraud and racketeering); Edwin Edwards, governor of Louisiana, was implicated in the "Koreagate" scandal by accusations of accepting a $20,000 bribe, which he denied and with which he was never formally charged. In 1980 Edwards was again implicated, this time in the FBI's "Brilab" investigation of political corruption in several Southwestern states, and most recently, in 1981 former Tennessee Governor Ray Blanton was convicted along with two aides on charges of conspiracy, extortion and mail fraud in connection with liquor license kickbacks.

Such corruption is not new to the American political scene, of course,[1] but fresh evidence of its continuing character, especially on state and local levels, has seen the light of day in the past several years.[2] The Watergate and associated scandals of the Nixon administration, which were a corruption of governmental power not for monetary gain so much as for the sake of greater political power, once again focused national attention on the moral improprieties of government officials. But the continuing unethical behavior on the part of certain state and local officials has also contributed to the calls since the late 1960s for more honest government, tougher laws and stricter enforcement against political wrongdoing, as well as a heightened sense of moral responsibility on the part of state, local and national office-holders and office-seekers.

Therefore, that governors of American states in the past decade would be sensitive to questions of proper conduct by themselves and their administrations is not surprising. Interviews with the fifteen former governors who left office since 1976 clearly support this.[3] This chapter investigates in what ways these governors were attuned to moral questions in state government and how they understood these issues. It argues that fundamentally, moral questions impinge upon the governors as managerial concerns.

Ethics and Morality

Before a closer look at the interviews, a brief definitional exercise is necessary. From E. E. Banfield,[4] "corruption" means either personal corruption or official corruption. Personal corruption occurs when an officeholder betrays the public interest for his private gain. For example, a governor might cause a contract to be given to a firm which will "kickback" money paid to him in return. Official corruption occurs when the officeholder serves the public interest as he understands it but in a manner which consciously violates a law or accepted standard of behavior. Perhaps the Nixonian abuse of "national security" to justify illegal wiretapping and burglary is a prime example of official corruption. George Benson's definition seems to combine the two notions: political corruption is "all illegal or unethical use of governmental authority as a result of consideration of personal or political gain."[5]

A second clarification is in reference to the term "code of ethics," which usually means a specification of acceptable behavior on the part of government officials. The term as used is not entirely accurate, although it has wide use in politics and in numerous professions. As often used, "code of ethics" really would better be called a "code of practice" or a "code of morality," spelling out specific behavior on the part of officials. For example, officials must annually and publicly report their income tax returns or file a financial disclosure form or refuse all gifts over $25.00 in value. In other words, the codes lay down the rules of governmental morality.

However, when one begins to ask why these actions are prescribed or proscribed, one moves from "morality" to "ethics," which is really the theoretical and conceptual exercise by which one attempts to go beyond the rules to the general principles, or a set of moral values, by which particular actions are permitted or prohibited. For example, when Reubin Askew talks of government service as placing the governor in a fiduciary relationship with the public, he is engaging in ethical discourse. If he then goes on to say that therefore he as governor should file full and complete financial disclosure, he is making a moral judgement.[6] By and large, the governors tend to think morally more so than ethically.

The line distinguishing ethics and morality is not always clear, of course, as the interviews reveal, nor is the relationship between the two as simple as the above paragraph might suggest. While a certain moral stricture might well be deduced from an ethical principle, the process can work inductively in the reverse. Certain problems that have not arisen before and that must be handled specifically may well generate thought that will produce new ethical principles that will serve as guides to future action. Therefore, the relationship between ethics and morality has a dialectical quality to it. This is especially true because morality often rests on custom or habit, and when one probes to find philosophical or valuational justification for a certain moral rule, he cannot always find that defense. Therefore, one might eliminate the rule, or alternatively, construct the missing justification. For the governors, this dialectical quality of the ethics-morality relationship is most apparent when they discuss the ambiguity present in many situations calling for ethical or moral judgement.

It's Not Easy to Decide

How then do these former governors understand the problem of ethics in government? The first question that might arise is how difficult is it to determine if a certain act or course of behavior is ethically or morally acceptable. Some see the situation rather straightforwardly. Reubin Askew: "We all know what is right and wrong. If you have to rationalize a wrong decision, you're in trouble."[7] For James Edwards, what is right and wrong is fairly easy to distinguish,[8] and Martin J. Schreiber adds that the ethics matter is "reasonably easy" to deal with, if one goes into office with a standard. "Once you do that [set a standard], I think it makes it a lot easier."[9]

But more of the former governors indicated the ambiguity present in determining acceptable behavior. Edwards, for example, also remarks that other people might differ with him on what is right and what is wrong.[10] Harvey Wollman observes that definitions of ethics can vary from abstract values to interpersonal relationships; therefore, an individual governor needs to enter office with his own well-developed conscience as a guide.[11] Jerry Apodaca states that whatever a governor does for a business in the state, e.g., deposit the state's money in a certain bank, some people will wonder if a deal was made between the governor and the bank.[12] Similarly, James Holshouser, Jr., speaks of "honest graft": a governor takes action Y through friend A rather than through person B because friend A can do the job as cheaply and efficiently as person B. Yet this behavior may well look as if predicated on a corrupt bargain.[13]

The note of ambiguity emerges strikingly but enigmatically in the Milton Shapp interview. Speaking of the negativism and sensationalism of the news media on matters of corruption in government, Shapp remarks that neither the press nor the public really understands how government works.[14] This is rather difficult to decipher, but one inference might well be that government officials may have to operate in certain ways that might seem corrupt, but are not and are necessary for the government to function.

Such a notion, by the way, has had scholarly precedent. For example James Q. Wilson in an important look at corruption in the states suggested that one explanation for its presence is that the separation of powers and the checks and balances mechanisms of American government engender efforts "to concert the action of legally independent branches of government through the exchange of favors."[15] Between Shapp's complaint and Holshouser's mention of "honest graft" there is latitude for ambiguity to emerge because the two men seem to suggest, as Wilson argues, that sometimes to make the gears of government turn, a little lubrication is necessary. Whether the problem is red tape to cut, too many agencies to go through, or too many permits to acquire, the temptation to grease the wheels may be irresistible.

This ambiguous character of many actions taken by governors and other officials may explain, then, why at the 1974 National Governors' Conference when there was a panel discussion on ethics, there appeared to be a tone of defensiveness permeating the remarks. (Granted, ascribing emotional states to speakers from a printed transcript is hazardous.) A rather extreme but somewhat typical attitude was ironically expressed by Marvin Mandel: we need to do something about "the corrupters, for without them there isn't too much corruption."[16]

Given this ambiguity, how does it manifest itself to these governors? Interestingly but not surprisingly, the difficulty inherent in judging morality and ethicality does not lie in convolutions of abstract thought but in concrete decisions. One example is the matter of gifts to a governor: is it right for him to accept them, or are they to be suspected as a prelude to something corrupt? For example, David Pryor feels any gift, especially money, should be reported quickly. But should it be accepted at all? What if personal friends give him a tackle box with lures: should he suspect their intentions?[17] Blair Lee notes the problem of distinguishing gifts to the state and those to the governor himself. Surely intra-family gifts should be exempt from reporting requirements, but what about two tickets to the University of Maryland football game? Does that mean he is now obligated to the university for some yet unspoken favor?[18]

Similarly, there is ambiguity with financial disclosure, enacted by many states in the past decade and endorsed by those governors who specifically mention it. But some wonder if it can be too stringent. Lee fears this especially for those who serve by appointment in lower level jobs or for parttime legislators, for whom disclosures of their financial records might reveal, unfairly, legal or business clients. However, Lee looks askance at the alternative: fulltime professional legislators.[19] James Exon extends the point: to some degree, financial disclosure is an invasion of privacy, but as a person committed to public service, he accepts the cost. But what about people a governor appoints to serve only a few years at his behest? How fair is financial disclosure to them, especially since many will be making a financial sacrifice taking a government salary.[20] His comment is echoed by several other interviewees: Apodaca, Robert Bennett, Edwards, and Holshouser, for example.[21]

The fear raised is that persons will refuse to serve in government if financial disclosure is made too strict, but the limited empirical evidence suggests this worry is overblown though not without foundation. The financial reporting requirements of the 1973 Alabama ethics legislation, which called for disclosure by any official in the state earning over $12,000 per annum, caused many municipal officials to threaten to resign.[22] But a report on the Ohio experience with its ethics legislation suggests financial disclosure has not driven people away; in fact, some have welcomed the opportunity to demonstrate their integrity. There have been no mass resignations, not even by uncompensated members of various boards.[23]

This concern with the ambiguity raised by financial disclosure requirements is found also in that discussion at the 1974 National Governors' Conference. Tom McCall of Oregon and Cecil Andrus of Idaho, among others, raised the matter of extending conflict-of-interest regulations too far, e.g., to include uncompensated commission members.[24] Mills Godwin of Virginia was worried that financial disclosure might be an invasion of privacy.[25] Jack Williams (Arizona), Philip Noel (Rhode Island), Dale Bumpers (Arkansas), and Winfield Dunn (Tennessee), all were disturbed that financial disclosure might harm part-time legislators economically and that the result might be full-time professional legislators.[26]

This aspect of the ambiguity factor is underlined by another detail mentioned several times, one which Exon called the "fishbowl life."[27] Political figures are constantly in the public eye, so that appearance of honesty is equally important, maybe more so, than its reality. This can lead to shows of ostensible morality in the form of financial disclosure which may obscure more subtle corruption. Askew sees disclosure as a big step but no panacea: it should at least keep officials out of clearly marginal situations.[28] Holshouser affirms that disclosure is "illusory" if the person in question is basically dishonest.[29] Again, from the 1974 National Governors' Conference, Williams seconded by Noel placed critical importance on the character of the people who serve in government: "No law will magically give birth to ethical men."[30]

There is also a miscellaneous resolution adopted at the 1975 National Governors' Conference which eliminated gifts to the governors from the host governor, his state, or "otherwise" except for "souvenirs of nominal value."[31] The "otherwise" went unspecified but one might easily infer that it referred to lobbyists, interest groups, or corporations, especially as it followed several Governors' Conferences in which the governors were provided with rather lavish treatment and gifts. The resolution suggests the governors as a body were concerned not only about whether they should accept these gifts, but also about their public image.

Further exacerbating the problem of appearance of honesty versus its reality is the occasionally misinformed or sensationalist character of the news media. Shapp was disgusted by the press once when front page exposure was given to a $1,400 misappropriation by a state employee, while a $330 million saving in state government was relegated to the back pages.[32] Dan Walker also criticizes the press in this regard. Paraphrasing: "My administration looked for fraud in the Medicaid program and found it. Then the press blamed us for it."[33]

The ambiguity the governors found in examining morality in government may in fact be inherent in representative government. First, in state government more than in national government, elected officials are less likely to be professional officeholders, so here the "citizen-politician" may still exist. The legislator serves only parttime and has other income, and the governor may well return to private life upon leaving office. Both have to make decisions on affairs that do or will affect their material well-being, and such decisions often appear rooted in the official's consideration of that fact, even if he solely decided the matter on its merits. Thus, how easily can a legislator who is an insurance agent sitting on the legislative insurance committee separate self-interest from the public interest? An energetic governor works hard at his state's economic development. Will not any number of grateful enterprises be ready to offer him employment when his term is over or select his law firm to represent them? Second, in representative government, elected officeholders openly and properly reflect certain interests, whether economic, political, or geographical. Is it necessarily wrong for them, once in office, to make policies in favor of these interests? The governors did not explicitly point to these qualities of representative government, but they do seem to silently underlie their discussion of moral ambiguity in government.

Where the Danger Is

Related to but distinct from the matter of ambiguity is the question: what is the major threat to the integrity of governors and other officials? Dukakis offers a framework within which to locate the threat: it is a function of the standards and guidelines a governor promulgates for his administration.[34] For Askew, the threat is more specific and explicit: cash, because cash leaves no trails.[35] The dominant opinion, however, focuses on the threat created by subtle pressures made and bargains offered.

Edwards was on guard for people offering a subtle quid pro quo, because "integrity is something that is pretty absolute and you can't be a little bit right."[36] Lee sees the ethics "cutting edge" as the subtle ways in which friends of a governor try to use that friendship, as in the case of Mandel, whom Lee thinks was taken advantage of by friends who were "not on the take but on the make."[37] Wollman is concerned with the corruption that comes because a governor just runs with the crowd, only wanting to retain office, rather than standing for some fundamental principles.[38]

Both Holshouser and Walker point to the opportunity for quiet, sub rosa deals in the regulatory, licensing and contracting activities of state government, e.g., alcoholic beverage control or highway bid letting. Walker notes that these areas of governmental action contain the "threat to efficient and fair operation of state government."[39] Interestingly, their insight here has found scholarly support in an examination of political corruption in economic terms by J. R. Shackleton. He argues that these powers of government constitute a scarce economic resource, so that suppliers of regulated and/or licensed products and services will create a demand for special treatment and at least some officials will supply it for a mutually agreed upon price.[40]

Precisely this concern for subtle corruption has been a prime motivation in the efforts by states, especially in the 1970s, to tighten their laws on campaign contributions, financial disclosure, conflict-of-interest, and lobbying. Further evidence of gubernatorial concern with subtle rather than crassly overt corruption is an examination of a summary of 1976 state of the state addresses.[41] The governors indicate awareness of widespread public cynicism and distrust, and they speak of less government, more efficient government, and a streamlined government.[42] Speaking of "accountability," eleven governors called for new or amended legislation restricting campaign contributions, tightening financial disclosure requirements, clarifying conflict of interest rules, and toughening lobbying regulations. Two others had proposals concerning open meetings and freedom of information, matters certainly related to preventing subtle corruption, and one other asked for the establishment of a special prosecutor's office.[43]

This gubernatorial concern with the threat of subtle corruption goes to the heart of their consideration of morality in government. Probably many of the former governors would concur with Askew's statement that government service places the officer in a fiduciary relationship with the public, i.e., that the officer holds the public's trust to serve it and not betray it. While crass offers of cash in return for favors might be easily resisted, more subtle corruption might be less easily withstood precisely because it might not always be recognized or acknowledged. This might be especially true with campaign contributions, conflict of interest matters, or lobbying activities.

But subtle or not, corruption can begin to weaken people's faith in government, because they believe that the officers of government are not serving the people's interest but merely pursuing personal or special interest goals. In time, whether or not corruption touches the governor himself, it may well seriously undermine his ability to govern. This subtle corruption then is not only ethically wrong per se because it violates a fiduciary relationship, but also because it weakens the governor politically and administratively, a line of thought which is probably in the governors' minds.

How to Prevent Corruption

One of the key questions in a governor's role as manager is span of control, and a similar question emerges with regard to morality. Should the governor assume responsibility for proper behavior only for his immediate staff, or should that responsibility extend to the whole state administration? On this count, there was little consensus. Apadaca, Askew, Edwards, Exon, Holshouser, and Wollman, for example, felt a definite responsibility for policing the behavior of their immediate staff, but saw as an impossible task taking direct accountability for the entire executive branch.[44] Bennett, Dukakis, Lee, Rampton, and Walker, on the other hand, felt to some degree an obligation to monitor the behavior of the executive branch personnel.[45] Bennett, for example, issued memoranda on the acceptability of various gifts and on the appropriateness of various political activities.[46]

However, the division is not clear cut. Those governors who accepted mainly a responsibility only for their staff were aware that what standards they declared for those persons had ramifications throughout their administration. Conversely, those governors who took on a sense of responsibility for the whole executive branch were not so naive as to believe their conceptions of acceptable practice would be necessarily followed by every state official.

What is important in this regard is the governor's setting forth a clear and well-defined standard of what he considers ethically acceptable behavior. Governors on both sides of the above question perceive this as a key preventive measure against corruption, though not foolproof by any means. Bennett declared a code of conduct for all state employees which actually extended then current legislation on conflict of interest and campaign financing.[47] Dukakis stresses the importance of announcing clear guidelines to all staff and employees, of setting a "general [moral] tone and attitude" for state government.[48] Exon notes the need to try to insure that government workers show no favoritism or engage in wrongdoing.[49] Lee, entering office after Spiro Agnew and on the heels of Marvin Mandel, felt an urgent pressure to set a high standard of morality, issuing an executive order with very strict, even "brutal" guidelines.[50]

The question that should be immediately clear at this point is: what is the source of the governor's code of conduct? But the answer is not clear from the interviews. A number of the interviewees did not really answer the question which sought to discover if they entered office with a code or set of expectations regarding proper behavior. Those that did, did not specify the source or really the nature and shape of those codes, i.e., the ethical principles underlying specifically permitted or prohibited behavior. One can only speculate that the governors' perceptions of acceptable practices were mixtures of personal preferences, community mores, precedent, careful thought, understanding of current legislation, and other elements. Less speculative is the conclusion that codes of conduct could differ markedly from one governor to the next, putting state employees, the legislature, the press, and the public generally in a confusing situation.

Assuming a governor does convey to his staff and administration a code of ethically acceptable behavior, he still has no guarantee that all the persons covered will faithfully follow those guidelines, as well as ones specified in legislation. That point carries these governors to a second preventative measure, albeit again not foolproof: the critical importance of selecting personnel who, to all judgements, are not only capable, competent and expert, but who are also fundamentally honest and trustworthy. Askew sets the foundation with his remark about government service being a fiduciary relationship with the public.[51] Holshouser adds that the public has to rely on a governor's and his appointees' sense of honesty, their character and their ability to spot problem behavior and eliminate it.[52] Schreiber apparently sought people who wanted to leave politics with "a good feeling" about themselves morally. His rule for them: "do what you feel is right and exercise common sense." This should help guide one through specific questions though the temptations will not disappear.[53]

Setting an overall tone and choosing personnel with integrity are the two basic measures these governors offer as preventive action. As was noted above, they also generally endorse legislation or have promulgated guidelines that set forth specific regulations concerning financial disclosure, gifts, campaign finance and the like. But clearly, they look beyond paper requirements or legalities; they seek persons with "self-imposed standards or norms of conduct . . . which are beyond those imposed by the written law."[54]

But How is All This Important?

At this point then, a helpful exercise might be to summarize the dominant findings thus far:

1. Morality in government as seen by the ex-governors is not simple, but an area of political life marked by ambiguity and difficulty in clearly distinguishing proper behavior from improper.

2. The ambiguity resides in concrete considerations: gifts, financial disclosure, invasion of privacy, appearance vs. reality, and the media handling of these matters. It would also appear to rest in the very nature of representative government.

3. The major ethical threat to governmental integrity is not so much crass offers of cash but subtle bargains and trade-offs.

4. A major problem facing a governor is whether he feels responsible for the behavior of only his immediate staff or of also the whole administration.

5. Two fundamental and primary measures of prevention of corruption that governors utilize are: (a) setting a tone of ethicality and promulgating clear guidelines of acceptable behavior; and (b) carefully appointing personnel who are honest and trustworthy.

6. Though a governor is likely to enter office with a code of conduct or set of expectations regarding proper behavior, the shape, nature and source of that code is unclear.

But having come thus far, let me ask what perhaps should have been the first question: how worrisome, relatively, is the problem of ethics and morality to the governors? Clearly it bears some weight, because the interviewees seemed to respond to the earlier questions with care and sensitivity. Unfortunately, the governors were not asked directly the question, but other evidence suggests that as a matter of daily routine, moral and ethical questions are of relative insignificance. For example, when one examines the proceedings of the National Governors' Conferences of 1973 through 1977 and a policy statement generated by the 1972 meeting, only in the Watergate year of 1974 did there occur any major examination by the governors of ethics and state government. The 1973 meeting did include a brief discussion on government and ethics, but it mostly referred to Watergate and national campaign financing and was in the context of a panel seminar on how the news media view the governors.[55] One intriguing note: the 1973 program listed a closed executive session in which morality in government was to be discussed.[56]

When the 1974 Conference did turn its attention to ethics, the seminar tended to become a "show-and-tell" session in which various governors related what they and/or their state had done in promulgating codes of proper conduct.[57] The governors did adopt an ethics resolution, which was couched in broad language about the need to restore trust in state government. Two key provisions were calls for campaign finance reform in the states, including pilot studies of public financing of candidates, and for "stringent ethical codes" including financial disclosure provisions, conflict of interest regulations, and independent enforcement. The resolution also urged states to legislate open meeting requirements and tighter registration of lobbyists in state capitals.[58]

What is interesting about this policy resolution is that it was not given separate, independent status, but placed in the larger policy resolution on management. This suggests the assembled governors in 1974 perceived moral violations and the treatment thereof as primarily a management control issue, not as an issue of underlying corruption significant in its own right. To some degree also, the governors seemed to deal with the matter as a political issue of the times. Also interesting is that the 1974 ethics resolution was again adopted by the 1975, 1976, and 1977 meetings, and it remains in the policy section on executive management and fiscal affairs. The later transcripts show no discussion of the resolution, suggesting the governors retained it more by inertia than by conscious deliberation.[59]

What all this suggests is an emerging though really unsurprising conclusion about governors and ethics: ethics as an independent philosophical issue is of relatively little import, as these men as a group are not philosophers or even moral crusaders. They are managers, politicians, problem solvers, and policy setters. Moral questions become important primarily as and when they affect and impinge upon these other roles. For example, as stated above, only in the climactic Watergate year of 1974 did there occur extended open discussion of moral issues at the National Governors' Conference, and the ethics resolution adopted then was retained in later years apparently by inertia alone. It is as if once the fever of Watergate passed, the governors' attention shifted to more immediately pressing matters. Moreover, when one reviews the six findings listed above, one is struck by the primarily practical orientation of the governors toward moral questions.

This pragmatic depiction of the governors might seem overly harsh, but it is not meant to be judgmental. For the governor as manager, moral questions are not philosophical issues. Rather they call for concrete and practical action that will not hamper the governor's administration of state government, harm him politically, or seriously undermine the public's confidence in state government. They are problems to be handled, not crusades to be fought.

Part IV. The Managerial Role

7. The Governor as Manager

Lynn R. Muchmore

All state constitutions describe the essence of the governorship in terms of the *executive* functions. The governor is "chief executive," with responsibility to "see that the laws are faithfully executed" by the cluster of organizations and sub-organizations that comprise the executive branch. Until recently, a substantial gap existed between the level of authority that governors enjoyed in practice and the much more expansive authority needed to control and direct the state bureaucracies. Lipson, writing forty years ago, alluded to the governor as a "figurehead" who was becoming a "leader" only as constitutions and statutes were amended to align gubernatorial powers with the needs of a true executive.[1] The rapid changes in state government that have occurred since 1960 extend also into the judicial and legislative branches, but the most visible and controversial change has been executive reorganization. Since 1965, twenty-two states have redesigned their executive branch, and in virtually all of these cases the result has been a consolidation of power in the hands of the governor.

While it is quite clear that the formal powers, obligations, and responsibilities of the governors have been modified in favor of greater executive control, it is more difficult to understand how these changes are being translated into a new pattern of policymaking and administrative behavior. Scholarly works on the governorship are relatively few, so that political scientists have little baseline information from which to draw contrasts. The governor's relationship to the executive branch has never been a simple one to describe or understand, and the literature is plagued by stereotypes that illuminate one aspect of gubernatorial behavior while obscuring other aspects that seem equally important. Some of the simpler models of the governorship have had far-reaching impact on the techniques and objectives of reorganization, and they have been adopted uncritically in the rhetoric of political campaigns as standards of gubernatorial conduct. One result has been a disturbing divergence between the kinds of executive performance that governors can be expected to achieve in reality and the somewhat exaggerated expectations that proceed out of administrative and organizational theory.

What is State Government?

Among the more appealing lines of reason that underwrite executive reorganization, for example, is the assumption that the executive branch can be treated as a single organization. As a single organization it will yield to the classical principles of management. Effective management requires attention to span of control and chain of command, principles that were routinely broken as state government grew in its topsy-turvy way through decades of expansion with no attention to central design. Organization, and with it management, could only be restored by sweeping away the old structures and beginning anew with a well-ordered hierarchy of departments and divisions ultimately accountable to the chief executive. Out of this comes the image of the manager-governor, whose vision of the public interest is the agenda that the organization is supposed to follow. The governor relates to the streamlined departments and bureaus as a superior dealing with subordinates, and he is given such important powers as appointment and dismissal to insure control.

The antithesis of this reasoning is simply that the state executive branch is not and cannot be a single organization, neatly constructed charts notwithstanding. Unity of organization implies unity of purposes and goals, and representative democracy insures that the objectives executive agencies are obliged to pursue will continue to arrive in a haphazard manner as new laws are written and old laws are changed to fit the legislature's interpretation of contemporary needs and problems. The executive branch is a collection of many organizations seeking many different objectives that cannot be neatly arranged because of the pluralistic interests they represent. There is and should be effective management in the executive branch, but in practice it is decentralized because of the enormous diversity of duties and responsibilities that have been thrust upon government by the public. The governor is a political leader with enormous influence among the organizations of the executive branch, but it is misleading to characterize him as a manager of the executive branch.

Both of these accounts are obviously caricatures, but the complexity of the governorship is made evident in the fact that each contains elements of truth. This is so, we argue here, not because some governors choose to be managers while others incline toward a different role—although differences in personal style are important. Rather it is so because no governor can deal with all elements of the executive bureaucracy in the same way. He may intervene directly in the affairs of some agencies, but only if he ignores others.

The Governor's Role

In practice he can neither manage the executive branch in the comprehensive and thorough-going way suggested by the first model nor can he totally escape the responsibility for central administration as suggested by the second.

The governor fulfills his executive role through a mixture of four relationships, a mixture that is determined in part by legal and institutional factors outside his control and in part by his own judgement. Over these relationships hover two fundamental facts that we will elaborate later. First, all governors are elected to represent the interests of the public, and as politicians they must nurture a belief by the public that they are in fact fulfilling that duty. Secondly, state government is a large and diverse machinery with enormous inertia that will outlast the administration of any governor. Unlike private sector executives, governors cannot persuade those responsible for day-to-day operation that the survival of the enterprise depends upon their support for their program.

Basic Stewardship: The Bottom Line

At minimum, governors want to insure that the business of any given executive agency is conducted in a way that cannot be labeled corrupt or grossly incompetent. The stigma of ethical breakdown in even the remotest bureau of the executive branch attaches in some degree to the governor, and exposure by the press can be politically expensive.

The pesticide applicator licensing program in a state department of agriculture may have little or no priority in the mind of the chief executive; in fact, he may be unaware that it exists. But if an inspector in that program is caught accepting payoffs and scandal follows, the governor will find it difficult to escape blame in the public mind, even though he has no direct control over the department or its personnel.

Former Governor Reubin Askew of Florida is among those who emphasize the "fiduciary" dimension of public office, in which the elected official becomes a trustee on behalf of the body politic.[2] Whether moved by a positive view of the governor as an elected trustee or by a more selfish determination to avoid the repercussions of bad publicity, governors define their relationship with many state agencies in terms of ethical discipline.

Response to Crisis

Beyond an assurance of integrity, governors must be concerned that executive agencies can respond to sudden demands that may be placed upon them by natural or man-made crisis. Many governors have found that disaster preoccupies their administration. Consider this summary by former Governor Milton Shapp of Pennsylvania, who reviews the major issues of his term this way:

> Starting in 1971, I had to come back from Puerto Rico and the National Governors' Conference because we had a flood in eastern Pennsylvania; then [Hurricane] Agnes in 1972. In 1973 we had minor emergencies, but nothing like Agnes. In 1974 there was a national truckers' strike in which I became heavily involved. In 1975 there was [Hurricane] Eloise, which was followed by a very severe winter. In 1976 we had very severe weather again; and in 1977 we had the Johnstown flood. In the spring of 1978 we had high snow drifts again. Between that and 1974 we had major ice storms in the western part of the state. We also had fires; both the West and the East had a drought one year. The gypsy moth came to visit us for about four years running.[3]

Preparedness is a much more serious concern in some areas than in others, but it is certain that wherever an emergency response is required the governor is viewed as the spokesman and the person in charge. If the response is ineffective or inappropriate the governor must account for the failure. He may have no day-to-day communication with the criminal justice agencies, and care little about the substance of criminal justice policy. But he has a vested interest in the capacity of his highway patrol to contain civil disturbance or the National Guard's ability to protect property and preserve order after a natural disaster.

The Administrative Functions

Gubernatorial relationship with much of the executive branch is administrative routine imposed by state or federal law under which the chief executive plays a perfunctory role. Some states require that the governor approve all public land purchases. Federal grant in aid provisions require that the governor select the agency that will be responsible for administering jointly funded programs, and that he approve for transmittal to a federal agency the formal plan of operations that will guide its execution. Typically, governors alone may exercise the power of extradition.

The administrative functions, together with the two levels of concern described previously, are the basis for what might be called a custodial relationship with the organizations of the executive branch. While custodial duties may require that the governor occasionally intervene in the affairs of a particular bureau or department, they do not define an active role on the part of the governor. He is a guardian of the public interest as that interest is defined by statute or other sources of governmental purpose and scope. He does not seek to redefine the ends of government; he only seeks to safeguard the integrity of the means. In most administrations the custodial relationship completely describes the governor's limited involvement with the bulk of the executive agencies, and in some administrations he does not step beyond it. Here the governor is a problem solver, and as such he deals with the office primarily from a reactive posture. Some candidly admit that the image of the governor's office as an indispensable hub around which turn the affairs of the executive branch is a gross exaggeration.

I've always said this—I think it's true—that if a governor didn't show up for work for six weeks the state would run very well without him if he had a good crew. It could go on for six months if you delegated authority to sign the 200 pieces of correspondence that go across the desk in a normal day— about 200 in our office. So a governor wouldn't have to do anything, really, if he didn't want to.[4]

The Managerial Relationship

While we have argued that the crucial custodial relationships are sufficient to describe most gubernatorial involvement with executive branch organizations, those relationships are peripheral to the executive branch reforms of the past two decades. Reorganization, and the procedural changes that have come with it, have been designed to place governors in a strong position to direct, control, plan, organize, evaluate, and coordinate the activities of the executive branch— to fulfill the role of manager in the classical sense.

Here the governor is looked to as an active and superior force who imposes upon the far-flung bureaucracy a coherent fabric of goals and objectives and then guides the executive machinery toward these. He is more than a problem solver concerned that government functions smoothly and without corruption; he is a policy maker who sets the agenda for executive action and shapes priorities that affect decision making at every level. These are the governors that Sabato refers to as "the emerging new breed."[5] According to the stereotype, the governor leads and the executive branch follows. The announced purpose of executive reform has been to build for the governors a bureaucratic structure that can be managed and to give the governors the capacity that is necessary for them to succeed.

Reality at the Top

How realistic is the management image as a standard for the contemporary governorship? How do the governors themselves use the newly awarded powers of appointment, the modern and more sophisticated budgeting systems, and the streamlined organization charts that are supposed to hold the key to expanded influence in the executive branch? Has structural reform really affected behavior, or is the same old game being played under modified rules?

That gubernatorial influence has been expanded follows these reforms almost by definition, and that expansion has been healthy. But resort to the language of management to describe changes in the governorships invites exaggeration. The custodial relationships continue to predominate, as they probably should. The most significant change has been wrought in the governors' self-perception. By endowing the governorships with institutional support for manager-like activity, we have encouraged governors to act like managers.

A Case in Point

Some of these difficulties can be illustrated by reference to an example those who have worked at the gubernatorial level will find uncomfortably realistic. Imagine a governor who has been elected to office in part because of an emphatic commitment to renewed and vigorous growth in rural areas and small towns. He begins his administration with a panoramic view of the executive branch, determined to use his powers as its manager to impress upon the organization this new set of priorities and goals. Perhaps he has experience in the business world, where he is accustomed to the management directives and decision memoranda that spell a major shift in marketing strategy or the adoption of a new product line. During initial conversations with state officials he finds these facts:

1. The Highway Commission of the Transportation Department decided more than a decade ago to favor the completion of urban interstate segments and reduce their commitment to new primary and secondary system projects. That principle has been applied consistently, and it continues through a six-year transportation plan that schedules funding years in advance.

2. The Higher Education Board has adopted a policy that calls for the phasing out of satellite campuses whenever enrollment falls below a target threshold; this in favor of investment in three urban campuses.

3. The business recruitment team of the Department of Industry no longer works with communities that do not have a county development corporatiou, after years of experience showed that the absence of local infrastructure undermined state efforts. Only a few rural counties have county development corporations.

4. The state legislature has enacted a law that prohibits rural electric cooperatives for servicing new business customers sited within five miles of any municipality whose population exceeds two thousand. Effectively, this means that new industry is denied the lower utility rates that might otherwise be available in rural areas.

5. Pursuant to federal environmental legislation, the Environmental Management Division of the Natural Resources Bureau has greatly strengthened restrictions on industrial waste disposal, so that the type of manufacturing business that the state finds easiest to attract must choose between the exorbitant cost of building its own treatment plants and the much less expensive alternative of linking into large urban systems.

This governor will realize after only a few months in office that the executive branch, however it is organized, obeys no coherent set of goals or objectives. The responsibilities assigned to government are not the single product of one well-organized mind. They are the cumulative debris of legislative battles, court compromises, interest group demands, bureaucratic tradition, and federal mandate that has arrived from different perspectives, for different reasons, and at different points in time. Each one has an organizational counterpart, and each organization or sub-organization has its own constituency. Few of these are as concerned about the overall architecture of government as they are with the narrow sliver of public interest they believe they represent. All respect the governorship in the abstract and all treat the governor personally with deference, but none rely upon the governor to furnish them with an agenda.

Suddenly the task that seemed before to require only a will and a commitment on the part of the governor becomes more complicated. The powers that have been granted to the governor under the rubric of "management capacity"—appointments, budget, central management—are hardly insignificant, and they can be used to advantage in the struggle to create and enforce a new sensitivity to rural industrial development. But the glitter of a neatly ordered "management process" begins to fade, and the old-fashioned skills of bargaining, negotiating and compromise grow more valuable.

Looking again at facts the governor found two of the five forces that contravene his goal originate outside the executive branch of state government. One is a statutory enactment by the legislature affecting utility rates; another is a federal regulation establishing environmental standards. Whether the governor can secure appropriate changes there is independent of executive branch structure, is immune to appointment or budget powers and has very little to do with staffing. Instead it depends upon a host of less tangible factors, such as the governor's ability to command the attention of the press, cordial relations with the president, his cabinet officers or members of the Congress, the level of political support he can muster in the legislature, and his skill at jockeying for advantage with the utilities interests.

The three obstacles that remain are internal to the executive branch and they take the form of policies established previously and for good reasons. Governors seldom have the opportunity to create policy in a void. Instead, they face the more difficult task of displacing old policy, and overriding the vested interests which that policy represents. Clearly that is the case here. Gaining control of the Highway Commission through appointment powers or coercing the Higher Education Board through budget review will not erase the accumulated history of transportation or education policy, nor can it diminish the political and economic costs that must occur if those policies are suddenly changed. The problem remains fundamentally the same no matter what management reforms have been introduced through executive reorganization, and the governor's success will depend upon political skills rather than management.

It is intriguing that former Governor James Edwards of South Carolina reviews his administration this way:

> I don't want to imply that I had a grip on things in the bureaucracy. No one ever has a grip on the bureaucracy. But we had complete cooperation, for the most part, from the Legislature. We went in with certain positive things that we wanted done and we accomplished them. The program speaks for itself. With the exception of reorganization of state government—and I never really thought that we would get that—we accomplished just about everything we set out to do. . . . I have no real disappointments for the four years.[6]

South Carolina has one of the worst organized executive branches in the nation. The governor does not control the budget process. When Edwards was governor he could not succeed himself. He has no central management staff. His appointment powers are limited, and many of the major departments of South Carolina government are headed by autonomous boards and commissions. Would Governor Edwards have accomplished more of his goals for South Carolina, one is forced to wonder, if he had had the benefit of the "management capacity" so highly emphasized in the reforms of the sixties and seventies?

8. The Political Nature of the Governor as Manager

H. Edward Flentje

The "governor as manager" has emerged as a dominant theme of contemporary governorship. While this theme has been sounded during past periods in this century, its current exuberance has raised governor as manager to the level of a major civic cause in state government. The power of this cause, its associated dogma, and other forces now reshaping the character of the federal system will likely leave their imprint on the U.S. governorship and on state government for many years to come.

A Civic Cause

The cause of governor as manager is founded on intelligence, advocacy, and dogma. A part of its foundation is formed on changes which are occurring in the office of governor and in those occupying the office. One prominent student of the "transformation of the American governor" has found governors serving between 1950 and 1975 to be "younger and better educated" with preparation for office "more thorough and appropriate" than ever before. Within the executive sphere, these governors have been successful not only in "orchestrating constitutional revisions and reorganizations but also in consolidating and fortifying their control of administration." Governors have gained "appointive powers where it really matters, at the top level in policymaking positions," and most institutional obstacles formerly in the way of governors "have been dislodged and swept away." As a result, fewer of this modern new breed of governors "are being defeated because of political and administrative incompetency".[1]

Governors have become more evangelistic in carrying the banner of governor as manager. For example, an examination of interviews of fifteen former governors who served their terms between 1965 and 1979 concludes that the managerial role seems to be "the most important facet of the office."[2] The governors interviewed were more emphatic. *Edwards of South Carolina*: "The management role is really where the meat of the governor's office is. . . . Without management, you have practically no leg to stand on." *Exon of Nebraska*: "To me, that's number one—being a good manager—more important, I think, than programs or anything else." *Rampton of Utah*: "If a governor is going to do his job, he has got to be the manager." *Walker of Illinois*: "What counts is management . . . we have to get the governors to concentrate on management." *Wollman of South Dakota*: "If a governor doesn't devote a high percentage of his time—over half of his time—just to executive management functions, he is really missing the boat."[3] Each governor interviewed elevated governor as manager from his own perspective; none denigrated its import.

The new enthusiasm for governor as manager now permeates the work of the governors' vehicle for collective action, the National Governors' Association (NGA). This enthusiasm is transmitted to new governors and to those assisting governors by NGA through biennial seminars for new governors and through *Governing the American States: A Handbook for New Governors*.[4] Over one-half of the NGA handbook by conservative estimate is dedicated to guiding governors in the managerial role. Chapters in the handbook include "Organizing the Governor's Office," "Staff Support for the Governor," "Selecting the Cabinet and Other State Officials," "Policy Development," "An Approach to Management," "The Budget: A Spending Plan and Policy Tool," and "Approaches to Reorganization."

In the chapter on an approach to management the handbook outlines management dogma for achieving hierarchical organization. The prescriptions provide guidelines for the relationship of governor to cabinet member, for avoiding staff-line conflicts, and for record keeping within the governor's office, among other matters. The chapter on approaches to reorganization tends to assume that a new governor will want to make "changes in the organization of state government" and outlines reorganization actions "to increase the Governor's executive authority and management capacity," such as expanding the governor's appointment power, reducing the number of statewide officials chosen by popular election, eliminating fixed terms of office for cabinet officers, ensuring appointees serve at the pleasure of the governor, and eliminating situations where boards and commissions operate state agencies.[5]

Values underpinning governor as manager are not new. Their U.S. roots are traceable to ideals of the progressive era in the early part of this century. These values are closely aligned with the purposes of classical bureaucratic organization:

1. *Hierarchical authority* provides the rationale for restructuring the executive branch of government and extending the authority of the chief executive to all executive branch functions;

2. *Division of labor* furnishes the logic for delineating essential staff and line functions and for organizing line agencies around major public purposes;

3. *Appointments on a merit basis* require definition of managerial and staff positions and selection of personnel for these positions more on considerations of managerial skill, experience, and competence than of loyalty to party, person, or ideology;[6]

4. *Efficiency and effectiveness* as the principal standards of performance for public agencies and programs point to a continuing search for clarity in public purposes and development of measures of public performance.

A more subtle yet real precept underlying governor as manager is that management could be or at least should be separated from politics. Politics is involved in the governor's legislative role, but once policy is adopted, implementation is a politically neutral process. Services are delivered impersonally without regard to political, social, or economic status. Governor as manager is free of political tasks and political impact.

Political Nature

The purpose of this chapter is to assess the political nature of governor as manager, that is, does politics have impact on the governor's managerial role? What are the political benefits and the political costs of an active gubernatorial role in management? These subjects are not well understood, nor are they well treated by those advancing the cause of governor as manager. Indeed, they have been given little attention.

Initial assessments raise questions as to whether a governor can nurture a political constituency by performing the role of governor as manager. For example, former Governor Walker believes that the administration of state government has more impact on the lives of people than legislative actions and therefore the governor's principal responsibility is management. He warns, however: "Nobody cares . . . whether you're actually managing state government. . . . It's not a political plus. . . . In terms of getting votes . . . you'd better spend your time somewhere else."[7] Walker concludes that it is tempting and safer politically to set your distance from the bureaucracy and let bureaucracy run its course.[8] These assessments closely coincide with my own conclusions as a participant-observer of the Bennett administration in Kansas:

> The substantive success of the governor's efforts at management improvement could not be translated into votes, for there was little, if any, real political support for effective management. Unlike almost any other area of state policy, there was no major constituency to whom management improvement was a salient issue. Indeed the situation was quite the contrary, as most organized interest groups pushed for objectives which militated against good management.[9]

A close observer of Governor Sargent's administration in Massachussetts similarly concludes that trying to manage certain departments "offers few political or electoral rewards for a political executive"; indeed, executive control, that is, changing the behavior of an agency, may be secured only at a cost of scarce political resources.[10]

The politics of governor as manager can be understood in part by examining the nature of administrative powers and bureaucratic politics in U.S. government. First, on administrative powers of U.S. chief executives, state constitutions have for the most part provided for the evolution of administrative powers which are separate, yet shared between the governor and legislature, and open-ended for the chief executive.[11] A governor's administrative powers are separate in the sense that they are derived from a governor's independent political base and may be exercised independently. They are shared in the sense that a legislature may also act in the administrative sphere if it so chooses— a situation which often creates a competition for the exercise of administrative power. The chief executive's administrative powers are open-ended in that they are most often ambiguously defined, for example, "the supreme executive power of this state shall be vested in a governor," without specific limits on gubernatorial action in the administrative sphere. In sum, this constitutional framework places the exercise of administrative powers largely in the political arena.

Gubernatorial exercise of administrative powers then immerses the governor in politics, state bureaucratic politics. Principal participants include state bureaucracies which "tend to be creatures of habit, inflexible and enmeshed in the process of administering ongoing programs. Around them emerge a complex of interest groups and legislative supporters, all committed to the survival and growth of extant bureaus and their programs."[12] These triangular alliances of state bureaus, organized clientele groups and legislative friends have evolved as one of the most potent forces in U.S. politics and are thought to be even more powerful at the state level than at the local or national levels.[13] These interdependent networks constitute a formidable political obstacle to gubernatorial direction of the bureaucracy as executive action may be challenged at any one or more points in the triangle. Any governor who takes seriously the job of governor as manager can expect to be contesting toe-to-toe with the iron triangles of bureaucratic politics.

While limited comparative data make it difficult to generalize on the political impact of an activist governor as manager, an emerging literature on individual governors and governorships gives mounting evidence that gubernatorial exercise of administrative powers incurs substantial political liabilities. This evidence is now examined in terms of four administrative powers commonly available to governors—the power of appointment, the power of command, the power of organization, and the fiscal power.

Power of Appointment. The power most fundamental to governor as manager is the power of appointment, the ability to select and to remove executive officials. Certain governors (Bennett, Dukakis, Rampton) making key administrative appointments on a merit basis in which primary consideration is given to managerial skill, experience, and competence caused antagonism within their own party organization. Merit-based appointment to cabinet positions also essentially precluded the use of patronage in those departments (Bennett, Dukakis) and, if appointees were from out of state or from outside state service, irritated state employees (Sargent).

Selection, however, is a joy compared to the political pains of removing key officials. Says Dukakis: "Nothing can bedevil an administration more than weaknesses among appointees."[14] Walker scored the quality and political impact of his appointees in this way: "If they're bad, you get more minuses for their being really bad than you get pluses out of their being good."[15] Outright firing of a department head in order to change policy direction in a department has the potential of unifying clientele groups, loyal bureaucrats and legislative allies to protest gubernatorial action and, if a replacement is not quickly in place, may lead to political havoc wrought by a runaway bureaucracy (Sargent).

The expansion of gubernatorial appointment powers has also largely precluded an option historically available to governors, that is, to take a "we-they" approach to the relationship of governor to bureaucracy. Governors may not be able to "view with alarm" a certain action taken by a state bureaucracy, for that bureaucracy is more likely than not susceptible to gubernatorial control.[16]

Power of Command. The power of command, the ability to direct the actions of state officials, has a number of dimensions. On a general level, state legislatures often give agencies broad grants of authority to carry out programs and thereby transfer the politically difficult job of defining programs and specifying purposes to the executive branch. Governors and their appointees are then placed in the position of drafting executive directives which narrow program purposes, exclude potential beneficiaries, and result in political liabilities for the governor.

On another level, the power of command involves directing personnel on a day-to-day basis. According to one somewhat frustrated former governor, Pryor of Arkansas, a governor "will spend almost as much time keeping his staff and his cabinet and the people around him happy as he does keeping his constituency happy."[17] Governors are also cast into resolving bloody battles among and between staff and agency personnel which ultimately results in deflated egos (Sargent, Shapp). Directing an agency to do something it is reluctant to do may lead to bureaucratic foot dragging and attempts to emasculate the directive (Sargent). Or directing an agency to turn down a federal grant may generate interest group pressure on the governor to reverse his decision (Bennett).

Another approach to the power of command is to delegate, but delegation too has its political costs (Rockefeller). A governor who delegates may be viewed as a weak manager by agency personnel and by the public but will ultimately be held politically accountable for problems which occur under delegation (Sargent).[18]

Power of Organization. The administrative power of organization, that is, the power to create and abolish offices and to assign and reassign purposes, authorities, and duties to these offices, is critical to governor as manager, for it may be used to confer organizational status and give certain programs, purposes and constituencies higher priority and easier access than others. For this reason gubernatorial proposals for reorganization commonly run into direct and immediate conflict with the iron triangles of bureaucratic politics, and many such proposals can only be found in the political graveyards of state government. State archives are replete with examples of these struggles which follow a pattern. Most often exercise of the power of organization will be vigorously opposed by elements in the legislature (Rockefeller), by interest groups (Bennett, Pryor), by elements within the bureaucracy (Apodaca, Rockefeller) or by combinations of these forces (Edwards, Rockefeller). Actions designed to strengthen a governor's control of administration will likely be denounced as a "power grab" (Rockefeller)[19] or as an attempt to import the ideas of out-of-state experts and associations.[20] The politics of reorganization are well summarized by former Governor Bennett:

> during the election campaigns there wasn't a candidate of either party . . . that didn't proclaim loud and clear that he was for reorganization, he was going to abolish unneeded activity, he was going to merge . . . duplicating departments, he in fact was going to streamline government. In the abstract, it is without a doubt, one of the finest and one of the most palatable theories ever espoused by a modern day politician. But in practice . . . it becomes the loss of a job for your brother or your sister, your uncle or your aunt. It becomes the closing of an office on which you have learned to depend for a small portion of your municipal economic sustenance. It becomes the doing away with an activity that is of personal economic benefit to you although it may be of little benefit to others. So there may in many instances be more agony than anything else in this reorganization process.[21]

Fiscal Power. The political nature of a governor's fiscal actions are generally better understood. For example, the political lives lost to gubernatorial tax measures is well known. Between 1951 and 1975, twenty-one incumbent governors were evicted from office through elections in which the key issue was a tax initiative of the governor.[22] Governors can survive a general tax increase, but the survivors list is a short one.

On the expenditure side most studies[23] of state budgetary processes show that state budgets result from a contest of competing interests—clientele groups, agency advocates, legislative spokesmen, and other political interests. This contest promotes decision rules for the budget process, most often a governor's principal management tool, which do not seriously question the existing operations of state agencies. The budgetary outcome is incrementalism and preservation of the governmental status quo. Governors wanting to enter this fray and seek substantial fiscal change will be required to expend considerable political capital and even then may be faced with embarassing budgetary defeats (Bennett, Edwards, Ogilvie).

Another political bugaboo for most governors is the periodic necessity to recommend salary adjustments for state employees which will likely be perceived as too little on the inside and too much on the outside (Dukakis). Those governors seeking to reward performance of middle and upper managerial personnel may also be stalemated by the political instincts of legislatures to spread limited salary funds to more employees at the lower end of the salary schedule and to reduce compensation for managers.[24]

Certain governors have recognized the political nature of the managerial role and formulated differing approaches to it. Evans of Washington, for example, concludes: "you must be a manager. But you also must be a political and issue leader. Those are two halves of being governor, and both halves are terribly important."[25] Somewhat similarly the thinking behind the Sargent and Walker administrations appears to be that political resources generated through non-managerial functions is essential to allowing a governor pursue an active and politically costly managerial role.[26] Rockefeller, however, preferred concentrating on policy rather than administration because of the political payoffs. In the administrative sphere he continually sought to cut his losses accepting compromise solutions to his often far reaching proposals. His political calculations were made in terms of achieving winning coalitions.[27]

By way of summary, then, governor as manager is not and cannot be separated from politics; gubernatorial management does not take place in a political vacuum. As with other gubernatorial roles governor as manager is immersed in politics, and in this environment the exercise of power, including administrative power, by a governor requires the expenditure of political capital. Active concentration on the managerial role, without concern for replenishing political capital, will dissipate a governor's political base and chart a sure course to political oblivion.

Advice to a Governor

State chief executives are confronted with choices daily. Nearly everyone coming in contact with the governor wants the governor to do something he would not otherwise do. This barrage of constituency demand, however, is "elastic and imperfectly formulated."[28] And in the final analysis a "governor has great freedom in defining his relation to his administration."[29] If, however, a chief executive desires to exercise leadership, he must be concerned with "promotion and protection" of values for the institution he heads.[30]

Purely political advice to a governor then would be: each administrative choice has political impact, and each affects a governor's political resources. In making these choices a governor may conserve or waste political influence; he may add to or detract from his political base. Each choice should therefore be assessed with a view to its effect on the governor's influence and political future.[31]

Such advice is in tune with U.S. politics and would likely contribute toward a governor's political survival. However, if a state's chief executive is not concerned with promoting and protecting the values underlying management, there are few other actors in a state political system who will take up this charge.

More balanced advice to a governor wanting to advocate good management might be as follows: Management goals should be an integral part of a governor's overall political strategy. This strategy should identify three or four key areas for primary gubernatorial attention and set priorities for gubernatorial achievement in each of these areas. This strategy should also identify those constituencies which should be nurtured through gubernatorial action. A governor should then develop within his administration the capacity for assessing both the political and the management impact of choices before him. Final choices should be made then in terms of their contribution to primary gubernatorial commitments tempered by calculations of political and management impact.

9. Governors' Views on Management

Robert Dalton

In 1981 the Center for Policy Research of the National Governors' Association published *Reflections on Being Governor*, a volume of debriefing interviews with fifteen former governors who left office in 1977 and 1979.[1] Consistently, the role of governor as manager emerged in the interviews as the prime function of the contemporary governorship. To illuminate how this role is seen from the inside, this chapter offers some selected comments by the former governors on their perceptions and their managerial role. The comments tend to fall into four basic categories: people, structures and processes, gubernatorial style of management, and keeping a proper perspective.

People

Time and time again, former governors emphasized the importance of the right person for the right position in order for the governor to have his policy goals carried out. Institutional structure, staff organization, and planning offices were not usually minimized, but the supporting cast emerged as a most important factor in the government's performance as manager. This importance of personnel is more than just the appointive power itself. Rather, it denotes the character of the people around the governor and how well he utilizes their respective talents.

It's the Who, not the What, that Counts[2]

Jerry Apodaca noted that "you simply need to pick people who are knowledgeable, who have good logic, who have the ability to make sound decisions and give good advice." Robert Bennett, to insure himself qualified subordinates, followed the slogan, "Hire an expert." Typical of Bennett's attitude is this comment about one cabinet secretary: "But this fellow was not an active politician; he was just a good craftsman in the area of economic development."

Other governors confirm the importance of personnel in the management of state government.

J. James Exon: Even more important . . . is that the success of any governor . . . is whether or not he can attract to him the right group of administrators to help him carry out his duties as governor.

Martin Schreiber: These [cabinet secretaries] were professionals who were selected not only because of their professional capability but also because of their sensitivity . . . and their compassion. They played a direct role in the success of this administration.

However an interestingly discordant note was struck by Dan Walker of Illinois:

> It doesn't really make all that much difference, as the public and the media perceive it, whether you have stars or mediocre people running the departments. So, in terms of history, it doesn't make that much difference. If they're bad, you get more minuses for their being really bad than you get pluses out of their being good. Does that convey my meaning? But, if you really care about management of programs and services to people, then it does become important. . . . So I would say to you that, even though you don't get a lot out of it, I would continue to fight to get super people to run the departments.
>
> One other footnote, if I may, on that score. You run a risk. The better the people you get, the more distance they place between themselves and you. They tend to adopt much more of that "we/them" syndrome that can be disaster to government.

In a Pinch—How to Get Your People into Position [3]

A key to any governor's management control of state government is having his major appointees into office early on. What happens if the state senate refuses confirmation of your cabinet secretaries? Milton Shapp met just such a test head-on:

> Then, I announced my cabinet positions. I was sworn in on January 17, 1971, at noon. There was a parade for an hour, and then my schedule called for lunch—and at one o'clock, the Senate was to go into session to confirm my appointments to the cabinet. At two o'clock, there was going to be a general reception in the House of Representatives for all the friends of the cabinet nominees—who at that point would all be cabinet officers. At 1:30, I was still on the reviewing stand, and had sandwiches and coffee brought out there—bands going by. I got a message from one of my aides that the Senate Committee on Appointments—the Nominations Committee—had adjourned without bringing out any of the names of my appointees to the various cabinet positions.
>
> So, I had my first crisis. About 2,000 to 2,500 people were there—friends, relatives and 17 to 20 people from the cabinet. Fortunately, the Attorney General, a man by the name of Fred Speaker, an attorney from Harrisburg whom I know very well, a Republican, had not resigned his post. So I called a meeting of all my top advisors, and we decided that what I would do was take my Secretary-designee for Welfare, Helene Wohlgemuth, appoint her Special Assistant for Welfare, and give her instructions to go on over to the secretary's office and sit at the secretary's desk and run things in my name. And my Secretary-designee for Agriculture, Jim McHale, would be designated Special Assistant for Agriculture to do the same thing, and so on across

the board. I couldn't do that with my Attorney General because of legal restrictions. So I had a meeting of all my cabinet-designees, and I appointed them all and just gave them a letter and signed it. They went over and started running things in my name. Fred Speaker, at my request, stayed on as Attorney General so I had an Attorney General, and so that when anything was challenged he could issue a ruling. After about a week, the Senate leadership came to me. I wouldn't say they capitulated, but the end of that meeting was that the appointments were all made. So, my first head-on clash with them showed that I was resolved to do things in a way that I thought fit.

Making Music, or Riding the Waves: Two Images of the Governor [4]

Governors are politicians, and one stock in trade for any good politician is the ability to manipulate the English language. Michael Dukakis and Calvin Rampton offer two striking images of the governor as manager.

Dukakis: I've got a colleague here at the Kennedy school who says you're really like an orchestra leader. You can't do it by yourself, and one of your most important jobs is to select the folks in the orchestra. And, you can't have all violins and all trombones. You have to have a variety of people. Whom you pick, how you pick them, and what kind of leadership and support, inspiration and motivation you can provide as a chief executive has a great deal to do with whether or not you are successful.

Rampton: [A] governor can shield himself from [getting burned by management]. I had subordinates who did my dirty jobs, like everybody else. If I felt a decision was necessary, but I knew it was not going to be well received, I had the decision announced by the department head. I don't think there is anything wrong with that. Being in the management role does not mean that you are going to be out there with your chest out taking the bullets all the time. You're more like the admiral of the flagship, sitting back in the bowels of the ship, letting someone else fire the shots—but you are making the decisions.

Structures and Processes

Not all of managing state government is working with people, for the very structure of state government and the processes by which state governments operate are important factors to be considered.

Is the Structure of State Government Important: Two Contrasting Views [5]

Blair Lee III of Maryland claims that it *is* important:

[The ability to manage the executive branch] depends more on the structure of government in a particular state than it does on the individual who is governor. There are some states that are so poorly set up that the best governor in the world still can't run the show effectively. . . . I think organization is *all*-important. [Emphasis in original.]

In contrast, Martin J. Schreiber of Wisconsin says that

lines—organizational lines and boxes—are nonsense, OK? More depends upon the individual responsible for a particular job than anything else. . . . You can have the most refined structure that anyone could envision . . . but if you have a fellow or woman in charge of the operation that no one can relate to—well, everything goes out the window then.

Is there need for some type of organization? Yes. Do I believe I should spend all of my time moving around the boxes? No, because anyone who does that ends up moving around the boxes to fit the people, rather than putting the people in who fit the boxes.

Plan, Plan, Plan[6]

Several of the former governors commented on the value of a central budget/planning/administrative unit, either as a separate cabinet department or as an office within the governor's staff organization. Fairly typical is Arkansas' David Pryor:

We had a new department called the Department of Finance and Administration, which combined both revenue collection and management and finance together. We called it DFA, Department of Finance and Administration. This one department was charged with the management of the entirety of state government. It was under this particular department that the budget department, the revenue department and some of the regulatory agencies found their home — and I found that they worked pretty well together. I found that it served the function for the first time of overall management by objective for state government.

We also went, during my second term as governor, to a new budget system—not exactly zero-base budgeting, but one that we called "priority budgeting." We did seek justification for budgets that the department heads and agency directors presented. Basically, I think it made them more accountable, and in the process it made our own administration more knowledgeable about some of the things going on out in the government.

So I would say yes, we did utilize this as a management tool, and I think it worked pretty effectively. We went through those four years without raising any taxes. We do have a constitutional amendment which disallows any deficit spending. During these particular four years, I think we slowed the growth of government because for the first time in a long time we had a handle on government. The agencies knew that we were going to be very strict on additional personnel and large amounts of additional appropriations. So I think as a management tool this department did help a great deal.

The Numbers Have It[7]

Decision making is a crucial factor in a governor's management style, and how he decides can be just as important as what he decides. James B. Edwards offers his method of picking among alternatives.

I find it very easy to make decisions if I have some statistical data that I have faith in, that I know are sound data. I was fortunate enough to have an administrative assistant who presented me with the statistical data on just about every issue, whether it be highway construction or legislative pay or higher education. No matter what the issue was, he would bring me the data in organized fashion. He would present the issue and present the statistical data on both sides of the issue. Then he would frequently have a recommendation as to which way we should go.

For the most part, it's pretty simple—most issues are pretty clear cut. On occasion, you get one where you could flip a coin and go either way. Those were the tough ones—when you weren't sure—when it wasn't a clear-cut decision. If it was clear-cut, there was no problem at all. There were those forces pulling and tugging, but we tried to close those forces out of our mind. On occasion, of course, we had to get political, and we would go in a direction we felt statistically we shouldn't go in. Or sometimes we would go in the direction of the statistics when the politics would dictate elsewhere. The statistics are much safer to go with than the politics, I find.

When you have a group of statisticians and research people who you know are not going to be advocates of one side of an issue or another, who're just going to present the raw facts, it relieves a lot of doubts that you may have about statistical data brought to you from some special-interest group. When you have your own people working for you, it makes it a lot easier. . . .

Just statistically, you'd say this is the way to go. Of course, human sensitivities come into some of these things. That type of thing is certainly a part of government today. Particularly today, you have to take those things into consideration. You can't always go with the cold, hard economic facts. You have to give help to people who are in need; you have to express some concern and some compassion for people—that all enters into government today. I think that's the difference between government today and government 25 or 30 years ago.

The Government as Business[8]

Different governors have different ideas on how to manage state government so as to make it work. One former governor with a straightforward notion of operating state government efficiently is James B. Edwards of South Carolina.

I tried to create a business atmosphere and employ business principles.

We balanced our budget, and we wound up with a $67-million surplus at the end of the four-year term. Now this is just a simple application of business principles to government. . . . We developed a computerized payroll/personnel system, payroll and personnel records back to back on a computer. . . .

That's just an example of the application of business principles to government. And it can work . . . Every business I know has to balance its books, at least not lose money annually.

Gubernatorial Style

How a governor approaches his or her job as the manager is a critical variable in the management equation. There are differing approaches and styles — each with strengths and weaknesses.

Should the Governor be a Generalist or a Specialist?[9]

According to at least two former governors, a prime managerial technique is to let the staff and cabinet officers deal with the nitty-gritty of policy implementation, while the governor makes the big decisions and provides overall guidance. First, there is New Mexico's Jerry Apodaca:

I've always been very skeptical of Governors who knew too much about some complicated issues — water, for example. In New Mexico we had Steve Reynolds. He's the most knowledgeable person in government on water and water rights and water litigation. He is a professional. He has been there through four Governors. I don't know if that's good or bad, but by and large I think it's okay. I never felt the need to sit there and study the issues of water to that detail. I think Governors face a danger when they become too specific, too detailed. You have some complicated issues that you ought to let some of the talent around you help decide.

Seconding that is Reubin Askew of Florida:

I think management is a very critical part of it. But the key to it is to try to get good managers along the way, because I think a Governor who gets too involved in the details of any particular program in operating a department under him is not making the proper use of his time. Everybody has a different way in which he works. I didn't get into too much detail because I conceived my role essentially as one of broad decision making. If you get tied up in the detail of too many problems, you will not have enough time or energy to make sure that you make the larger decisions. . . . But in the final analysis, I think the Governor must be someone who sets the tone, and then looks to other people to minister under some type of supervisory mechanism.

Nonetheless, there was at least one contrary position, expressed by Milton Shapp of Pennsylvania:

Now, most governors don't operate this way. I have talked to a number of governors. They meet with their secretaries. "You handle this, Joe. You handle this, Alice." That's the way they do it. I didn't do this. . . .

But when the governor wants to implement a program along the lines I am talking about, it leads to a lot of involvement by the governor's office. The governor's office, then, and many times even I personally, would have to get involved in battles between departments.

Target Your Issues [10]

Any governor faces a host of issues and problem areas that demand solutions. But no one governor—no one administration—can realistically expect to resolve all those difficulties. One management tool to deal with this situation: set your sights on a realistic number of issues and concentrate your attention. Two former governors offer their thoughts.

Dan Walker: If you take on too many big issues and crises or problems, those people get spread so thin that some of those issues go down to the next level of staff. And when you get down to the next level, that staff just isn't as good as the top level, so those problems don't get as good a treatment. So one of the smart things to do, I think, is to pick a manageable number of issues that you can have your staff concentrate on, bring those to fruition, and pay the price for letting some of the others go their way without gubernatorial attention.

Harvey Wollman: But one day I wrote down 15 things that I'd really like to do, and we set priorities on about six. I said then that we would spend the bulk of our time — like 80 percent of our time — on these, and we disciplined ourselves to stay on track. We never got sidetracked to the point where we neglected something and regretted it later. I think that's pretty good advice for any new Governor coming into a governorship. He should take inventory based on his experience — what he knows and what he feels that he would really like to do — and make a list. And then he should sit down with a group of very close advisors to review the list and to decide what he wants to zero in on. The people tend to respond to that.

Keep Your Perspective

Finally, governors must develop their own sense and feel for what is going on not only in state government but in the state. Each governor undoubtedly has his or her own way of keeping their perspective. Here are two especially unique approaches.

Don't Trust the Bureaucrats[11]

Information flow to the governor is crucial to his effective management of the state bureaucracy. Unfortunately, the bureaucrats sometimes may have different goals than the governor and this may affect the quality and quantity of information the governor receives. Dan Walker had a particularly unique way to keep himself aware of this problem:

> For the first year of so of my administration, I used to carry a piece of paper with me in my pocket to meetings with bureaucrats, particularly middle-level bureaucrats. I don't use that as a perjorative term, although I know it sounds that way. Well, halfway through a meeting I would take that piece of paper out of my pocket and look at it. On it was written, "The bastards are lying." Well — they are. Not consciously, not consciously at all, but the system produces an intense desire to tell the boss, the elective guy particularly, what you think he wants to hear instead of what he really wants to hear.

"Get a Worm's-Eye View of a Bird"[12]

One way for a governor to manage state government effectively so as to meet the felt needs of the citizenry is to insure he knows what those felt needs are, what the real problems are. Milton Shapp found an effective way to do this, but let him describe it:

> One of the most effective things we did — and I would recommend to every governor — is set up a hot line. A citizen of Pennsylvania had a toll-free hot line directly to Harrisburg. . . . We had a government hot line, and any person who had a problem with a service needed could pick up the phone and dial us. I had a staff of about 30 people working in there. It was a great management tool because it enabled us to find out what was going on at the level where state services were being delivered or not being delivered to people.
>
> I would have meetings with my staff and my cabinet and sub-cabinet people and heads of agencies, and we would discuss problems — whether it be delivering of welfare checks, or whatever. But the point where government services are delivered to the people, we never saw in my office; I would be dealing with the top people who then would implement these programs.
>
> Now, a bird's eye view of a worm is entirely different than a worm's eye view of a bird. The people who don't have the services are looking up at this bureaucracy, and they see the underbelly of the bureaucracy. They know that they have impure water because somebody in the Department of Environmental Resources, or whatever, or some building, has screwed the water supply in the area, and they can't get anybody to do anything. They call the governor's hot line, and it goes to the top of the agency. The way I ran it, the

head of the hot line would keep a check on what was going on in the department. I had people on my staff working with them. We didn't let the bureaucracy push it into a corner. There had to be a final resolution of every call — back to the person — that the problem was taken care of or why it couldn't be taken care of.

So, the hot line became a management tool in my administration. . . . You've got to put the pressure on, and you have to have people from the governor's office who are going to insist that if something is found to be wrong, it gets corrected in the system. We cut out so much red tape because of the hot line it's almost unbelievable. Again, using the worm's eye view of that bird, we were able to see what was happening at the point of delivery of services, and you never see that in the governor's office unless you have that type of information coming from the people.

Conclusion

A comprehensive conclusion about the governor as manager is not possible from these selected quotes, though they do offer insightful and perceptive thoughts. But beyond the fact that at least some governors are quite adept with the English language, perhaps two things can be elicited from the remarks. First, whether the comments reflect hindsight after the fact or foresight before entering office, they seem to indicate that the governors place a high premium on the personal traits of pragmatism and flexibility. Second, though there are commonalities in their remarks, each governor manifests his own uniqueness in carrying out the function of manager, and, to a certain extent, appears to regard this uniqueness itself as a managerial strength.

10. Appointment Power: Does It Belong to the Governor?

Thad L. Beyle and Robert Dalton

> The power most fundamental to the president's administrative role is the power of appointment . . . a necessary, though not sufficient condition for presidential direction of the federal bureaucracy, as other administrative powers in large measure flow from it.[1]
>
> —H. Edward Flentje

One of the first sets of decisions facing a governor-elect on that Wednesday morning in November is the appointment of personnel to key positions in his administration. Similar to Flentje's view of the presidential level, the power of appointment is fundamental to a governor's administration, especially in relation to the state bureaucracy. But, the appointive power also extends to the governor's legislative role as promises of appointments to high-level executive positions and to the state judiciary are often the coin spent for support of particular legislation.

Background

The history of state governors' appointment powers is one of growth from very weak beginnings. Early state executives were provided few powers at all, due partly in reaction to the abuses of British-imposed colonial governors and to the desire to lodge power in the state legislatures.

During the period of Jacksonian democracy, more electoral control for the people and the "plural executive" became the goals with many state executive branch officials achieving office by election rather than by gubernatorial appointment. Patronage and the "spoils system" grew during this period, as did the length of the ballot, creating a fractionalized executive. Popularly elected administrative officials and their departments were outside direct gubernatorial control, and less restrictive tenure limitations often gave them greater staying power than the governor.

To this was added the ad hoc proliferation of state agencies established to meet emerging problems brought about by changing social and economic conditions during the nineteenth century. These agencies were often headed by boards and commissions, whose members were not necessarily appointed by the governor. This diluted gubernatorial power was the background for such twentieth-century reforms as an executive budget authority, the item veto, executive reorganization, and greater gubernatorial appointive powers.

The academic literature has long held to the importance of the governor's appointment power for administrative control,[2] and recent empirical studies continue to underline this importance.[3]

The Contemporary Governor

The surveys of Lipson, Ransone, and Sabato generally agree that contemporary governors with their increased powers—including appointive—are able to exert greater control over the executive branch than earlier governors. Lockard's discussion of three modern, strong governorships—New York, New Jersey, and Massachusetts—finds that one common element is enhanced gubernatorial appointive powers.[4]

Governors themselves also hold to the importance of their appointive powers. Former Governor Terry Sanford of North Carolina calls for fewer elective offices and boards or commissions controlling the administration of departments, thereby allowing the governor to use his appointive power to bring back to him the slices of executive authority that have been handed to others.[5]

From a series of interviews with fifteen former governors who have left office since 1976, it is clear the governors are well aware of the political and administrative significance of their appointive powers over top policymaking positions.[6] Dukakis feels a governor's success "depends heavily on the quality and caliber of people he appoints." Exon agreed. Shapp so realized the importance of his appointees that when the legislature held up confirmation of his cabinet, he named them "special assistants" and sent them to run their respective offices in his name. Rampton, a vigorous opponent as governor of the fragmenting symptoms of "picket fence federalism," saw his appointment power as a counter and check on these trends.

In sum, the gubernatorial power of appointment is a most significant weapon in a governor's arsenal. From rather weak beginnings and a complicating historical development, the governors are now seeking greater appointive power and achieving it—but not without some continuing problems.

State Government Reorganization

A twentieth-century reform goal in state government has been to eliminate the plural executive and provide greater gubernatorial appointive powers through reorganization. Over the past six decades there have been three separate waves of reorganization—beginning in 1914, 1937, and 1965. In the most recent period, twenty-one states have undergone major reorganization, while most other states reorganized one or more departments.[7]

As the Advisory Commission on Intergovernmental Relations notes:

> The reorganization activity that began during the 1960's resulted from pressures on the states to establish the policy, organizational and fiscal machin-

ery to enable them to meet the demands made by an increasingly urban population. They also sought to rationalize functional responsibilities, to create clearer lines of authority, and to increase accountability.[8]

Sabato indicates the basic purpose of all reorganization activity is to simply "increase the accountability and efficiency of government by giving the state governor the authority to match his responsibility in the executive branch." In major reorganizations the number of agencies is reduced drastically, the governor's span of control (number reporting directly to him) is reduced, the governor's appointment power is enhanced to cover most agencies, and a clear chain of command established.[9] Or so the theory goes.

We will explore the impact of this latest wave of state reorganizations on two aspects of gubernatorial appointment power: the continuation of elected plural executives in the states and the specific areas and functions in which the governor's appointive power has changed. The value of gubernatorial enhancement undergirding these state government reorganizations, for both major and minor efforts, should be reflected in greater appointive powers for the governors.

The Impact of Reorganization on the Plural Executive

It is clear that the most recent reorganizations have not changed the status of the plural executive appreciably. While there have been some downward shifts in numbers of separately elected officials, the main finding demonstrated in Table 10.1 is the similarity in these numbers for 1965 and 1980.

However, there are some significant shifts that should be highlighted.

Lieutenant Governor. Beginning as recently as 1953 in New York, there has been a rapid growth in the number of states having the governor and lieutenant governor run as a team. This has been especially true since 1966 when the number rose from seven to twenty-one. This shift coincides with an upgrading of the job of lieutenant governor from part-time to full time and a movement toward seeing the lieutenant governor as a part of the executive branch rather than as a hybrid "executive-legislator."[10]

Auditor. The decline in separately elected auditors has been more than offset by a rise in legislatively selected auditors. While the National Municipal League's "Model State Constitution" calls for the governor to be the only statewide elected official, more recent reorganization approaches consider that in the interest of accountability the auditor should be outside gubernatorial control, preferably chosen by the legislature.[11]

Education. For the past few decades there has been a decline in the number of separately elected superintendents of public instruction, but this has almost been offset by the rise in separately elected school boards. Thus while there appear to be shifts, in fact education was overseen by separately elected officials

Table 10.1. Separately elected executive branch officials, 1965–80

Official	1965	1980	Change
Governor	50	50	—
Lieutenant Governor[a]	38	42	+4
Attorney General	42	43	+1
Treasurer	40	38	−2
Secretary of State	39	36	−3
Auditor[b]	29	25	−4
Superintendent of Education, Public Instruction[c]	22	18	−4
Board of Education[c]	9	12	+3
Secretary of Agriculture	13	12	−1
Controller	9	10	+1
Insurance Commissioner	10	8	−2
Land Commissioner	7	6	−1
Secretary of Labor	6	4	−2
Commissioner of Mines/Minerals	4	1	−3
Public Utility Commission	14	11	−3

Source: The Book of the States, 1966–67 and *1980–81* (Lexington, Ky.: The Council of State Governments, 1966 and 1980).

a. Lieutenant governors and governors ran as a team in seven states in 1965 and twenty-one states in 1980, representing a +14 change.

b. During the same time period, the number of states in which the legislature selects the auditor increased from eleven to eighteen.

c. Two of the four states, Alabama and Kansas, switched from electing a superintendent to electing a board of education.

in thirty-one states in 1965 and in thirty states in 1980. (This is down from thirty-four states in 1947.) Thus, governors in thirty states still lack direct policy control and administration in public education.

Other Offices. For the remaining offices there may be less than meets the eye in the data contained in Table 10.1. Some of the offices that are separately elected do not carry major policy or administrative responsibilities (e.g., secretary of state, treasurer) or represent some of the still-potent politics of the nineteenth century (e.g., land, mines, and minerals). Some of the offices such as agriculture, labor, and insurance seem to be more representational in nature with each interest having an elected representative to head an agency. Further, the major functions of state government as they have evolved during the twentieth century (human services, health, transportation) are already under gubernatorial appointive control, except for education as noted above.

So it is that calls during a state's reorganization effort to reduce the plural executive and its attendant problems often fall on unresponsive ears, the power actually gained being judged not worth the political effort. In fact, in reviewing which states switched their mode of selection from elected to appointed (and vice versa in some states), there was no relationship between that decision and whether or not a state went through a major reorganization.

Table 10.2. Average gubernatorial appointment power by functions[a] and by reorganization status,[b] 1965–67 and 1980

Function	1965–67	1980	Percent change
Management			
Reorganized	3.15	3.37	+4.4
Unreorganized	3.35	3.24	−2.2
Administrative			
Reorganized	2.44	2.60	+3.2
Unreorganized	2.06	2.65	+11.8
Police/safety			
Reorganized	3.67	3.56	−2.2
Unreorganized	4.06	3.62	−8.8
Regulation			
Reorganized	3.39	2.82	−11.4
Unreorganized	3.27	3.14	−2.6
Human services			
Reorganized	2.68	2.84	+3.2
Unreorganized	2.53	2.95	+8.4
Development			
Reorganized	2.26	2.77	+10.2
Unreorganized	2.65	2.95	+6.0

a. See figure 10.1 for detail on functions.
b. See note 20 for listing of the twenty-one reorganized states.

Reorganization and Gubernatorial Appointment Power

Looking first at the changes in gubernatorial appointment powers between 1965-67 and 1980, we can see several general trends (see Figure 10.1).[12] First, governors have increased their control over the human service and development agencies, the so-called policy output side of government. They are now, on the average, able to appoint these agency heads with the approval of both houses of the legislature rather than having separately selected boards and commissions do so. They have similarly gained increased control over the administrative services component of state government, although still at a slightly lesser level than the policy output areas.

Second, there is a clear trend to reduce singular gubernatorial control over the police/safety and regulatory agencies toward that level noted for the policy output agencies. In the past, governors had considerable appointive power over these functions, but the more recent changes are, on the average, bringing both houses of the legislature into approving these gubernatorial appointments. Finally, there is virtually no change in gubernatorial control over the management-related agencies, although their power here is second only to that they wield over the policy/safety agencies.

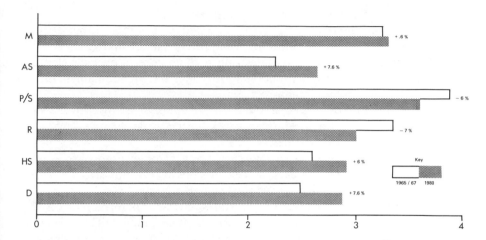

Figure 10.1 Average gubernatorial appointment power by functions, 1965-1967 and 1980.

Key: **M:** management (lieutenant governor—team, administration, budget, personnel, planning); **AS**: administrative services (purchasing, taxation, general services, pre-audit); **P/S**: police/safety (adjutant general, disaster assistance/civil preparedness, police/ highway patrol); **R**: regulation (banking, commerce, labor/industrial relations, insurance, public utilities); **HS**: human services (employment, health, mental health, welfare, corrections); **D**: development (agriculture, highways, natural resources).

The scores for gubernatorial appointment power are derived in much the same manner as that set forth by Joseph A. Schlesinger in "The Politics of the Executive," pp. 222-223. He created a six-point index based on the following methods of appointment of state officials using the governor's involvement as a reference point: 0 = elected by popular vote; 1 – appointed by department director, by board, by legislature, by civil service; 2 = appointed by director with governor's approval, or by governor and council; 3 = governor appoints and both bodies of legislature approve; 4 = governor appoints and one body of legislature approves; 5 = governor appoints alone. The scores can range from 0 (no gubernatorial appointment) to 5 (solely gubernatorial appointment power). For each of the functions, the 50-state average score was derived and is presented in this figure. This varies somewhat from the approach Schlesinger took. He totaled raw scores of sixteen separate offices by state, and then using arbitrary cut points between these summed scores, assigned to each state's governor an overall appointment score ranging from 1 to 5. The only variation from this scoring system was for the lieutenant governor where an attempt was made to incorporate the unique aspects of that office into a similar range of scores: 0 = no lieutenant governor; 1 = lieutenant governor chosen by legislature; 2 = lieutenant governor has other major executive responsibilities but is elected at same time as governor; 3 = lieutenant governor and governor elected at the same time; 4 = governor and lieutenant governor run as team in general election; 5 = governor and lieutenant governor run as team in primary and general election. For ease in understanding the percentage change figures presented above, the bars are in percentages rather than the change in actual derived score. Percentage change = actual derived score change, divided by 5, the maximum possible change in the scores.

As for the differences between those states that have undergone a major reorganization during the period versus those that have not (see Table 10.2), the following was found in relation to the general trends noted above:

1. Governors in reorganized states gained more control over development agencies than in any other functional grouping, but still remained slightly behind their counterparts in non-reorganized states.

2. Governors in reorganized states lost more appointive power over regulatory agencies than did their non-reorganized peers, while the reverse was true for police/safety agencies.

3. Reorganization did enhance managerial control for governors, while governors of non-reorganized states saw their powers over administrative services enhanced to the level of their reorganized state counterparts.

In sum, there were changes in the states in the appointive powers they provide governors—some related to reorganization, some not. There were also changes in some functions such as police/safety which gave the legislatures a greater role in the governors' appointive powers. The changes reflected in Table 10.2 for a single fifteen-year period are fairly strong and if continued indicate a centralizing trend in which the governor and the legislature are gaining more control over who runs state government at the expense of separately chosen boards and commissions and some separately elected officials. What must not be overlooked here is the symbiotic relationship between the governors and the legislatures. Gubernatorial reform via reorganization and increased appointment power have gone hand in hand with legislative reform. Both branches have increased their appointment power generally and necessarily.

Gubernatorial Appointment Power in the 1980s

The most recent selection procedures for state administrative officials across the fifty states are presented in Table 10.3. Of the 1,992 administrative positions covering up to forty-eight functional areas, 932 or 46.8 percent are appointed by the governors, 761 or 38.2 percent are appointed by other actors or institutions (boards, agency heads, or the legislature), and 299 or 15 percent are separately elected. For gubernatorial appointments, only slightly more than one-third of his or her appointments (34.5 percent) do not need confirmation by some other body or institution (the legislature, a board or council). There is considerable variation among the states as to the percentage of officials the governor may appoint, ranging from a low of only 8 or 20.5 percent in South Carolina to a high of 33 or 86.8 percent in New York.

Looking at the configuration of gubernatorial appointment powers across the states in 1980, we can see several patterns (see Table 10.4).[13] Arguments are made in the literature that there are differences in state governments and gubernatorial powers according to the region of the country and the size of the state. And we find support for these statements.

Table 10.3. How state administrative officials are selected

State	Total officials[a]	Separately elected[a]	Appointed, but not by governor	Appointed by governor		Appointed by governor— no confirmation needed	
				Number	Percent of total officials[b]	Number	Percent of total appointed by governor
Alabama	37	8	15	14	38.9	14	100
Alaska	45	2	29	14	31.8	3	21
Arizona	39	6	17	16	42.1	5	31
Arkansas	38	6	17	15	40.5	5	33
California	40	7	4	29	74.4	11	38
Colorado	37	5	15	17	47.2	2	12
Connecticut	43	5	17	21	50.0	2	10
Delaware	42	6	16	20	48.8	2	10
Florida	41	9	18	14	35.0	1	7
Georgia	35	8	18	9	26.5	5	56
Hawaii	19	2	3	14	77.8	0	0
Idaho	40	7	15	18	46.2	7	39
Illinois	31	6	3	22	73.3	2	9
Indiana	37	7	8	22	61.1	21	95
Iowa	40	7	6	27	69.2	2	7
Kansas	43	6	20	17	40.5	0	0
Kentucky	42	8	18	16	39.0	16	100
Louisiana	41	10	6	25	62.5	2	8
Maine	41	1	25	15	37.5	6	40
Maryland	42	5	18	19	46.3	4	21
Massachusetts	46	6	16	24	53.3	23	96
Michigan	41	4	23	14	35.0	1	7
Minnesota	41	5	10	26	65.0	4	15
Mississippi	35	11	10	14	41.2	13	93
Missouri	40	5	24	11	28.2	0	0
Montana	43	6	19	18	42.9	7	39
Nebraska	43	8	13	22	52.4	6	27
Nevada	44	6	22	16	37.2	16	100
New Hampshire	39	1	14	24	63.2	3	13
New Jersey	40	1	17	22	56.4	0	0
New Mexico	37	6	12	19	52.8	6	32
New York	39	3	3	33	86.8	9	27
North Carolina	44	10	13	21	48.8	20	95
North Dakota	40	12	15	13	33.3	10	77
Ohio	43	5	16	22	52.4	1	5
Oklahoma	39	8	17	14	36.8	5	36
Oregon	42	6	24	12	29.3	2	17
Pennsylvania	44	5	11	28	65.1	10	36
Rhode Island	42	5	17	20	48.8	12	60
South Carolina	40	9	23	8	20.5	3	38
South Dakota	44	7	16	21	48.8	4	19
Tennessee	43	2	21	20	47.6	20	100
Texas	39	6	24	9	23.7	4	44

Table 10.3. (continued)

State	Total officials[a]	Separately elected[a]	Appointed, but not by governor	Appointed by governor		Appointed by governor— no confirmation needed	
				Number	Percent of total officials[b]	Number	Percent of total appointed by governor
Utah	39	6	15	18	47.4	3	17
Vermont	41	6	13	22	55.0	5	23
Virginia	37	3	4	30	83.3	0	0
Washington	44	9	18	17	39.5	4	24
West Virginia	40	6	15	19	48.7	3	16
Wisconsin	32	6	12	14	45.2	2	14
Wyoming	38	5	16	17	45.9	16	94
Totals	1,992	299	761	932	—	322	—
Avg. number per state	39.8	6.0	15.2	18.6	—	6.4	—
50-state percentage	—	15	38.2	—	46.8	—	34.5

Source: The Book of the States, 1980-81 (Lexington, KY.: The Council of State Governments, 1980), pp. 195–97. A total of forty-eight separate functions/departments/agencies are contained in the data for each state. However, all states have one or more officials with multiple responsibilities, and some states indicate no such function or agency exists.
   a. Includes the governor.
   b. Less governor.

It is clear that southern governors have a differing level of appointment powers than their counterparts in the rest of the country. While there are some variations between regions according to the function involved, it is the southern states that are consistently at variance with one or two other regions, or with all non-southern states. The direction of the differential is for the southern governors to have less appointive power than their peers in other states, supporting the long-held view that southern governors continue to hold less formal powers than other governors.[14]

As to size of state, it is interesting to note that population size as such does not relate to any consistent patterns in gubernatorial appointment power, nor does the size of the state government bureaucracy, except in regulatory and human service agencies where the larger the bureaucracies the less is gubernatorial appointment power. However, it is with the size of state and local government expenditures that an intuitively sensible relationship is found: the greater the expenditures per capita by state and local governments, the greater is the gubernatorial appointment power in the management and administrative services functions. As state governments become more complex and larger (as measured by expenditures), the governor's managerial role becomes enhanced.

Table 10.4. Gubernatorial appointment powers, 1980: by region and size of state[a]

Functions	Avg. score	Region[c]					Population size[d]			Bureaucracy size[e]		Expenditure size[f]		
		West	Mid-west	North-east	South	Non-South	Small	Med.	Large	Less than 150 per 10,000	More than 150 per 10,000	Less than $1,150 per capita	$1,150 to $1,450 per capita	More than $1,450 per capita
Management	3.3	3.6b	3.5b	3.2	2.9b	3.4b	3.4	3.0	3.4	3.4	3.3	3.0b	3.3	3.6b
Administrative services	2.6	2.8	2.6	3.0b	2.3b	2.8b	2.5	2.6	2.8	2.9	2.5	2.4b	2.5	3.0b
Police/safety	3.6	3.3b	3.8b	3.6	3.7	3.5	3.2b	4.0b	3.6	3.7	3.5	3.7	3.6	3.6
Regulation	3.0	3.1b	3.1b	3.3b	2.6b	3.2b	3.0	2.8	3.1	3.4b	2.8b	2.7	3.0	3.1
Human services	2.9	2.5	3.2b	3.3b	2.7b	3.0	2.8	2.7	3.2	3.3b	2.7b	2.6	3.0	3.0
Development	2.9	2.9	2.8	3.4b	2.5b	3.0b	3.0	2.8	2.8	3.0	2.8	2.4b	3.0b	3.0b

a. See Figure 10.1 for key to detail on functions and methodology for determining gubernatorial appointment power scores.

b. Indicates those gubernatorial appointment scores which were discernibly different from other appointment scores on the particular variable.

c. Regions consist of following states: West—AK, AZ, CA, CO, HI, ID, MT, NV, NM, OR, UT, WA, WY; Midwest—IL, IN, IA, KS, MI, MN, MO, NE, ND, OH, SD, WI; Northeast—CT, DE, ME, MA, NH, NJ, NY, PA, RI, VT; South—AL, AR, F—, GA, KY, LA, MD, MS, NC, OK, SC, TN, TX, VA, WV.

d. Size of state based on 1975 population estimates, divided into thirds.

e. October 1978 figures from the U.S. Bureau of the Census. *Public Employment in 1978* reported in *The Book of the States, 1980–81* (Lexington, KY.: The Council of State Governments, 1980), p. 271.

f. 1977–78 per capita direct general expenditure of state and local governments from U.S. Bureau of the Census, *Government Finances in 1977–78*, in *The Book of the States, 1980–81*, p. 306.

Like the proverbial gun behind the door, what we have discussed so far is the potential of gubernatorial appointment power, rather than the actual exercise of that power. The sample of governors interviewed and the extant academic literature diverge at this most critical point—the practical considerations of whom to choose, how to choose, from where to choose and the constraints on this appointive power. The academic literature is largely concerned with asserting, proving and measuring the impact of appointive powers in much the same manner as we have here. The governors accept these powers as given and are more interested in the constraints placed on them and processes they have to undertake in order to carry out their increasingly significant managerial role.

The Impact of Civil Service Reform

The civil service movement is a major reform, crafted in response to the excesses of the "spoils system," and has had an impact on gubernatorial appointive power. Patronage, the power of appointment to many and widely varying posts in the state bureaucracy, has declined, being replaced by a more professional state bureaucracy. Of interest are Lipson's, Ransone's, and Sabato's views that contemporary governors by and large prefer this trend and that several recent governors have in fact pushed for civil service reform and the reduction of patronage powers.[15]

The interviews with the fifteen former governors uphold these views. The governors felt that, on balance, the current situation is more positive than negative. Civil service regulations generally did not interfere with making top level appointments, reduced nepotism, and provided continuity of state personnel. The governors felt they saved much time and many headaches and were freed to concentrate on key appointments, major issues and their general managerial role. Moreover, since they downplayed their partisan roles and since patronage and party building go hand in hand, their acceptance of civil service is reasonable.[16] Moynihan and Wilson found that patronage in New York under Governor Harriman (1954–58) did little as a vote-producing operation, was of only limited help in controlling state government, and was of greater service, though still limited, in controlling the party.[17]

The governors did lodge two basic complaints however: that civil service protection may well induce laziness, mediocrity, and unresponsiveness to gubernatorial direction and that it does interfere with removing incompetent employees or even moving personnel to more appropriate jobs for their skills. They all desired greater flexibility for the governor and the removal of more of the top levels of personnel from civil service protection. Recent U.S. Supreme Court decisions tend to be working against the latter goal.[18] One current governor's frustrations may be indicative of even broader problems, however. After years of "abuse," Pennsylvania's extensive patronage system was changed to a civil service system. Governor Thornburgh now finds civil service sheltering many crucial policy-making positions, thereby insulating some of the bureaucracy from his policies and administration.[19]

Thus, civil service reform both frees and restricts the modern governor. Freedom is perceived in the reduction of onerous personnel matters governors face. Restrictions lie in the protection from political and gubernatorial intrusion the reform provides for those in the bureaucracies—often up to the very highest levels.

The Process of Gubernatorial Appointment

As for the qualities the governors are seeking in appointees, they listed as their most important criterion *management and administrative skills.* In an era of fiscal constraints, both Askew and Dukakis saw the key to good management as the recruitment of good managers to work for you. Walker and Exon wanted those with an "ability to administer," and Schreiber appointed those who "could run their own show (because) you have to give your top people their tether and have confidence in them."

Secondly, these governors sought *experience, expertise, and competence* in the field of their charge. Bennett wanted "craftsmen," expert in their field since he was "trying to get the job done." Askew looked for "professional competence," and Exon sought those who could develop "realistic, workable programs." *Prior experience* was clearly important, as both Askew and Edwards noted they retained holdovers from the previous administration—even some of the opposing party—because of their proven experience in their positions.

A third important criterion was the governors' desire for appointees to have at least a *basic commitment to the administration and its policy direction.* Wollman, not wanting mere "yes men" but preferring a team atmosphere of mutual support, tried to ensure that he and his key appointees were "on the same wavelength." Edwards recruited those sharing his basic conservative philosophy, while Apodaca mentioned loyalty to his administration as important. In a few words, they seek out basically loyal persons who are competent to carry out the governor's policy direction.

In addition, the governors looked for a variety of other qualities, of which two groups stand out. One was *intelligence, common sense, and good judgment.* Exon wanted people who "could think," Holshouser sought "common sense," Lee recruited "bright" staffers, and Wollman looked for persons with "just plain intelligence." The other set of qualities was *sensitivity to people, compassion, and a sense of fairness* especially in the human services areas. Askew made "empathy to people and constituencies" a standard, and Dukakis watched for "sensitivity to people and constituencies." All in all, the governors looked for administratively skilled persons with intelligence, flexibility, understanding of human needs and foibles, and the willingness to follow the governor's overall policy direction.

What ever happened to partisanship or patronage? Party affiliation, as such, was not a criterion for appointees. At first surprising, this becomes less so as one understands the governors' views on partisanship in general, when they play down its importance and in particular when they play down their own role as party leaders.[20] In choosing personnel, party membership was not made a requirement nor was the appointee's affiliation always determined, though Holshouser and Walker tried to build their parties through appointments to a degree. Nor did the party apparatus have much influence directly, though Shapp used it for minor appointments, and Rampton for appointments to citizen advisory boards which by law were required to have members of both parties. In fact, Bennett, Dukakis, and Rampton all antagonized their parties because they used the party so little in their appointments.

Yet consistently, these governors admit a great majority of their appointees were of their own party. Assuming the governors were not deceitful in downgrading party affiliation as a criterion, why is this so? In part, of course, the governor is most likely to know best the qualified members of his own party. Further, there might be a spillover from the criterion of loyalty to the administration: other things being equal, who is most likely to be loyal but members of the governor's party? Therefore is not loyalty to the administration a cleaner surrogate for party affiliation? Exon summarized it best: "I didn't appoint people to policy-making positions whom I thought [would try] to destroy my administration. If there were no difference between two people for a given post, I'd appoint the Democrat."

In theory the governors held high performance standards for their potential appointees, but the concepts of loyalty and partisanship are still significant parts of the selection process.

The questions concerning how to exercise the appointment power unearthed a series of ad hoc processes all focusing the *final* decision on the governor. The processes varied from being entirely staff based, to a designated head of the search process, to merit selection boards and agencies and others, all used to seek out names and screen the applicants down to a selected few (or one) for the governor's final action. As to sources, none was dominant, ranging from reviewing existing and stimulating resumes from interested people, to a predecessor's recommendation, to searching the private sector, to friends and acquaintances—often out of the campaign organization.

These questions of selection process and sources of appointees must be answered by the governor-elect in the early transition, at precisely the time when he is tiredest from the long campaign, when the most demands on his time and attention are being made, and when he has the fewest defenses to protect him (an office staff of special assistants, schedulers, patronage aides, and a personnel department). There is little in the academic literature to provide guidance except for some of the "watch out for this" case study literature on gubernatorial transitions[21] and certain recent National Governors' Association publications.[22] However, from the governors' own commentaries, they too often started from scratch, creating their own processes, and relearned the lessons of their peers.

Conclusion

It is clear that gubernatorial appointment power is a significant tool in the governor's arsenal of weapons. Long touted as such by outside observers, governors also give it a high rating.

However, rather than being a uniform grant of authority for a governor, appointment power varies across the range of state activities, as it does also across differing states according to their location and size. On the average, we find governors being able to appoint most officials with the approval of both houses of the legislature. This reflects a trend away from also sharing or losing the power to boards and commissions or separately elected officials.

The wave of state government reorganizations occurring over the past decade and a half has increased some gubernatorial appointment powers such as in the policy output agencies, while reducing it in the police/safety and regulatory areas. Thus, reorganization is not just a one-way street to enhanced gubernatorial power, but leads to some shifting of powers among functions and agencies according to the wisdom of the day.

Finally, we must highlight the need to move beyond the question of what level of gubernatorial appointment power a particular governor or group of governors has, to questions concerning how such power is used. Here we find the greatest interest among former governors and less support from the literature. The power of appointment can be expended in various ways, through differing processes, to achieve many goals. These questions must be addressed as we seek out and evaluate gubernatorial performance and not just gubernatorial potential.

11. The Gubernatorial Appointment Power: Too Much of a Good Thing?

Diane Kincaid Blair

It is clear that gubernatorial appointment power is a significant tool in the governor's arsenal of weapons. Long touted as such by outside observers, governors also give it a high rating.[1]

An ample appointive power has been repeatedly identified by observers and governors alike as an essential component of an effective administration. It is therefore somewhat surprising that questions about the actual exercise of the appointive power seem to elicit so many rueful recollections from those very governors who simultaneously embrace the power's efficacy.[2] The adverse aspects of the appointment power are even more frequently and vehemently articulated by those aides who have assisted governors with the appointive process.[3]

What explains the aura of disappointment which surrounds practitioners' discussions of the appointment power? Does it reflect mere distaste for this particular kind of decision making? Or does it indicate more fundamental problems, which merit additional attention and concern?

Gubernatorial Views on Appointments

To be sure, many of the appointive problems which governors recount have long been familiar to students of state politics and public administration. The potential pool of qualified appointees sometimes proves disappointingly thin,[4] while "many of the individuals who were looking for patronage were not individuals you'd like to patronize."[5] The ever-present possibility of scandal or embarrassment is evident in governors' warnings to get police checks on possible appointees,[6] to avoid appointing those with "weird hangups,"[7] to find appointees with "the ability to keep your head down and stay off the front page."[8]

Difficulties occasionally arise when square pegs are placed in round holes: "I think I made mistakes in some of my choices, not necessarily as it regards the man or woman, but as regards the position";[9] "Sometimes you make a bad decision about where a person fits."[10] Governors also refer to the problems created when appointees perform contrary to expectations, that "usually you can expect a change in that person, for the better or for the worse";[11] and, "The better the people you get, the more distance they place between themselves and you."[12]

Still another theme is the inevitable anger of those who were denied the appointments they sought: "[I] got into a lot of hot water because I refused to appoint some of the more prominent Democrats around the state";[13] "I now have twenty-three good friends who want on the Racing Commission. Soon I'll have twenty-two enemies and one ingrate."[14]

While governors have tried to facilitate the appointment process with a variety of advisory mechanisms, the advisory apparatus itself can apparently lead to difficulties: "I had the county chairman of the Democratic executive committee in each of the counties as a member of this advisory commission. . . . My second term, I just abolished them . . . too frequently I would have to justify not taking the advisory committee's recommendation";[15] "Once they (a county delegation) actually come to you with a request, you've lost";[16] "I think screening committees are bad";[17] "One thing I will never do again is go to the blue-ribbon (search) committee."[18]

The detrimental side of the appointive process is strongly suggested by an Arkansas governor's expression of relief that, "We have it better here; at least the governor isn't involved in judgeships."[19] Even more explicit are the laments that "nothing can bedevil an administration more than weakness among appointees. Because if you pick wrong in one or two or three key cases, you find you're spending 90% of your time trying to deal with those weaknesses";[20] and, "If they're bad, you get more minuses for their being really bad than you get pluses out of their being good."[21]

Aides' Views on Appointments

The inimical aspects of the appointive process are expressed even more forcefully by the staff members who participated therein. Their comments are liberally sprinkled with phrases like "geographic paranoia," "greedy legislators," and "those who see a new governor primarily as an instrument for getting rid of good people." They speak of constantly having had to "nag" the governor to fill openings, and of the whole process as a "necessary evil," "an incredible waste of time." Their suggested rules of procedure include few "Thou shalts" and many "Thou shalt nots": Do not consult too widely; Do not delay, thereby letting pressures and expectations build; Do not let applicants or their supporters see the governor personally; Do not make appointments at the front end of a legislative session. The most frequently suggested guideline is simple, but unmistakably ominous: Do not embarrass the governor. In fact, the observation of one aide encompasses the attitude of all: "We always began by looking for the most qualified person; we usually wound up going with the one least likely to embarrass the governor."[22]

While these candid comments identify some of the specific hazards inherent in the appointive process, they still do not wholly answer the questions raised at the outset. Why, given the universal agreement that "gubernatorial power of appointment is a most significant weapon in a governor's arsenal,"[23] do those who have employed these weapons sound so much like the victims thereof?

Volume of Gubernatorial Appointments

One explanatory factor, only hinted at above, may well be the sheer volume of appointments which most governors must make. Wyner, in 1968, referred to "the average governor making approximately 400 statutory appointments, plus appointments to many more advisory boards and commissions."[24] Sabato, in 1978, notes that "each state government, even the smallest, includes scores of boards, agencies and commissions and requires the appointment of thousands of persons."[25] In a 1980 study of California, a state supposedly free of patronage, Bell and Price note that the governor has about 170 appointments to make of heads and administrators of agencies; another 2,200 appointments of part-time members to over 300 state councils and commissions; about 160 judicial appointments in the average four-year term; and appointments to fill vacancies in otherwise elective positions, including those in local governments.[26] These staggering numbers are confirmed by contemporary governors themselves.[27]

Here, perhaps, lies at least a partial answer to the questions raised. While political scientists have traditionally measured the appointment power in terms of freedom to name the heads of major agencies,[28] such appointments are only the tip of the iceberg, both in visibility and in value. The importance of having one's "own" Budget Director or Health Department Director is so clearly advantageous in terms of policy imprint, administrative control, and political loyalty as to clearly outweigh whatever ill will may be raised in the appointment process. What, however, is to be gained from having one's "own" person on the Oil Museum Advisory Commission, or the State Capitol Cafeteria Commission, or the Criminal Justice and Highway Safety Information Center Advisory Board? Indeed, since many statutes only permit gubernatorial appointment of one individual annually to a multi-member board, even having one's "own" person on a University Board of Trustees, or State Highway Commission, may only provide a reliable informant, or an occasional transmitter of gubernatorial preferences. All too often, the only immediate consequence of many such appointments is the anger of the individual being replaced (since virtually everyone serving on such a commission develops a strong proprietary interest therein), and the resentment of those individuals who wanted to be named but were not.

The Appointive Process

Not only can political credit be squandered in the process, but the drain on time and energy can be consequential. While the "key" appointments are usually made early in the gubernatorial term, filling the thousands of lesser offices is an ongoing, unending operation, and although the position itself may seem petty to most observers, it may hold towering significance for those who desire it. The calls and correspondence to the governor's office on only one such appointment can be voluminous, and frequently demand (literally) the governor's personal attention.

Whereas "key" appointments are characteristically made by the governor personally, with a minimum of consultation and checking,[29] the clearance mechanisms for minor appointments can consume inordinate quantities of staff time — a fact which may help to explain why appointment aides are even more critical than the governors themselves. Thousands of recommendations must be solicited and/or acknowledged. At the lowest levels of appointments, (local vocational-technical school advisory committees, for example, or local water districts), nobody in the governor's office may be personally acquainted with any potential prospects; indeed, they may be unable to locate easily anyone who is.

Whether the prospect is a known quantity or not, even minor appointments usually require an elaborate clearance procedure with the appropriate legislators, campaign coordinators, relevant county party chairmen, affected professional or interest groups, and often members of the commission to which a new member is being named. All of those consulted must also be advised of the final outcome. The process of checking out potential appointees frequently precipitates additional nominations, thereby generating additional clearance procedures and lengthening the list of those ultimately to be disappointed.

Political Consequences of Appointments

If, as suggested above, the policy consequences of such appointments are frequently negligible, do the possible political benefits still result in a net plus to gubernatorial power? Again, these thousands of minor appointments are a decidedly double-edged sword. The governor may envision numerous possible political benefits to be reaped from a "good" appointment: the abiding gratitude of the appointee, which hopefully will translate into active political support and generous campaign contributions in the future; the indebtedness of an "interested" interest group; the favorable publicity which may ensue from the naming of some clearly meritorious individual; the applause for egalitarianism which may accompany the appointment of previously neglected minorities. A shrewd appointment may induce the legislative support of a recalcitrant senator or representative; may forestall the future candidacy of a potential opponent, or bind the wounds of a previous opponent; may demonstrate one's solidarity with party machinery, or one's sensitivity to a particular area or county, or one's flair for originality and independence.

Even this partial list of potential political benefits should be instructive: in extraordinarily fortuitous circumstances, a single appointment may accomplish several desirable purposes. Inevitably, however, some considerations — perhaps equally essential to the governor's political posture — must be not only ignored, but thwarted.

Indeed, even within one of these politically advantageous purposes lies a threatening host of possibly disadvantageous consequences: placating one legislator may arouse the jealousy of another; naming a woman for "equity" purposes may anger blacks; rewarding one county with an appointive plum may offend the geographic sensibilities of another area; indeed, satisfying one faction within a county may insure the undying hostility of another faction within that same county. If the governor bows to pressure from nurses (rather than doctors) for a seat on a health advisory board, there still remains the potentially explosive choice between registered nurses and practical nurses. Theoretically, there should ultimately be enough appointments to satisfy all; practically, it does not work that way. Interests and individuals wanting representation on the Board of Private Investigators and Private Security Guard Agencies cannot be placated with a seat on the Committee for Purchases of Workshop-Made Products.

Conflicting Expectations Surrounding Appointments

What confounds the appointing process even further is that whatever considerations finally prevail at the gubernatorial level, these inevitably differ from the purposes and expectations of those who are seeking gubernatorial appointments. Here, as well, an almost infinite panorama of possibilities exists.

Probably most prevalent is the coveted prestige which a gubernatorial appointment is seen to confer. For many appointment-seekers, this is the prime consideration (which helps to explain the dangerously wounded egos of those passed over). Other aspirants may have more specific axes to grind: the opportunity to influence, however slightly, decisions in behalf of one's ideals (protect the environment, promote schoolbook censorship), one's personal concerns (encourage awareness of spinal cord injuries, improve the status of women), one's professional ties (tighten up licensing requirements for realtors, weaken the standards for cosmetology inspections), one's economic interests (get more state funds deposited in savings and loan associations, encourage more state promotion of tourism), or one's locale (obtain a community college in the county, build a four-lane highway in the area). Others may be seeking a political stepping-stone, or at least a forum from which to speak and make useful contacts; still others may desire various "perks" for themselves (per diem pay, travel expenses, good parking at football games, racing passes) and/or their friends (inside information on jobs and contracts). Gubernatorial aides report an astonishing number who confide that they just want a legitimate excuse to get away from home occasionally!

By now, the reasons for the rueful tone which permeates practitioners' discussions of the appointment power may be more apparent. At the upper levels of administration, good appointments do produce, or at least have the strong potential for producing, highly beneficial results. At the lower levels, where the vast majority of appointments are made, the decision-making process is elaborate and exhausting, the policy consequences may be negligible, and the political consequences are frequently a net minus.

Conclusion

In his comprehensive treatment of contemporary governors, Sabato notes that patronage, i.e., the awarding of salaried state jobs to the party faithful, has markedly diminished, and further concludes that:

> The decline of patronage has been judged, somewhat surprisingly, as a boon for governors, since it has liberated them from a tedious, time-consuming, and frustrating chore that is outmoded in the modern political system. At the same time the governor has gained appointive powers where it really matters, at the top-level in policy making positions.[30]

Perhaps it is time to do some equally vigorous pruning of the hundreds of non-salaried positions on advisory boards and councils and commissions to which governors must annually appoint thousands of individuals. How many of these entities are equally "outmoded in the modern political system"?

Many were originally established as "buffer boards," to protect agencies from the ravages of the spoils system. With the decline in patronage and growth of professionalism, their continued necessity is at least questionable. Others owe their origins to the once-felt necessity for "patron" boards, to build enthusiasm and credibility for a new state venture. If the service has acquired popularity and legitimacy, the patrons may no longer be necessary; if not, it may be time to abandon the quest. Many existing committees are enduring memorials to the classic response to a bothersome interest or problem: form a committee to study it. The resulting committee continues to require periodic appointments, but accomplishes little else. Some citizen boards were mandated by federal or state laws, now obsolete, or reflect a since-spent passion for citizen participation. In many other instances, while a totally legitimate function may exist, the necessity for gubernatorial involvement in the appointive process may be much less persuasive.

To summarize, while there is universal agreement on the necessity of ample gubernatorial power to appoint top level administrators, there is some evidence that the power to make appointments to thousands of lower level positions is so excessive as to be counterproductive. In that sense, perhaps governors possess too much of a good thing.

Part V. The Legislative Role

12. The Governor and the State Legislature

Thad L. Beyle and Robert Dalton

The governorship is many things, . . . and the governor must play many social roles and must learn to help the public keep them individually identifiable. The governor is chief of state, the voice of the people, chief executive, commander-in-chief of the state's armed forces, chief legislator and chief of his party. No man acting alone could play so many roles.[1]

The governor is, ex-officio, probably the single most powerful legislative leader in state. He must worry about both the substance of legislative programs and legislative strategies, in order to get favored programs passed and prevent passage of measures he opposes.[2]

The legislative role of the governor is one of several roles, yet many observers of state government regard it as the role around which others revolve. A governor who fails to develop a positive relationship with the legislature may find his executive budget, his programs and policies, or his key appointments tied up in legislative committees or mired in petty controversy. To avoid such embarrassment, a governor must be willing to commit substantial time and energy; in fact, interaction with the legislature is one of the most demanding responsibilities of the office.

Trends in the legislative-executive relationship are difficult to analyze, in part because the conflict and confrontation that draw so much media comment are often but a sideshow that obscures fundamental changes. There are reasons for antagonism between the two branches. The "separation of powers" doctrine is widely espoused but difficult to interpret and apply to specific problems, so it can easily be misused to transform a minor difference about functions or responsibilities into a major confrontation over "principle." The governor has a statewide constituency, and his view of the public interest may be devoid of specifics. The legislator answers to a smaller group of voters whose concerns are more sharply defined, and he may be less interested in the broad sweep of state policy than in the particular impact of a state program or project on his own district. Such differences in perspective are easily exaggerated, and the separation of powers doctrine is irrelevant to the bulk of ordinary legislative business. But neither can they be entirely dismissed. The conciliation and progress that has led to constitutional revision, tax reform, structural reorganization, and other advances in state government should not obscure the fact that the legislative-executive alliance is a fragile one that will not be sustained without effort.

The discussion that follows presents some of the views of the governors themselves as expressed through the surveys conducted by the National Governors' Association and through the series of in-depth interviews with former governors. Unlike many other topics, legislative-executive relations seem to enjoy little consensus. All agree that it is a dimension of state government that is changing rapidly, but opinions vary widely about the substance of the change and about its long-term implications for the performance of state government.

One further trend is apparent: the impact of intergovernmental relations on both institutions. It may have been true once that sitting in a governor's chair or a legislative seat could occur without much concern with other governments— national, state, or local — except your very own government. This is no longer obviously true as governors and legislators must contend with metropolitan areas, councils of government, multistate activities and the various parts of our national government from the president, the bureaucracy, the Congress and the courts. In some ways the state legislatures and governors must cope jointly with the problems and potentials these intergovernmental actors and activities present. The power conflicts in the state capitols have been superceded by the myriad of power conflicts inherent and operating in our federal system, between the states and the federal government.[3] Again, this is not to downplay the existence of internal state level power struggles which still surface, especially when there is divided party control between the governor and the houses of the legislature. We do intend to point out the larger conflict lodged in our federal system of government.

Governors View the Legislature: The Chief Legislator Role

To anyone participating in or observing gubernatorial politics, it is abundantly clear that the relationship to the legislature is of relatively high priority, and it must be addressed immediately by a new governor. Most new governors face their legislatures within the first month of their administration. The state of the state address, the governor's budget, specific programmatic legislation, special messages on high priority programs, oversight of agency bills, and responses to bills introduced by individual legislators head a series of specific policy and budget decisions which a newly-elected governor must make —almost from the day after the election forward.

Over the course of an administration, governors gradually routinize their relations with the legislature in order to reduce the burden on them personally and their office in general. Nevertheless, governors find interaction with the legislature one of the more burdensome activities they face. In the survey of all governors' offices in 1976, appointment secretaries and schedulers indicated that working with the legislature consumed a major portion of gubernatorial time (16 percent on the average), second only to managing state government (29 percent). Sixteen incumbent governors, responding to a separate survey made similar estimates of working time allotted to both managing state government (27 percent) and working with the legislature (18 percent). Twenty-two of fifty-five former governors responding to the question about aspects of the job they found most difficult and demanding, indicated that working with the legislature was most difficult — second only to the interference with their family life.

During 1978 and 1979, in the interviews conducted with former governors who had left office since 1976, several of the governors proceeded through nearly two hours of discussion concerning modern state government without any substantial mention of the legislature, while others raised the subject almost immediately. This fact overlay the diversity of opinion among governors about the importance of legislative relations to their executive performance. The relationship is perceived as difficult, yet necessary. Governor Shapp includes the behavior of the Pennsylvania legislature on the list of crises that shaped his administration; after storms, floods, and infestations of the gypsy moth, he cited "man-made disasters, such as dealing with the legislature."[4]

At the other extreme Governor Walker argued that governorships should be evaluated with no reference to legislative success. "Most of the people in the State of Illinois, and I think this is true across the country, are much more affected in their daily lives by the operation of the administrative and executive part of government than they are by ninety percent of the bills that go through the General Assembly."[5]

Several governors described their relationship with the legislature in terms of specific battles, such as tax reform measures or budget items. But the modal viewpoint is probably that expressed by Governor Apodaca of New Mexico: "Even in the legislature, I felt we were always in control over our programs."[6] His statement is consistent with the sixteen incumbent governors who say they agreed with this statement offered in an NGA survey of 1976: "The governor should be the most significant single force in the legislative process with a legislative program of his or her own and efforts to get it passed."[7]

Governors View the Legislature: Some Problems in the Relationship

Some of the problems in the executive-legislative relationship are structural in nature. Governor Exon faced the unicameral, non-partisan legislature of Nebraska without nominal party support, so he had to create new coalitions to cope with each significant issue. Governor Shapp had a legislature that could ignore his proposed budget, whereas Governor Lee's budget could only be reduced by the Maryland legislature, not increased. Governor Edwards not only faced a heavily Democratic general assembly in South Carolina, but also a legislature which was relatively more powerful than he, constitutionally. He could not succeed himself, and many state agencies were controlled by boards or commissions whose members were selected by the assembly. Akin to this is Governor Holshouser's complaint that an elected council of state member, by virtue of his independence from the governor and his relationship with key legislators, forestalled Holshouser's policy goal of competency testing in the North Carolina public schools.

Some problems are more political in nature. Governor Dukakis continually faced and was not able to find an effective way to deal with some of the permanent ideological factions of Massachusetts' Democrats in the legislature — liberals, conservatives, moderates and those specifically representing rural, urban and suburban constituencies. Governor Walker claimed he faced a permanently hostile coalition, the Daley loyalists, and was unable to create a legislative power base within his own Democratic party, let alone lead the party. Some, like Governor Pryor, had an easier job, as both he and the legislature were not only Democratic but worked together. Governor Askew claimed the key to getting legislation passed was to set aside questions of party politics and attempt to persuade legislators on the basis of issues.

Split party control focuses the partisan issue more directly. Governor Shapp's image of the legislature was that of a board of directors, but with a large contingent on that board playing for his party's competition — the Republicans. Both Edwards and Holshouser, Republicans, faced overwhelmingly Democratic legislatures which occasionally created conflict. Yet both noted they tried to downplay partisanship, out of necessity.

It was at the personal level that the most positive bridges to the legislature were built by the governors. At least eight of the fifteen governors had served in their legislatures previously and had developed a sense of what was legislatively possible and how legislators would react to given proposals. Governors Edwards, Holshouser, and Bennett (Kansas) — all Republicans — especially indicated the importance of this background for their administrations. This prior legislative experience had developed friendships in the legislature to which they could turn for advice and counsel.

This latter point should be broadened to indicate that the legislature was one significant source of advice to governors on given issues. Governors indicated that in addition to keeping the legislative leadership informed about pending issues, they gather advice in discussions with the legislative leadership. Governor Schreiber suggested "in general (the legislators) furnish the most realistic sounding board that the governor could hope to have."[8] However, other governors indicated the advice sought was less on the substance of proposed policies as on the political aspects: "How will bill X do in the general assembly?" "Will policy Y be acceptable to the citizens of house district 58?"

Thus the governors' views of their legislative role are complex and indicate just how difficult fulfilling that role is. The constraints are structural, political, ideological and personal. Yet these were also the sources of strength that governors could call on to help in their relationship with the legislature. What emerges from the interviews is a picture of a relationship in which the legislatures are often friendly to the governors, but occasionally hostile. To paraphrase Governor Schrieber, a governor has to work with the legislature in order to realize his policy goals, so a governor might as well try to make the relationship as smooth as possible.[9] This is not done easily. These governors leave an overall impression that they struck a positive relationship with their legislatures, and the absence of gubernatorial criticism is something of a contrast to the visions of animosity often conjured up by the press.

Governors View the Legislature: Some Reservations

Recent literature indicates the resurgence of state legislatures. The National Conference of State Legislatures (NCSL) feels state legislatures have evolved over the past two decades into "full partners in the formulation of state policy." This was accomplished, NCSL indicated, in a three stage process: (1) the removal of certain constraints on legislative activity; (2) the adoption of procedures and practices designed to expedite the legislative process; and (3) the development of "interest and capability for reviewing and analyzing the activities of government and overseeing the performance of the executive branch."[10]

The Council of State Governments reports that state legislatures have been in the process of consolidating their reforms — "the removal of constitutional restrictions on legislative activity, compensation, and session time" — while concentrating increasingly on evaluation and oversight activities, thereby "making more effective use of legislative time and resources."[11] Some legislative observers feel the growth of the executive oversight and review function by state legislatures has been the greatest single change over the past decade.[12]

Jewell and Patterson discuss means by which legislators control executive agencies: statutory authorization, approval of appointments and legislative vetoes. However, they note that a number of problems undermine the legislative oversight function, that oversight by investigation is rare and that legislative fiscal control is still relatively weak.[13] On the other hand, several recent studies find that legislative oversight of administrative agency rule making has been increasing, raising constitutional questions of separation of powers and political questions of who sets and administers public policy.[14]

A cautionary note was sounded by several governors on the increasing strength and capability in the legislatures. Several were apprehensive about the balance of powers between the executive and the legislative branches, the encroachment by the legislature upon the rightful domain of executive authority and interference in matters of administration. Governor Askew was concerned about the enlargement of legislative staffs: "[They] wind up staffing the legislative branch in order to give it some independence. Then the staff has got to have something to do. So they wind up really usurping the authority of the executive branch. . . . That is unfortunate."[15]

As legislatures grow more responsible, professional, and expertly staffed, governors such as Askew and Walker mentioned the tendency of some state legislatures to go beyond establishing policy to trying to implement it, occasionally in the guise of "oversight." Governor Walker noted a further problem:

bureaucrats begin to pay more attention to key legislators than to their line supervisors, obscuring lines of responsibility and actually worsening the problems of inefficient bureaucracy.[16]

In a related area, some of the legislatures have taken steps to develop a more "meaningful role for themselves in the implementation and management of federal policies and programs."[17] Such activities as review of federal funds flowing into the state and state agencies and review of administrative rule making have been supported by court decision and constitutional changes.[18] As to this intrusion into intergovernmental relations, Governor Askew was fearful of the legislature's attempt to interfere with the spending of federal grant money, even when federal law expressly delegates that as a gubernatorial responsibility.[19]

In sum, while legislative reforms and resurgence may be creating a partnership, the governors often see the intrusion of legislative activities into previously executive areas as a problem and a threat.

Conclusion

What emerges from this sample of interviews and other data from governors, former governors and their staffs is the substantiation of the continuing importance of the governor's legislative role in state government. Unlike the governor's political party role which has been declining significantly in most states, governors generally perceive themselves as the key legislator, with legislative relations at the heart of their administration. They face constitutional, ideological, political and personal constraints, but in these also lie strengths on which they can call.

Of importance is the general sense that conflict is not necessarily at the base of the gubernatorial-legislative relationship but that there is a partnership involved in which mutual accomodation and cooperation are major components. Here we would like to restate an important but often ignored fact of government: governors and legislators spend most of their policy-related efforts trying to work with and orchestrate existing policies to achieve some goal, and spend comparatively little time creating policy that is altogether new. Gubernatorial and legislative activities then are somewhat systematic processes (i.e., the budget) by which the principles guiding governmental action are arranged and rearranged to achieve some version of the public interest. The larger contours of state government organization, policy and commitment are generally agreed upon; it is the specifics of how the policy is implemented and the order of priorities which can cause conflict.

The new locus of tensions and potential conflict between the two major actors in the states lies in the resurgence of the legislatures. Of particular significance here is the development of a legislative oversight effort and intrusion of legislatures into intergovernmental relations questions especially through their budgetary powers. Both have raised gubernatorial concerns.

Finally we must call attention to the findings presented elsewhere on the declining importance of the governor's role as political party leader. Morehouse's findings have highlighted the influence of the governor's role as party leader in relations with the legislature, and that it was in his legislative relations that the political party role may have been most important.[20] While there are certain qualifications attached to research findings on this question,[21] her basic thrust has been accepted by other researchers.

However, with the declining strength of political parties in the states — due to the impact of the mass media and single issue politics, among other reasons — governors have less formal political structure and partisan attachments on which to call. The party is now only one among several potentially useful instruments available to the governor in his working with the legislature.

13. The Governor as Chief Legislator

Thad L. Beyle

This chapter more closely examines how a governor carries out his/her responsibilities of being the chief legislator. In order to understand better the legislative-executive relationship from the gubernatorial perspective, staffing the governor's offices for working with the legislature, developing the governor's legislative program, gubernatorial lobbying, use of the veto, and gubernatorial involvement in legislative elections are discussed.

Staffing the Governor's Office for Legislative Liaison

Virtually all governors' offices have an individual who serves as the governor's legislative liaison or assistant. However, there is sufficient variation in the titles for this role that only eleven of the thirty-seven respondents (30 percent) included "legislative" among the words in their official title. This suggests that those fulfilling this role in the governors' offices also fill other roles such as executive assistant, administrative assistant, legal advisor, or counsel, even though only two respondents indicated spending less than 50 percent of their time on legislative activities. Of course, the frequency and length of legislative sessions have much to do with the work load of these legislative assistants.

Those performing the role were generally in their thirties (average age thirty-five years), were male (88 percent), had college degrees (94 percent), and had law degrees (65 percent), although others (25 percent) had postgraduate degrees in history, political science, or social work.

There was little pattern in the backgrounds of those serving in this liaison capacity. For example, a few came from the governor's campaign staff (26 percent), and a few had served as legislators (24 percent), as former legislative staff members (38 percent), as civil service employees (12 percent), or as locally elected officials (18 percent). Further, forty-one percent had served only one session as legislative assistants, with another 35 percent having served two sessions, indicating that three out of four assistants had served two or less sessions in the role. At the other extreme, three reported serving five sessions and one as many as eight sessions as legislative assistants for the governor.

The attitudes and opinions of the responding legislative assistants on executive-legislative relations are shown in Table 13.1.

While all respondents agree that a governor needs a fulltime legislative assistant, especially while the legislature is in session, there is considerably less agreement as to whether the legislature should be made more effective (better

Table 13.1. Opinions of legislative assistants[a]

Opinion	Agree	Indifferent, no opinion	Disagree
I don't see how any state can get along without at least one full-time person in the governor's office to deal with legislative relations, at least during the legislative sessions.	35	1	0
Our legislative branch needs stronger standards on such subjects as disclosure and conflict of interest.	20	3	8
Our legislators should be paid more.	17	4	10
Our executive branch needs stronger standards on such subjects as disclosure and conflict of interest.	14	4	13
Our legislature needs more staff.	14	5	14
Agency bureaucracies have more impact than they should on what goes on in the legislature at the expense of elected officials such as the governor and legislators.	11	3	17
The legislative recommendations of the governor are not given as much weight in the legislature as they should be.	13	0	19
On balance, a small group of legislators has more influence on agency budgets than the governor does.	9	1	22
Our legislative sessions should be longer.	4	1	27

a. While there were thirty-seven states which responded to this request for information, not all responded to each item.

pay and larger staff), and little support for having the legislature stay in session longer. The legislative assistants were naturally more likely to see the need for higher ethical standards in the legislature than in the executive branch. On power relations questions, the respondents were split on their views: only a few see a small group of legislators more dominant on agency budget questions than the governor; slightly more feel that the governor's legislative recommendations do not carry as much weight in the legislature as they should; and some perceive that the bureaucrats in the agencies have more impact on the legislature than do either the governor or legislators.

There were some variations in these responses, depending on the size of state represented by the respondents. Those from smaller states were more likely to see the need for stronger ethical standards and more pay for legislators, and to feel that the governor's legislative recommendations are not given as much weight by the legislature as they should be.

Respondents from states with greater gubernatorial power were less likely to feel that better ethics are needed in the executive branch and that the legislature does need more staff.[2]

Developing the Governor's Legislative Program

Table 13.2 presents data on the development and presentation of what is called the governor's program. While some governors may not wish to have

Table 13.2. The governor's legislative program[a]

	Frequencies	Percent
DEVELOPING THE PROGRAM		
Have a somewhat formalized procedure by which each agency is asked to submit recommendations, which are then reviewed and the agencies advised of what is approved for submission.	22	60
Have a more informal procedure by which the agency heads check with legislative liaison or the governor on what is appropriate to submit.	12	35
Have no procedure at all. Agencies generally make their own decisions.	2	5
IDENTIFYING THE GOVERNOR'S PROGRAM		
A list of bills recommended for enactment by the governor.	29	90
Distinguish between the governor's program and the departments' or agencies' programs.	28	78
A prepared summary of the governor's legislative recommendations.	27	84
Submit draft bills to implement every item in the governor's legislative program.	20	56
No list of bills, but extracts from messages and press conferences indicating legislation recommended by the governor.	8	22
Do not use a concept of "governor's legislative program" as such, although the governor does from time to time take positions on legislation.	6	17
The budget or the state of the state message contains recommendations or summary.	3	8
PRESENTING THE GOVERNOR'S PROGRAM		
Governor presents state of the state message.	36	(35 in person)
Governor presents budget message.	35	(23 in person)
Governor presents other messages[b]	21	(13 in person)

a. While there were thirty-seven states which responded to this request for information, not all responded to each item. The frequencies are the actual number of states indicating agreement with the statement; the percentages represent the percent of responses agreeing to that particular statement.

b. Forty-five separate messages were reported, twenty-five presented in person. Some of these messages were reported by the same governor so that only thirteen governors in twenty-one states reported in person on these forty-five messages. Subjects of the messages included energy (five), transportation (two), corrections (two), economic recovery (two), health care (two), social services (two), growth and development (two), and closing address or prorogation (four). Two states reported at least five separate gubernatorial messages.

such a concept used, especially since observers can track the legislative success or failure of their administration, thirty-four of the thirty-six states responding indicated there was a procedure for developing a governor's program—although for 35 percent it was an informal process.

For many, the governor's program is usually contained in broad brush strokes in the state of the state message, the budget message, special messages on particular topics of highest concern to the governors (60 percent reported their governor doing so), or in positions the governor or his staff take in personal interviews or at news conferences. However, most states further specify the contents of such a program by identifying it as a list of bills (90 percent of the states), issuing a prepared summary of the program (84 percent), and distinguishing it from state department or agency bills (78 percent).

Thus, across most of the states there is a discernible process by which a governor's program is developed and presented to the legislature. Governors in the larger states were slightly more likely to have a more formal procedure by which the program is developed, and to submit draft bills to implement each item. Governors with less formal powers were more likely to maintain a distinction between their own and agency bills. A report by the National Governors' Association (NGA) addressed this latter situation.

> The Governor's power to review draft agency legislation before it is submitted to the legislature is generally not based in statutes of the State. Rather, it is part of the overall supervisory relationship between the Governor and the agency director. In circumstances where the governor's supervisory power is limited, as with agencies that are headed by other elected officials or by boards or commissions that are not particularly responsive to the Governor, the Governor's legislative review power also tends to be limited. The Governor's review power may also be avoided by lower-level agency personnel who work with interest groups that are capable of having legislation introduced without the endorsement of the Governor.[3]

Less power and less control therefore mean more distinction between the governor's own program and those of the agencies. However, even these governors are not without recourse as they are able to use their executive budget power to review agency legislative requests.

The Governor and Lobbying

The governor of Ohio, and other high-level Ohio state officials, recently decided to register as lobbyists before the legislature under that state's lobbyist disclosure law which defined a "legislative agent" as one who spends "at least a portion of his time influencing legislation." This registration as a lobbyist highlights the fact that the state administration and the governor are the chief lobbyists before the state legislatures. This part of the governor's role is moving beyond the presentation of the state of the state, budget, and other messages, to working with individual legislators and legislative committees on pending legislation throughout the legislative session.

Tables 13.3, 13.4, 13.5, and 13.6 present the activities which are performed by the governor and staff in this role. Clearly the main differences are whether lobbying, working on the legislative calendar, recruiting witnesses for hearings, encouraging agencies and others to lobby, and providing questions for legislators are performed routinely or occasionally. Preparing legislative floor speeches is where many legislative assistants draw the line as to the extent of their activities. However, the larger gubernatorial staffs are considerably more likely to write floor speeches for friendly legislators.

Table 13.3. Legislative activities of governor's legislative assistant/staff[a]

	Often	Sometimes	Never
Lobby with individual members	31	4	1
Discuss legislative calendar with leadership	22	12	1
Recruit witnesses to testify before committees	16	16	3
Encourage agencies and interest groups to lobby	15	14	6
Provide questions for friendly legislators	13	20	2
Prepare floor speeches	2	19	13

a. While there were thirty-seven states which responded to this request for information, not all responded to each item.

Table 13.4. Lobbying[a]

	Yes	No
Does legislative liaison have floor privileges when legislature is in session?	21	14
Do you have rules regarding lobbying by state agency heads or other state staff?	20	15
Nature of rules:		
Must clear positions in advance with governor's office.	4 states	
Traditionally staff and agency heads don't oppose governor's bills or "linger" near the legislative chamber.	2 states	
They are discouraged from these activities but expected to be on call for testimony.	2 states	
Registration and reports are required where legislative liaison is not included in job description.	2 states	

a. While there were thirty-seven states which responded to this request for information, not all responded to each item.

Table 13.5. State's tradition on governor/staff testifying before legislative committee[a]

	Will testify upon request	Rarely	Generally no, but depends	Does not testify	Would refuse strong request to appear
Governor	7	2	2	15	2
Executive assistant/ chief of staff	27	1	1	2	—
Legal counsel	24	1	1	1	—
Press or news secretary	10	1	1	16	—
Yourself (legislative assistant)	22	2	2	3	—

a. While there were thirty-seven states which responded to this request for information, not all responded to each item.

Table 13.6. Policy for dealing with individual legislators[a]

	Yes	Percent
Governor has an open door for legislators. He will always see them; no major efforts are undertaken to divert them to staff members.	27	75
Some significant attempts sometimes taken to handle legislators who wish to see the governor by having staff members handle their problem; but if a legislator does not find these satisfactory he always has the option of talking to the governor.	6	17
Combination of 1 and 2 above.	2	6
There are some circumstances where individual legislators will not get to see the governor even if they insist on it.	1	3

a. While there were thirty-seven states which responded to this request for information, not all responded to each item.

Sixty percent of state legislatures represented here accord the governor's legislative assistants floor privileges, especially in those states in which the governor has less formal powers.

Finally, as to the personal involvement of the governor in lobbying, the responses indicate that the governor and his/her news secretary are least likely to testify before the legislature, leaving that activity, if it is to be carried out by a member of the office staff, to the executive assistant, legal counsel, or legislative assistant. If there is personal testimony by the governor, it appears to occur more frequently in the smaller states. The governor rarely goes directly to the legislature to lobby. Rather, lobbying by the governor takes place on his or her "turf"—the governor's office or mansion—or in special messages. It is the staff which goes to the legislature.

Governors without considerable formal power rely on techniques such as clearly distinguishing their own program from agency initiatives or by placing more rigid rules on agency lobbying in the legislature without gubernatorial clearance. They also rely on one of their most important formal powers—the executive budget authority—indicating that the formal/informal power distinction blurs in fulfilling the gubernatorial role.

During the legislative session, governors use various means to ensure close contact with members of the legislature, whether they are legislative leaders or rank-and-file legislators and regardless of their political party affiliation. Over two-thirds of the responding states reported they used traditional formats for meetings between the governor, legislative leaders, and rank-and-file legislators.

The most common of these are dinners at the Governor's mansion for legislators, a reception at the mansion at the time the legislative session opens, breakfast meetings with the legislative leadership, weekly luncheons or office meetings with the leadership of the governor's party during the legislative session, and social gatherings near the end of the session.[4]

As a general rule, most governors' offices allow a legislator to see the governor almost any time he wishes, although in eight states the staff tries to intervene depending on the issue involved and the governor's time schedule. Only one state reported there were circumstances where legislators would be refused access to the governor. Further evidence on the prevalence of this rule is found in the responses of seventy-two incumbent and former governors to the following proposed policy advice for new governors: "Keep an open door policy for legislators." Only two of these governors did not agree with this policy statement.

The Governor and the Veto

The most direct power the governor can exercise vis-à-vis the legislature is the use of or threat to use the veto. Of course there are differences in the veto power extended to governors, from total bill veto to item veto to item reduction power to amendatory veto to no veto at all (as in North Carolina).

The first question facing the governor is whether to use the potential veto power during the legislative process. Should the governor commit in advance to sign or veto a particular bill, in answer to either a reporter's or legislator's query? Should the governor do so as an explicit part of his negotiating strategy with the legislature, since the mere threat of a veto can be a considerable weapon in securing defeat of a bill?

As the responses of both the legislative assistants (1976) and the former governors (1979) suggest, well over one-half of the governors take the general position that they never decide in advance whether to sign or veto a bill (see Table 13.7). Three-quarters of the remaining legislative assistants indicate each case is handled on its merits, which view is echoed by the former governors. Both indicated that governors from the larger states were more likely not to take a general position on the use of the potential veto and handle each case on its merits as were the former governors who had served in the 1970s.

The second question facing the governor regarding the veto is the philosophy undergirding its actual use (see Table 13.8). While there is not exactly agreement on when the veto should be used, responses of the legislative assistants and former governors indicate there is nearly complete agreement that constitutionality or budget balancing are not the sole reasons for exercising a veto. Only five former governors dissented from this view. However, 10 percent of the legislative assistants and nearly 30 percent of the former governors feel a governor has "a kind of super no vote." There is an even split among the assistants and a 60 percent majority agreement among the former governors when asked if the political consequences of a veto should be taken into account even when a "bad" bill is involved. Obviously the political consequences impinge on the governors personally to a greater degree than on the legislative assistants. Finally, there is considerable support (74 and 92 percent respectively) for the more restrained position the bills should be signed unless the governor has very strong objections.

Table 13.7. Threat of the veto[c]

	Legislative assistants[a]		Former gov.[b]	
	Yes	Percent	Yes	Percent
How does governor/legislative assistant answer questions as to whether the governor will veto certain legislation if it passes?				
Answer the question always to the best of knowledge.	4	11	5	29
Take a general position that the governor never decides in advance on whether to veto a bill.	20	55	13	62
Take no general position like the two above but handle each case on its merits.	12	33	12	71

a. While there were legislative assistants from 37 states who responded to this 1976 survey, not all responded to each item. The frequencies are the actual number of states indicating agreement with the statement; the percentages represent the percent responses agreeing to that particular statement.

b. These represent the responses of 25 former governors to a 1979 survey. One former governor was unable to answer these questions as his state did not provide the governor with a veto.

c. For the questions on the threat of the veto the legislative assistants were given a forced choice of selecting one answer, the former governors were allowed to answer each yes or no. Hence the data frequencies and percentages are noncomparable but illustrative.

Governors' legislative assistants from the smaller states and from governors' offices with less formal powers were considerably more likely to agree with the restrained position. This suggests there are underlying restraints on the exercise of the veto power, no matter what its constitutional form may be. In other words, even when a governor has the constitutional right to veto legislation, he or she may be unable to do so in practical terms.

A further problem facing the governor is captured in the "hard case" veto situation presented to the legislative assistants, where a veto would be politically unpopular and would not accomplish the termination of the legislation because it would be overridden by the legislature. Their responses indicate that even in the face of such adversity, the veto would be used by governors to stake out their position or objections. However, this is not a problem to all governors, as overriding a veto is unusual in most states.

For example, in all the 1977–78 legislative sessions, governors vetoed 5.2 percent of all bills passed by the legislatures, and only 8.6 of those vetoed bills were then passed into law by a legislative override. There were no legislative overrides of gubernatorial vetoes in twenty-four states, while in twenty-four others overrides did occur. The number of vetoes ranged from only two in Montana (1.6 percent) and Vermont (0.8 percent) to 274 in Illinois (18 percent) and 155 in New Jersey (30.1 percent).[5]

The overall rates of 1977–78 vetoes (5.2 percent) and veto overrides (8.6 percent) compares with the 1947 figures of 5 percent of bills being vetoed and 6 percent of these being overridden.[6] While the rate of gubernatorial vetoes has

Table 13.8. Governor's veto philosophy[c]

	Legislative assistants[a]		Former gov.[b]	
	Agree	Percent	Agree	Percent
A decision to sign or veto should be based solely on grounds of constitutionality or balancing the budget and the governor should not interpose his or her feelings or position on the question.	0	0	3	14
The considerations that go into the decision to sign or veto legislation should be the same as those that go into a decision on whether to propose a particular bill. All "bad" bills (ones for which the governor would not vote were he a legislator) should be vetoed—PERIOD.	3	10	6	29
In considering whether to veto legislation, the presumption should be that all "bad" bills (as defined above) should be vetoed. However, this presumption should not lead to vetoes in all cases, as political consequences of vetoes need to be taken into account.	14	48	12	60
A decision to sign or veto is not the same decision as one a legislator would make to support a particular bill. The presumption should be that a bill which has passed both houses should be signed unless the governor has a very strong objection to it.	23	74	22	92
Hard case veto: If the administration were confronted with cost-increasing legislation that was very popular (e.g., a tax-relief bill), but which you opposed, and were as certain as one can be in this world that the veto would be overridden, would the governor veto the bill?	28	90	20	91

a. While there were legislative assistants from 37 states who responded to this 1976 survey, not all responded to each item. The frequencies are the actual number of states indicating agreement with the statement; the percentages represent the percent of responses agreeing to that particular statement.

b. These represent the responses of 25 former governors to a 1979 survey. One former governor was unable to answer these questions as his state did not provide the governor with a veto.

c. For the hard case veto those who responded "probably yes" were folded into the "yes" category. (Legislative assistants—21 "probably yes," former governors—2 "probably yes.")

remained constant over the three decades, the rate of legislative overrides has grown nearly fivefold indicating a recent escalation in legislative-executive conflict over legislation.

The final set of questions facing the governor regarding the veto concerns the procedures established to advise the governor on his or her decision, and how those affected by the decision are involved in the process (see Table 13.9).

Table 13.9. Governor's veto procedure

	Legislative assistants[a]		Former gov.[b]	
	Yes	Percent	Yes	Percent
Governor or staff requests comments on legislation from agencies.	34	94	19	86
Legislative liaison/staff examines legislation and makes recommendation.	33	94	22	96
Legislative liaison/staff requests comments on legislation from affected parties or interest groups.	31	86	19	86
Routinely receives opinions from attorney general.	16	44	11	50
Assume that unless you hear from the affected agencies to the contrary that they concur in the governor signing the bill.	12	39	9	43
Puts the burden of identifying the legislation and initiating comment on the agencies.	9	30	2	10
No formalized procedure; each bill handled separately.	4	15	Not asked	

a. While there were legislative assistants from 37 states who responded to this 1976 survey, not all responded to each item. The frequencies are the actual number of states indicating agreement with the statement; the percentages represent the percent of responses agreeing to that particular statement.

b. These represent the responses of 25 former governors to a 1979 survey. One former governor was unable to answer these questions as his state did not provide the governor with a veto.

Nearly all states rely on the agencies to provide comments, although several also indicate that they actually put the burden on the agencies to initiate comment, or that unless agencies speak up, the assumption is they concur in the governor signing the bill (more likely in smaller states).

Almost all responding states request comments from affected parties or interest groups and approximately one-half of the states routinely receive opinions from the attorney general on the bills, the latter situation most prevalent among the larger states. Only four of the legislative assistants reported no formal procedure, with each bill handled as an individual case.

Once the governor has made a tentative decision to exercise the veto power, almost all states reported that affected legislators are notified of decisions, as are the affected agencies and agency heads (see Table 13.10). However considerably fewer states indicated they have an appeals process to the governor's decision and very few allow the option of a public hearing under any conditions. Thus, while the courtesy of notification prevails across the states, in a good proportion of those states responding, the legislative assistants and former governors indicated that once a decision on a bill is made by the governor, it stands. In sum, the veto power and process is a more narrow gubernatorial power and not an overall executive branch power, although members of the administration outside the governor's office are involved throughout.

Table 13.10. Governor's veto notification procedure[c]

	Legislative assistants[a]		Former gov.[b]	
	Yes	Percent	Yes	Percent
Notify the affected legislators of your intentions.	32+	88	20	83
Notify the affected agency of your intentions, if the agency head would have problems with the decision.	33+	92	19	86
Is there an appeals process for agency?	18	60	8	36
Is there ever a public hearing?	3+	9	1	4

a. While there were legislative assistants from 37 states who responded to this 1976 survey, not all responded to each item. The frequencies are the actual number of states indicating agreement with the statement; the percentages represent the percent of responses agreeing to that particular statement.

b. These represent the responses of 25 former governors to a 1979 survey. One former governor was unable to answer these questions as his state did not provide the governor with a veto.

c. Legislative assistants were more qualified in their answers to this series of questions. For the three answers marked with a (+), some indicated the governors generally did so (included in the "yes" category) or sometimes did (not included in the "yes" category).

The Governor and Legislative Elections

Another method to directly influence the legislature is to take an active role in legislative elections and in the selection of legislative leaders. The method is obviously fraught with potential problems. The NGA report stated the dilemma facing the governor in his or her own party's primaries:

It can be argued that the Governor must be active in contested primaries within his own party in order to make sure that the party fields strong candidates, to support his faction or wing of the party, to unseat legislators who wear his party's label but do not support his programs, and to fulfill the role of party leader. On the other hand, it can be argued that the Governor should never be active in his party's legislative primaries because his involvement would be viewed as intervention in the free choice of the local voter, because such action is not conducive to party unity under the Governor's leadership and because the person he supports may lose and he may, therefore, be confronted with legislators of his own party against whom he campaigned.[7]

As can be seen from Table 13.11, governors are split on this dilemma, with 21 percent playing a hands-off role, 15 percent an activist's role, and 64 percent agreeing that selective involvement is appropriate.

The case for involvement in general elections should not normally pose a problem for the governor, as the option of not participating at all in general elections is not realistic from the governor's position as chief party leader. If there is a question, it is over how extensive his involvement will be. This is reflected in the responses of the legislative assistants, with 50 percent indicating an activist involvement and 41 percent a selective involvement. Only three (9

Table 13.11. The governor and legislative elections[a]

	Agree	Percent
PRIMARIES IN THE GOVERNOR'S PARTY		
The importance of fielding strong candidates who are reasonably disposed toward the governor's policies warrants active participation by the governor and/or staff in the candidate selection process in the governor's party.	5	15
In a few select cases, involvement by the governor and/or staff is appropriate.	21 (5)	64
Under no circumstances should the governor or top staff ever be involved.	7	21
GENERAL ELECTIONS		
As leader of his party, the governor is obligated to campaign as much and as hard as his or her schedule will permit.	17	50
Some involvement by the governor, such as endorsing candidates of his or her own party, is appropriate but a major campaign effort is not.	14 (3)	41
The governor should not participate in any major way.	3 (1)	9
LEADERSHIP SELECTION		
Leadership selection is critical to a successful administration. The governor can and should play a very active role.	0	0
Because the selection of legislative leaders in the governor's own party will have an effect on management of the state, the governor should be consulted, should feel free to express his or her opinions and those opinions should be accorded some weight.	7	21
The selection of leadership is strictly an internal matter of governance for the legislature. The governor should play absolutely no role in the process.	26	79

a. Some of the respondents and governors had not been in office long enough to pass through the cycle of party nomination, general election, and leadership choice, so they were asked to "speculate" on "what you think that policy (governor's) will be." These are indicated in parentheses ( ) beside the numbers, and are included in the overall frequency. While there were thirty-seven states which responded to this request for information, not all responded to each item. The frequencies are the actual number of states indicating agreement with the statement; the percentages represent the percent of responses agreeing to that particular statement.

percent) indicated that the governor did not participate in any way in the general elections.

Finally, as to the governor's role in the selection of legislative leadership, the responses suggest that governors by and large stay out of this aspect of legislative politics (79 percent) or take a relatively moderate role of expressing their views (21 percent). No legislative assistant indicated his governor takes an active role. However, experienced watchers of state government and politics surely must question just how valid this latter finding is. For example, one legislative assistant commented as follows:

I . . . find it very difficult to accept a judgment that a governor plays no role in the selection of legislative leaders. The governor's ability to communicate, albeit on a very *personal* basis, with key legislators to make his preferences and annoyances clear, cannot be avoided. It is probably safe to say that a governor will make no public endorsement or comment on a struggle for legislative leadership. It is probably also safe to say that it is rare that a governor will let someone else perform this function for him even on a discreet basis. I think it is unlikely that the governor actually remains neutral in most situations.[8]

In this area, where gubernatorial political power runs squarely into the separation of powers doctrine, politics or political involvement by the governor is not necessarily reduced; rather, it is kept at a less visible level.

Governors most and least active in legislative elections were found to be from states with less formal gubernatorial powers at their disposal, while those moderately active tended to be from states with the higher rankings of power. This relationship suggests that there is a subtle balancing of political and formal gubernatorial powers, especially in gubernatorial involvement in legislative elections. "Weaker" governors dare not enter the electoral thicket as they may fear that losing will further weaken them, while strong governors need not enter as they have other powerful weapons at their command relative to the legislature.

Conclusion

This chapter has presented data on the governor's legislative role from the perspective of the governor's office. This role is of major importance to the governor and staff, and, while there are slightly varying modes of fulfilling that role across the states, the clear message is how similarly the governors approach and carry out their legislative role.

Of interest is the sometimes subtle interplay of formal and informal power bases that the governor can call upon and use in relations with the legislature. Perhaps more important is that governors are not inclined to deal with the legislature on a power basis—overt, hard-sell lobbying, use or threat of vetoes, campaigning for election of friendly legislators or openly advancing favorable legislative leaders. Instead, the emphasis is more toward bargaining, personal contact and interaction in many forms to achieve success in legislative goals.

The American state governor, for the most part, undertakes his legislative role in a most active manner, using all possible tools and approaches available.

14. Governors and Lieutenant Governors

Thad L. Beyle and Nelson C. Dometrius

States established the office of lieutenant governor partly in emulation of the national model of the vice president and partly due to their own colonial experience with absentee governors.[1] The major function of the office is to provide for a competent successor should the governor be unable to fulfill his or her duties. All other functions, with the possible exception of some ceremonial roles, could be performed by other state officials. Understandably, most analyses of the office of lieutenant governor have focused on keeping the office filled for possible transition to the governor's chair, or trying to upgrade the caliber of men or women selected as lieutenant governors.

However, suggestions for doing away with the office have recurrently been put forward. The thrust of these suggestions is captured in Warren Isom's observations in the late 1930s:

> The office of lieutenant governor has been the object of a great deal of scoffing because, among other things, it is said that in the 33 states in which he is presiding officer of the senate he has little power as such. . . .
>
> The fact that it [lieutenant governorship] is not found in 13 states is evidence that it is not an essential office, and the fact that governors are overworked in many states where the office exists, is indicative that it is not as useful a device of government as it might be.[2]

Despite this and similar plaints, the office has gradually been adopted by other states. At the turn of the century, thirty-five states had the office, thirty-eight in 1950, and forty-one in 1975, with four other states designating the secretary of state as lieutenant governor. Obviously, states feel there is utility in the office of the lieutenant governor.

Governors View Lieutenant Governors

This chapter will bring the views of a new set of actors to bear on the question of the usefulness of lieutenant governors—the governors themselves. The objectives are to identify: (1) how lieutenant governors are utilized by the governors, and (2) what factors might help account for the varying roles they play in different states.

Rather than continuing the more usual commentary on transition or qualities of the persons involved, this chapter will focus on the lieutenant governor's official duties. There are two rationales for this approach. First, the lieutenant governor's qualifications as a competent, potential successor to the governorship are presumably shaped by his or her training in the lieutenant governor's office itself.

Second, while the focus on transition is important, it is also important to understand those functions performed by lieutenant governors who may never accede to the chief executive's position. In particular, how do governors utilize the resources which lieutenant governors represent?

In 1976, a questionnaire was sent out to about 200 incumbent and former governors, from which seventy-four (sixteen incumbent and fifty-eight former governors) responses were obtained.[3] One of the questions asked of the governors was whether they gave any assignments to their lieutenant governors other than those constitutionally or statutorily mandated.[4] As Table 14.1 indicates, nearly 45 percent did make some assignments and 32 percent did not, while 24 percent did not have a lieutenant governor on whom to rely. Further, there were several tendencies in making or not making assignments to lieutenant governors. Lieutenant governors were more likely to have been given assignments by their governor if: (1) they served in the northeast or midwest; (2) they served with governors with high formal powers; (3) they served with governors who were Republicans; (4) they served with governors who had previously been lieutenant governors.

There is also at least one interactive effect going in the other direction—they received fewer assignments if they served in the south and for Democratic governors. The one-party dominance, the overriding importance of the Democratic Party primary, and the one-term gubernatorial limitation—all parts of southern gubernatorial politics—have virtually assured that the lieutenant governor will be a political competitor for the gubernatorial chair.

There are obviously many other explanations as to why lieutenant governors are seldom fully utilized. What we wish to investigate more fully here is whether certain specific conditions lead to a governor's greater or lesser use of his lieutenant governor. The two conditions to examine are: (1) the lieutenant governor's method of selection, and (2) the statutory and constitutional obligations of the office.

Selection Method

The selection process is the first step in developing the later relationship between the governor and lieutenant governor. A few states follow the presidential model of nominating both candidates as a ticket by convention, but most states select the two candidates independently through primary elections. The most significant recent change in this process has been the growing number of states requiring the team election of the governor and lieutenant governor. Beginning with New York in 1953, the number of states which require that the governor and lieutenant governor run as a team in the general election has now grown to twenty-two. Four states—Kansas, Florida, Maryland and Montana—further require that the two candidates run as a team in the primary election.

Table 14.1. Gubernatorial use of lieutenant governors

Question: "Did you make any assignments of continuing responsibility to your lieutenant governor?"

| | Number responding to question[a] | Made assignments to lieutenant governor | | | | No lieutenant governor | |
| | | Yes | | No | | | |
		Percent	Number	Percent	Number	Percent	Number
Total sample	(72)	44.4	(32)	31.9	(23)	23.6	(17)
Region[b]							
Northeast	(16)	56.3	(9)	6.3	(1)	37.5	(6)
Midwest	(17)	58.8	(10)	41.2	(7)	0.0	(0)
South	(21)	28.6	(6)	47.6	(10)	23.8	(5)
West	(18)	38.9	(7)	27.8	(5)	33.4	(6)
Size of state							
Largest third	(20)	45.0	(9)	35.0	(7)	20.0	(4)
Middle third	(30)	50.0	(15)	30.0	(9)	20.0	(6)
Smallest third	(22)	36.7	(8)	31.8	(7)	31.8	(7)
Gubernatorial power[c]							
High	(17)	70.6	(12)	11.8	(2)	17.6	(3)
Medium	(32)	28.1	(9)	46.9	(15)	25.0	(8)
Low	(23)	47.8	(11)	26.1	(6)	26.1	(6)
Party affiliation of governor							
Democrat	(41)	36.6	(15)	39.0	(16)	24.4	(10)
Republican	(29)	58.6	(17)	20.7	(6)	20.7	(6)
Other	(2)	0.0	(0)	50.0	(1)	50.0	(1)
Time of gubernatorial tenure							
Pre-1970	(37)	40.5	(15)	37.8	(14)	21.6	(8)
Post-1970	(35)	48.6	(17)	25.7	(9)	25.7	(9)

Length of gubernatorial service				
Less than 4 years	(36)	47.2 (17)	36.1 (13)	16.7 (6)
More than 5 years	(36)	41.7 (15)	27.8 (10)	30.6 (11)
Governor was a lieutenant governor				
Yes	(12)	58.3 (7)	25.0 (4)	8.3 (1)
No	(60)	41.7 (25)	31.7 (19)	26.7 (16)

a. Two of the 74 governors responding to the questionnaire did not respond to this particular question, so the sample size for this table and analysis is 72 usable responses.

b. The states were grouped as follows for regions: *Northeast*—Connecticut, Delaware, Maine, Massachusetts, New Hampshire, New Jersey, New York, Pennsylvania, Rhode Island, Vermont. *Midwest*—Illinois, Indiana, Iowa, Kansas, Michigan, Minnesota, Missouri, Nebraska, North Dakota, Ohio, South Dakota, Wisconsin. *South*—Alabama, Arkansas, Florida, Georgia, Kentucky, Louisiana, Maryland, Mississippi, North Carolina, Oklahoma, South Carolina, Tennessee, Texas, Virginia. West Virginia. *West*—Alaska, Arizona, California, Colorado, Hawaii, Idaho, Montana, Nevada, New Mexico, Oregon, Utah, Washington, Wyoming.

c. Power of the governor was based on an updated version of Joseph A. Schlesinger's index of formal powers including appointment power, budget power, tenure, and veto. See Schlesinger, "The Politics of the Executive" in Herbert Jacob and Kenneth N. Vines, eds., *Politics in the American States* (Boston, Ma.: Little, Brown and Company, 1971), p. 232. Using Schlesinger's scale, which runs from a low of 7 to a maximum of 20, the categories are high (20-18), moderate (17-14), and low (13-7).

Table 14.2. Lieutenant governor use by party differences[a]

		Lieutenant governor's political party			
Assignments made by governor to lt. governor		Same as governor		Different from governor	
		Percent	Number	Percent	Number
Yes	(32)	65	(26)	40	(6)
No	(23)	35	(14)	60	(9)
Total	(55)	100	(40)	100	(15)

a. Sixteen of the 72 usable gubernatorial responses came from states without a lieutenant governor's office and another had a vacancy in that office; all 17 are excluded from this table and analysis.

The major rationale behind the team election of the governor and lieutenant governor is to avoid the embarrassment of these two individuals being of different parties. Eugene Declercq and John Kaminski's study, covering the period of 1950 to 1975, found that party divisions existing between these two offices were as great as 25 percent in 1966 but, due to increasing use of team elections, dropped to 18.7 percent in 1975.[5] Our own sample has a party split in 27.3 percent of the cases.[6] If there is concern about preparing the lieutenant governor for the governorship, it hardly seems reasonable that a governor will include a political opponent in significant policy-making or publicity-generating activities of state government. Table 14.2 confirms these suspicions, as there is a strong difference between the use made by governors of lieutenant governors based on whether they are or are not of the governor's party—65 percent used if of the same party while 40 percent used if not of the same party.

Obviously, requiring a team election eliminates the problem of a party split between the two top offices, but does it contribute any more to the role of the lieutenant governor? Most states require team balloting in the general election only.[7] Consequently, the governor may have little control in the selection of his running mate even though they are of the same party.

Does the requirement that they sink or swim together lead these individuals to cooperate during the campaign and possibly build a basis for later cooperation while in office? Table 14.3 shows a strong tendency in this direction since, when looking only at cases where the governor and lieutenant governor are of the same party, lieutenant governors are still used more often in states which require a team election (80 percent vs. 50 percent). The evidence is not conclusive, however, since even in those states where there is no team election, one half the governors gave assignments to their lieutenant governors. To explore this issue further, we will examine the impact of office duties on the use of the lieutenant governor.

Office Obligations

In an attempt to provide for full utilization of the lieutenant governor, many states have constitutionally or statutorily attached various duties to the office.

Table 14.3. Lieutenant governor use by team election, controlling for party similarity[a]

Assignments made by governor to lt. governor		Governor-lieutenant governor team election			
		Yes		No	
		Percent	Number	Percent	Number
Yes	(26)	80	(16)	50	(10)
No	(14)	20	(4)	50	(10)
Total	(40)	100	(20)	100	(20)

a. This table includes only those cases (40 of 72 usable responses) where both the governor and the lieutenant governor are from the same political party.

The job of presiding officer of the senate is very common, and some states have taken this a step further by making the lieutenant governor a true legislative leader, primarily by giving him or her the power to select legislative committees and their chairpersons. However, the most recent trend is in the opposite direction. States such as Alaska have provided that their lieutenant governors will serve as secretary of state, thus making them administrative officials.

Each of these approaches provides the lieutenant governor with substantial duties, yet there are potential drawbacks. First, state government reorganizations have consistently been concerned with consolidating state activities under the governor. Making the lieutenant governor either an administratively or legislatively powerful official may mitigate the effects of this consolidation. Such officials are highly visible alternatives to the governor, and they have the tools to damage the governor's program either in the legislature or from within the administrative branch. Governor-lieutenant governor feuds are not unknown. Governor Edmund G. Brown, Jr., recently asked his state's supreme court to void an appointment made by his lieutenant governor while he was out of the state and to limit the use of powers by the lieutenant governor unless absolutely necessary. However, the court ruled in December 1979 that the lieutenant governor may exercise the powers of governor when the governor is out of state. Providing lieutenant governors with a substantial constitutionally mandated role in state policy making may prepare them to be more effective managers. However, at the same time, it may also make the governor's job of directing and coordinating state government more difficult.

A second problem with constitutionally mandated duties is that while providing for the current use of the lieutenant governor, they do not necessarily provide well-rounded training for acceding to the office of the governor.[8] This could be mitigated if the governor assigns the lieutenant governor extra tasks to complement his other duties. Further, as Sabato notes, "The abolition of his legislative duties has helped to make him a firm and integral part of the executive branch, with his allegiance clearly owed to the governor rather than a house of legislators.[9]

Do the obligations of the office make a difference in the assignments made to

Table 14.4. Lieutenant governor use by legislative duties of the lieutenant governor[a]

Assignments made by governor to lt. governor		Legislative duties					
		None		Presiding officer only		Presiding officer and appoints committees/chairmen	
		Percent	Number	Percent	Number	Percent	Number
Yes	(32)	91.7	(10)	53.6	(15)	43.8	(7)
No	(23)	8.3	(1)	46.4	(13)	56.3	(9)
Total	(55)	100.0	(11)	100.0	(28)	100.0	(16)

a. Sixteen of the 72 usable gubernatorial responses came from states without a lieutenant governor's office and another had a vacancy in that office; all 17 are excluded from this table and analysis.

the lieutenant governor? While there were no cases with a secretary of state as lieutenant governor in the data, the evidence involving lieutenant governors with legislative duties (Table 14.4) indicates that the answer is yes. Over 90 percent of those without any other duties are given assignments by the governor, contrasted with about 44 percent of those with substantial legislative responsibilities.

It is not surprising that a lieutenant governor with many legislative duties might not be called upon to perform tasks for the governor. It is intriguing, however, that even having the minimal role of presiding officer also makes a difference in the extent to which a lieutenant governor is used (53.6 percent vs. 91.7 percent). Surely lieutenant governors might be willing to perform other tasks, but the governors seem less inclined to use them than lieutenant governors with no legislative duties.

While a possible reason for this finding is that governors are leery of appearing to violate the separation of powers, this concern has seldom stopped governors in the past. A more likely explanation is that a governor can avoid the responsibility of making assignments to his lieutenant governor if he already has other prescribed duties, but pressure from the press or public cannot be sidestepped if the governor is the sole source of a lieutenant governor's duties. This point is further supported by those cases where we would assume the governor had little desire to work with his lieutenant governor—cases where there is a party difference between the two officials. In the one case where the lieutenant governor had no other obligations, the governor assigned him duties. In the fourteen situations where the lieutenant governor had some legislative duties, only five (35.7 percent) were given assignments by their governors. Obviously, such a small number of cases makes any conclusions suspect, but the findings are supportive of the conclusions drawn from all the cases.

Thus far, the evidence indicates that recent changes in the states will promote greater utilization of lieutenant governors by governors. The trend in the states is to adopt team election requirements and, concurrently, greatly reduce the lieutenant governor's legislative role.

Types of Duties Performed

Simply making assignments for the lieutenant governor is only one concern. Another is to know the manner of assignment. The governors surveyed were asked to list the kinds of assignments they made to their lieutenant governors (see Table 14.5). Some indicated up to five separate assignments, with liaison assignments and policy/management assignments being mentioned equally by the total sample (37.3 percent). Ceremonial assignments were somewhat less frequent (25.4 percent).[10]

Again, there are certain tendencies in the types of assignments made by governors to lieutenant governors.

Liaison assignments were made to a greater extent by governors in the northeast and midwest, in the larger states, by those with high formal powers, by Republicans, and by those who served longer terms in office.

Policy and management assignments were made to a greater extent by governors in the south and west, in the smaller states, by those with low formal powers, by Democrats, by those who have served in the 1970s, and by those who previously served as lieutenant governors.

Ceremonial assignments were made to a greater extent by governors in the west, by those with moderate formal powers, by those who had served prior to 1970, and by those who had not served previously as lieutenant governors. There was a general trend away from assigning ceremonial duties. As Sabato notes, "Ceremonial activities attract a great deal of publicity; publicity builds name identification; non-controversial, harmless public activities tend, in fact, to build favorable identification."[11]

Of concern is whether the factors examined in the earlier section—team election, party difference, and extent of legislative duties—also determine the type of duties performed by lieutenant governors.

Political party affiliation of these two top actors in the state does make a difference in the type of duties assigned. There is a direct relationship: when the governor and lieutenant governor are of the same party, there are more liaison and fewer ceremonial assignments; the reverse is true if they are of different parties (see Table 14.6). This trade-off between liaison and ceremonial assignments is even greater when the two are not only of the same party, but run as a team in either the primary or the general election (see Table 14.7).

Unlike the findings on gubernatorial assignments to lieutenant governors, the legislative duties of the lieutenant governor are not as significant in determining the type of assignments made (see Table 14.8). There is a tendency for governors to make more policy management and fewer liaison assignments to lieutenant governors who have legislative responsibilities. This is especially true when the governor and the lieutenant governor are of the same party. However, when these two actors are of different parties, no specific assignments are made unless

Table 14.5. Type of assignments given lieutenant governors by governors

	Number of respondents	Number of assignments made	Type of assignments[a]					
			Liaison		Policy/management		Ceremonial	
			Percent	Number	Percent	Number	Percent	Number
Total sample[b]	(72)	(67)	37.3	(25)	37.3	(25)	25.4	(17)
Region[c]								
North	(16)	(23)	43.5	(10)	30.4	(7)	26.1	(6)
Midwest	(17)	(24)	45.8	(11)	33.3	(8)	20.8	(5)
South	(21)	(11)	27.3	(3)	45.5	(5)	27.3	(3)
West	(18)	(9)	11.1	(1)	55.6	(5)	33.3	(3)
Size of state								
Largest third	(20)	(21)	52.4	(11)	23.8	(5)	23.8	(5)
Middle third	(30)	(31)	35.5	(11)	38.7	(12)	25.8	(8)
Smallest third	(22)	(15)	20.0	(3)	53.3	(8)	26.7	(4)
Gubernatorial power[d]								
High	(17)	(27)	44.0	(12)	29.7	(8)	25.9	(7)
Moderate	(32)	(20)	35.0	(7)	35.0	(7)	30.0	(6)
Low	(23)	(20)	30.0	(6)	50.0	(10)	20.0	(4)
Party of governor								
Democratic	(41)	(29)	27.6	(8)	44.8	(13)	27.6	(8)
Republican	(29)	(38)	44.7	(17)	31.6	(12)	23.7	(9)
Other	(2)	(0)	0.0	(0)	0.0	(0)	0.0	(0)
Tenure								
Pre-1970	(37)	(27)	37.0	(10)	25.9	(7)	37.0	(10)
Post-1970	(35)	(40)	37.5	(15)	45.0	(18)	17.5	(7)
Length of service								
Less than 4 years	(36)	(30)	30.0	(9)	46.7	(14)	23.3	(7)
More than 5 years	(36)	(37)	43.2	(16)	29.7	(11)	27.0	(10)

Governor was a lt. governor

Yes	(12)	(15)	40.0	(6)	46.7	(7)	13.3	(2)
No	(60)	(52)	36.5	(19)	34.6	(18)	28.8	(15)

a. These responses were grouped into three categories as follows: *Liaison assignments*: Chair conferences and committees (11); legislative liaison (9); sit in on conferences (5); local government liaison (2); party liaison (1); federal liaison (1); and satellite governor's office (1); *Policy and management assignments*: industrial development (5); kept lieutenant governor briefed and ready to assume governor's chair (3); general policy assignments (3); acting governor when governor is out of state (2); investigative matters (2); reorganization (2); interagency relations (2); specific assignments when governor out of state (2); energy policy (1); general management (1); growth policy (1); and serving as "my right hand man" (1); *Ceremonial and other minor assignments*: ceremonial (16); and other occasional assignments (1).

b. See footnote *a*, table 14.1.

c. See footnote *b*, table 14.1.

d. See footnote *c*, table 14.1.

Table 14.6. Type of assignment by party differences[a]

Type of assignment given lt. governor by governor		Lieutenant governor's political party			
		Same as governor		Different from governor	
		Percent	Number	Percent	Number
Liaison	(25)	40.7	(22)	23.1	(3)
Policy/management	(25)	37.0	(20)	38.5	(5)
Ceremony	(17)	22.2	(12)	38.5	(5)
Total	(67)		(54)		(13)

a. Sixteen of the 72 usable gubernatorial responses came from states without a lieutenant governor's office and another had a vacancy in that office; all 17 are excluded from this table and analysis.

Table 14.7. Type of assignment by team election, controlling for party similarity[a]

Type of assignment given lt. governor by governor		Governor-lieutenant governor team election			
		Yes		No	
		Percent	Number	Percent	Number
Liaison	(22)	43.2	(16)	35.3	(6)
Policy/management	(20)	37.8	(14)	35.3	(6)
Ceremony	(12)	18.9	(7)	29.4	(5)
Total	(54)		(37)		(17)

a. This table includes only those cases (40 of 72 usable responses) where both the governor and the lieutenant governor are from the same party.

the lieutenant governor has some legislative responsibilities, in each case here—presiding only.

Again, the evidence indicates that team elections lead governors to assign more significant responsibilities to their lieutenant governors. The trend to team elections for these two executives does fit with more liaison, or "speaking on the governor's behalf," assignments. There is less impact of the lieutenant governor's legislative role, primarily since this was a major determinant on whether any assignments were given at all.

Conclusion

This research has demonstrated that more than governmental structure and good intentions are needed to ensure more adequate and relevant use of lieutenant governors in the states. How they are selected, partisan differences with their governors, and obligations of their office all interact on the uses governors will make of lieutenant governors.

We also realize that personality variables are excluded from the analysis.

Table 14.8. Type of assignments to lieutenant governor by legislative duties and party differences[a]

Type of assignment given lt. governor by governor		Legislative duties			
		No		Yes	
		Percent	Number	Percent	Number
Overall					
Liaison	(25)	42.9	(9)	34.8	(16)
Policy/management	(25)	28.6	(6)	41.3	(19)
Ceremony	(17)	28.6	(6)	23.9	(11)
Total			(21)		(46)
Governor/lt. governor—same party					
Liaison	(22)	45.0	(9)	38.2	(13)
Policy/management	(20)	30.0	(6)	40.9	(14)
Ceremony	(12)	25.0	(5)	22.7	(7)
Total			(20)		(34)
Governor/lt. governor—not same party					
Liaison	(3)	0.0	(0)	25.0	(3)
Policy/management	(5)	0.0	(0)	41.7	(5)
Ceremony	(5)	0.0	(0)	33.3	(4)
Total			(0)		(12)

a. Sixteen of the 72 usable gubernatorial responses came from states without a lieutenant governor's office and another had a vacancy in that office; all 17 are excluded from this table and analysis.

They are obviously important in this governor-lieutenant governor relationship. While personality variables may be significant, there was no way in which to measure them except when volunteered.

We do not want to suggest in this chapter that all states should move in one direction in terms of how they view their lieutenant governors. The 1976 version of *The Lieutenant Governor: The Office and Its Powers* suggests there are four main models of a lieutenant governor's role: (1) traditional, (2) executive, (3) legislative, and (4) administrative. The suitability of each is dependent upon the state's needs and characteristics.[12]

We are suggesting that states should first determine what role their lieutenant governor should perform. If a state wants the lieutenant governor to play an active role and to be suitably trained for succession, the results of this research based on the views of former and incumbent governors suggest that the most effective way of accomplishing this end is to reduce political and administrative blocks between the governor and the lieutenant governor. This leads to team election of the governor and lieutenant governor, reducing a lieutenant governor's involvement in the legislature, and his or her becoming more a part of the gubernatorial administration. As state governments reorganize their structures and responsibilities, locking in certain constitutional or statutorial duties may have short-term positive effects, but may have other, longer-term effects of a not-so-positive nature. A more flexible approach to defining the lieutenant governor's role is suggested, so states are not faced with the dilemma of Lieutenant Governor David O'Neal of Illinois. O'Neal, who had served since 1976, resigned in August 1981 to return to private life. He indicated the office was a confining job which should either be strengthened, made part-time or abolished.[13]

His action, leaving the state without a lieutenant governor until 1983, pinpoints an alternative possibility that some states may wish to consider: doing away with the office altogether. Allen Pease, who served in the Maine governor's office for many years, would prefer eliminating these standby offices (including the vice presidency at the national level) "rather than spend a great deal of effort in neutralizing these offices or in making them useful to the Chief Executive."[14] It might well be worth investigating the experiences of Maine and the six other states without the office of lieutenant governor to see what if any differences exist in how state government operates.

Part VI. The Structural Role

15. Governors' Offices: Variations on Common Themes

Thad L. Beyle

The number of employees working directly under the president has been growing steadily since New Deal days when only a few dozen people served in the White House entourage. . . . The most disturbing aspect of the expansion of the presidential establishment, as it is often called, is that it has often become a powerful inner sanctum of government, isolated from tradition, constitutional checks and balances.[1]

While there has been much concern voiced about particular personalities and styles of White House staff, more recently the concerns have focused on the growth in size itself, on the power of non-accountable (publicly) officials, the uses to which the staff are put, on how the office is organized, and on what alternative staffing models might be available for use.[2] Cronin lists the following factors as significant in the changes seen in the office: the expansion of the role of the presidency itself tied usually to emergencies; the distrust of the permanent government by the presidential establishment; the need for higher level coordination for policy consistency and conflict resolution; the inclusion of interest group representatives within the White House staff; the development of a large public relations apparatus; and, the abdication by Congress of significant authority to the president.[3]

In the states, observers have also noted that governor's offices are becoming larger, gubernatorial staffs are increasing in size and in actual and potential influence; and, in some states, a more institutionalized organization is developing around the governorship itself. While not rivaling that of the presidency it is instructive to compare the concerns of those viewing the national executive office with the trends now at work at the state level, with states moving from personalized governorships to more institutionalized (and less personalized) offices of the governors.

Organizing and Managing the Governor's Office

An early decision facing the new governor is how to organize and staff his immediate office. Over the years, views of what size and type of staff governors need have changed. An early survey of the office in the states had only scattered references to office staffing and organization.[4] In the 1950s, Scace pleaded for more staff indicating that governors should be surrounded by approximately five men of loyalty, competence, and especially versatility, each of whom would be charged with specific responsibilities but flexible enough to handle a number of different tasks.[5] Howe reported changes in the Pennsylvania governor's office in which a secretary to the governor coordinated his staff and a Secretary of Administration supervised administrative agencies. Under each secretary were several persons with fairly narrowly defined responsibilities.[6]

Ransone, in one of the classics on the office, devoted a whole chapter to staffing and organizing the governor's immediate office. He contrasted Nevada and California as to the degree of formalization of gubernatorial staff organization, inferring that the informality in such offices as Nevada's was "doomed" to move toward the formalization found in California. He also noted that a chief of staff or executive assistant was required to provide adequate coordination of the office staff in the larger governors' offices.[7]

A decade later, a forty-eight state survey indicated that only eight states (17%) had no clearly designated chief of staff, with thirty-six of the states (75%) having formally designated a chief of staff. In the others a press aid or chief secretary doubled up on their roles in providing staff leadership. They also found that once "the need to formalize the line of authority within the office" in a chief of staff there was considerably less need to formalize other staff members' interactions.[8] Another study conducted at about the same time concluded that in general, governors' offices were becoming more structured, specialized, formalized, and hierarchical. Interestingly there was a partisan differential: "Democratic staffs are more loosely structured, involved in more functions, less formal, and more reliant on their judgment in reaching their own decisions." The Democratic gubernatorial staffs were also smaller than their Republican counterparts.[9]

By 1976, the National Governors' Association (NGA) reported that not more than five states lacked an executive assistant/ chief of staff.[10] Thus institutionalization as measured by establishing a formal authority line from governor to a chief of staff had become the rule in governors' offices.

There is of course the debate over whether such an organizational arrangement places too much power in the hands of a non-elected official or officials. One side of the argument is articulated by Tropp who compared gubernatorial and mayoral staffs. He found that growth in size, complexity, and power of such staffs has led to an inordinate conception of power in a select circle around the chief elected official, that cabinet secretaries and major department heads have been derogated as the staff "interposes" itself between these officials and the governor or mayor, and that the chief executive is cut off from alternative and valuable sources of information and public contact. Moreover, there is too much "groupthink" and sycophancy around these chief executives. He calls for, among other measures, a reduction in staff size, complexity, and control and access to the chief executive.[11] Sprengel was bothered by this earlier, suggesting that by proximity to the governor and control of information, the staff could become "executive substitutes, assistant executives, or executive alter egos" in total submission of self to the governor."[12]

These concerns were also voiced by one-quarter of the former governors (thirteen of fifty-one responding) who answered no to the question as to whether they would advise new governors to have an executive assistant or chief of staff through whom most of the agencies and immediate staff would report on most occasions.[13] Their stated reasons were: need to allow direct access to the governor (seven former governors); governor needs to know what is happening (four former governors); governor needs to develop working relationships with them (two former governors); and, governor needs to work on the problems to administer (two former governors). In some of their own words:

> Especially immediate staff [should report directly to the governor]. The inflow of ideas, solutions, opportunities must be varied and diverse. The filter principle is inevitable but if a governor can't accomodate the direct reporting of administrative/finance/legal/press/political [aides] and at least his party chairman, he is becoming the alter ego of his own subordinate.

> The governor should let it be clearly known that he is accessible at all times to key staff members and to his cabinet. The executive assistant should be just that, the governor's assistant who is available when the governor isn't or is otherwise engaged.

The case for an executive assistant is made at several levels; the sheer necessity for someone to be in charge of the office and staff, to ensure that everything is being done that should be done, to conserve the governor's time and energies and to coordinate various activities. NGA also reported that "regardless of the role envisioned, one person nearly always assumes the role of cabinet coordinator and staff director. He or she is usually the executive assistant."[14] Three-quarters (thirty-eight of fifty-one responding) of the former governors answered yes to the need for new governors to have an executive assistant. They indicated that an assistant brings order to the situation and acts as a filter (seven former governors); gives the governor time to think (six former governors); can often serve in a governor's place (five former governors); can handle routine matters and send major problems to governor (four former governors); and more simply, the governor needs help (four former governors). In some of their own words: "Impossible to make yourself available to all. Too time-consuming to have to listen. Need a good strong executive assistant that you can trust to fulfill these duties." "Relieves governor of much time-consuming work and enables him to establish *his own* priorities for attention."

However, some former governors provided warning signals on making sure the executive assistant is capable, always allowing ultimate access to the governor, have more than one such assistant, and for the governor to keep on top of things even with such assistance.

Analyzing some of the 1976 NGA data, Williams admitted that the executive assistant can dangerously control the flow of information and access to the governor, but found an opposite phenomenon occurring. Viewing the executive assistant as a "gatekeeper," he constructed a "gatekeeper index" to measure the strength of the position and found that governors who spend 40 percent or more of their time on political and public relations functions are more likely than other governors to have a strong executive assistant/gatekeeper, and that they are more likely to encourage public contacts. He thus argues these governors use strong executive assistants to "protect them from administrative detail," and thereby the gatekeeper role may, paradoxically contribute to more open gubernatorial administration.[15]

Nevertheless, Tropp, Williams and some governors all speak uneasily of the potential negative impacts on governors that the Nixon-Haldeman White House organizational model presented the country. And others argue for a more political model in which access is relatively open to the chief executive. In former governor and President Jimmy Carter's initial concept of the presidency, the chief executive is at the center of "spokes of the wheel" with all information, advice and concerns coming to him. There is obviously tension between these two different approaches to organizing the office.

Size of the Governor's Office

Recent studies also document the growth in size of gubernatorial staffs. In 1956 Ransone found an average staff size of eleven (both clerical and professional), with a range from three to forty-three.[16] By 1976 the National Governors' Association reported the size had increased to an adjusted average of twenty-nine (both clerical and professional), with a range from 7 to 245. Three years later this had grown further to an adjusted average of thirty-four full-time employees, with a range of 6 to 262.[17] Looking at the growth of professional staff only, during the twelve year period 1956–68 alone the average grew from 4.3 to 7.3.[18] Unfortunately, the NGA data do not distinguish between professional and clerical staff, so the 1968 figure is the latest available.

While it is clear that the size of the governors' offices do vary with the size of the state, it is also apparent that governors' staffs tend to be proportionately larger in the smaller states. This indicates a certain minimum size necessary to perform the activities and responsibilities of the governor's office. The NGA suggested that in 1976 "the normal Governor's staff size is twelve persons plus four more for each million persons in the State's population."[19] The fact that these figures may underestimate the actual size of the governor's staff is suggested by the three states in 1979 reporting considerable use of borrowed personnel from state agencies and the twenty-six others which made some use of such personnel.

This growth is also reflected in the size of the governor's office budget, which by NGA data grew from an adjusted average of $672,000 in 1976 to $1,177,350 in 1979. While the growth of gubernatorial staffs accounted for a portion of this increase, the fact that the average cost per staff member rose from $23,000 to $36,000 over the three year period suggests it is costing more to attract and keep the staff needed for the modern governor's office.

Governors queried about the size of their own offices did not seem to be concerned over this growth in size. Of sixteen incumbent governors asked about staff size in 1976, only one preferred a smaller staff while six felt they needed even more staff in a wide variety of activities. None of fifty-four former governors responding to the 1976 survey felt their staffs were too large, with eleven indicating they needed larger staffs.[20]

By all available indicators, the governor's offices in the fifty states have been growing in much the manner the White House has, and for some of the same reasons. Some growth can be accounted for by increases in the traditional activities of the governor. For example, as the population has increased so too has the volume of mail focusing in the governor's office. While comparative data are not available, in 1976 thirty-six states' governors' offices averaged almost 200 cards and letters per day—and approximately as many phone calls.[25] This requires considerable staff assistance to handle such volume. Twenty-nine of the forty-one offices responding in 1979 indicated one or more persons in the office primarily involved in traditional political activities, and one suspects the other offices do also but are leery to answer such a question directly. And there was an average of 3.5 persons performing press duties in the forty-one offices, ranging from a half-time person in a small state to thirteen in one of the larger offices. Clearly some of the traditional gubernatorial functions of working with the public, press and politics are still of significance in the size of the office.

However, it is in some of the more policy related areas of concern and responsibility that we find some of the major reasons for growth. Certainly the crises facing presidents with their national and international aspects rivet the attention of the media and the public to the president's actions and reactions. And he has increased his staff in these areas accordingly. Governors too can face dramatic crises, although not of the same scope, i.e., a weather or environmental disaster, a volcanic eruption or earthquake, a major fiscal crisis or civil disturbance. These crises engender their own particular policy and administrative responses across the states which often are forgotten or placed in mothballs once the crisis has passed.

Over the past two decades however, the governors have had to cope with an intergovernmental crisis which has focused problems, demands, functions, planning, and programs on the governor's office. Between 1962 and 1980 federal grant-in-aid programs increased from an estimated 160 to over 500, and the federal grant-in-aid dollar has risen from $7.9 billion to $91.5 billion.[22] Not all these programs or dollars flow into or through state government, let alone the governors' offices, but a sufficient number do to make the planning and use of them by the state a major gubernatorial concern.

This has led to several organizational and gubernatorial staff changes. Since coordination becomes an important need, and at the highest levels of government, states have reorganized into fewer agencies and departments (twenty-one major reorganizations since 1965), have established cabinet systems (36 states by 1979)[23] and have revamped their budgeting and planning processes. In the governors' offices themselves several changes are seen. There is increasing use of agency liaisons or aides concerned with the programs and activities that cross cut several agencies or departments. Two-thirds of the governors' offices listed such a person in the *1976 Directory of Staff Assistants to the Governors* and in 1979 over 80 percent of the forty-one reporting states indicated an average of 3.67 people per office involved in federal-state relations.[24] Included in these figures are some of the thirty states which maintain state offices in Washington, D.C., for federal-state purposes. Approximately half of the states reporting in 1979 also indicated there was at least one person on the governor's staff involved in policy development activities. Thus part of the growth of gubernatorial staffs can be attributed to the intergovernmental position of the governor and what to some governors must have seemed an intergovernmental crisis.

The Governor's Extended Office

There is growing awareness that merely looking at an organization chart depicting the governor's office or reviewing the governor's office budget seriously underestimates the real size and capability of the governor's staff. We noted before that many offices reported use of borrowed personnel from the departments and agencies of state government. In fact only nine of the forty-one reporting states in 1979 indicated *no* use of such personnel. Augmenting scarce staff resources with such borrowed personnel, paid from an agency's budget, can increase gubernatorial ability and reach.

Of even greater importance is the governor's reliance on the budgeting and planning agencies in carrying out his duties. These two agencies, often viewed as "two of the most important among those central management organizations commonly employed to reinforce his executive leadership," increasingly have been moved closer to the governor and his staff by the governors themselves.[25]

While these offices are by nature management oriented, they also can expand the governor's policy effort from merely coordinating and providing liaison activities to policy development. This is especially important vis-à-vis the intergovernmental problems governors face. In fact NCA surveys in 1979 indicated that budget offices provided the governor with a source of management support and as a lobbying base for the governor's programs in the legislature, while planning offices provided assistance where various types of intergovernmental questions were involved.

Governors must address questions on budgets and policies early in their administration, indeed early in the transition process. Organizationally they must decide several questions. The first is how close to the governor's immediate office the budget planning/policy offices should be. If not in the immediate office should they be lodged within a cabinet level department (i.e., administration or finance) or freestanding outside a cabinet official's line of authority? For example, in 1978 the governor of North Carolina moved his Office of State Budget and Management from the Department of Administration into his immediate office, making the State Budget Officer one of his two executive assistants. (His salary was still paid by Administration.) Governor James Hunt indicated that he "pulled the budget closer to the governor's office [because] if you know what you want to do programmatically, you've got to have the budget close to you."[26] As the governor's liaison to departments and agencies the budget officer has both the normal budgetary and the additional political clout of the governor. The governor also recast the state planning office in the Department of Administration into a policy development office.

This trend toward creating a policy planning, analysis and/or development staff is fairly recent among the governors and as Flentje has noted "while no stable organizational pattern has emerged, most of the staffs are located in the state planning office, the central budget agency, or the governor's office."[27]

A final question facing governors is whether the budget and planning or policy offices should be separate or combined into a state-level Office of Management and Budget (OMB) with an interest in overall state policy, including those policies for which a financial dimension is not paramount. In recent years governors have moved in this direction, raising the number of state OMB style staff agencies from seven in 1975 to nineteen by 1978.[28] Although the definition of each state's version of what such an OMB should be varies, the general trend is unmistakable and one which greatly enhances the governor's power through his extended office, much as the president's power is increased by his OMB.

> The policy staffs most commonly assist the governor in preparing the annual legislative program, coordinating executive branch planning, conducting special studies of new or existing state policies, and overseeing intergovernmental relations. They may also conduct economic and demographic analyses, assist in local development projects, draft executive orders or carry out a host of semi-related activities. The most critical function of these staffs, however, is to provide the governor an independent source of advice on a broad range of state policy issues.[29]

How Well Does the Governor's Office Work?

Evaluation of an organization's activities and performance is a difficult task as there are so many perspectives one can use, i.e., the citizen, the party leader, the agency head, the legislature, the media, the office staff itself, and finally the governor. Here we will attempt to evaluate the governor's office from the

Table 15.1. Former governors' views on office functions[a]

Staff function	Responses			Overall index score[b]
	Worked well	Not bad	Worked poorly	
Legal (other than attorney general)	24	7	1	4.30
Budgeting	38	12	2	4.23
Appointments (boards & commissions)	35	14	1	4.20
Agency liaison	34	17	0	4.17
Office management	32	19	1	3.99
Legislative relations	33	17	3	3.92
Staff coordination	31	19	2	3.89
Press relations	32	19	3	3.84
Scheduling	28	18	4	3.70
State/local relations	25	26	1	3.65
Recruiting agency heads	23	25	1	3.62
Federal/state relations	24	23	5	3.41
Planning	20	19	9	3.07
Legal services (from attorney general)	24	16	13	3.02
General political liaison	12	32	7	2.75

a. Responses were received from fifty-eight former governors; however, not all governors answered all the questions in the survey or all the items in this question, hence the varying number of responses per item.

b. The index score was created by scoring the responses: Well = 5; Not bad = 2.5; Poorly = 0, and dividing by the total number of actual responses to the item.

perspective of former governors and some on-site visits to selected governor's offices. All the data were collected between 1976 and 1981.

Views of Former Governors

Obviously with the changes that have occurred in the governors' offices recently, it is important to find out just how well these offices function. The most critical evaluator of how well the office worked is the governor himself. Was he pleased or not with staff performance? In the 1976 survey of former governors the following question was posed: "As you look back, please try to think about which staff functions were performed well and not so well, on the average, during your tenure." Fourteen separate functions were listed, one of which had two options. The answers to this question will give us a cross-sectional evaluation of the performance of the major functions performed in the governors' offices. (See Table 15.1.)

The former governors' views present several interesting findings. First, it is apparent that the former governors generally felt the various functions of the office were performed adequately or better. On a scale of 5 (worked well) to 2.5 (not bad) to 0 (worked poorly) there was a range of scores averaging from 4.30 to 2.75—all above a "not bad" rating. However they did feel that some functions were performed better than others. At the upper end of the scale (worked well) were some of the more routinized activities facing the governor: legal services (excluding those provided by the attorney general), budgeting, appointments to boards and commissions, and agency/department liaison. Toward the lower end of the scale were those which are considerably less routinized and often have some political overtones: federal-state relations, planning, legal services from the attorney general (forty-three states separately elect this official), and receiving the lowest rating, general political liaison. Clustered at the midpoint of the scale were the remaining functions of managing the office, legislative liaison, coordinating the immediate office staff, press relations, scheduling the governor's time, state-local relations, and identifying and recruiting agency heads.

Thus routinization or lack thereof in the offices is an important factor in the governors' evaluations. This suggests that the growth and greater institutionalization of the governor's office presents a governor with greater support for his roles and responsibilities. The other factor of note is the low standing of political liaison. In part Sabato indicates this can "reflect the politically devilish and unavoidable consequences of the tough decisions which come across a chief executive's desk. . . . (and) is a commentary on the least 'manageable' part of a governor's administration."[30] It further suggests there are political costs involved in this institutionalization—costs that may prove to be personally damaging to the governor and his political ambitions. In fact, four of the seven former governors indicating political liaison worked poorly did subsequently lose a statewide election for either the governorship or the U.S. Senate.

Looking at the gubernatorial responses more closely, specifically at their own attributes or at the type of states they governed, provides some further points of interest. First, as to gubernatorial attributes themselves—party affiliation, time of service, length of service—there is not much variation in their views, at least none greater than ±10% on the 0–5 scale.

However, there are some interesting variations in the governors' views depending on the type of state in which they served (±20% on the 0–5 scale), especially tied to state size and region. The larger the state in population the better were the federal-state relations and planning functions for the governor. In those states ranked between 11 and 30 in 1975 population estimates governors felt appointments, legislative relations, and legal assistance from the attorney general were performed better than their counterparts in other states.

The regional divisions also indicate some intriguing patterns. Southern former governors felt their basic managerial functions of budgeting and planning were below par while their western counterparts saw some internal functions such as office management and staff coordination, their own scheduling and political liaison as not being performed as well as other governors did. However the latter group of governors really focused their attention on how poorly intergovernmental relations worked for them.

Thus in further defining how various functions were performed in different

Table 15.2. Who advises the governor: "I would have been better off listening to them."

Role	More	Less	Neither	% Neither	Advisory score[a]
Executive assistant	7	6	30	69.8	0.08
Immediate family	12	1	29	69.0	0.85
Budget staff	10	3	28	68.3	0.54
Agency heads	10	4	27	65.9	0.43
Legislative leadership (opposition)	7	7	26	65.0	0.00
State party leaders	10	4	26	65.0	0.43
Personal secretary	13	2	27	64.3	0.73
Legislative liaison	10	6	26	61.9	0.25
Influential citizens	13	4	23	57.5	0.53
Legislative leadership (own party)	10	8	22	55.0	0.11
Press secretary	13	6	23	54.8	0.37
Close personal friends	10	9	22	53.7	0.05
Newspaper editors	13	10	18	43.9	0.13
Volunteered: lobbyists	6	—	—	—	—

Source: These data were obtained in the 1976 survey of 58 former governors from the following question: "Below we have listed various types of individuals who normally offer advice to Governors. In retrospect we would like to see whether former governors as a group feel you would have done better as governor if you had paid less or more attention to the advice of:"
a. Score derived by the following formula: (more − less)/(more + less). Score values can range from +1.00 (more) to −1.00 (less).

types of states we find that the region of the country and the size of the state are the most significant variables. In particular it is those states facing the greatest change and growth, the so-called sunbelt states of the South and West, in which governors felt deficiencies in the critical management and intergovernmental functions of their offices.

Advising the Governor

Governors obviously obtain both solicited and unsolicited advice from many sources, and establish their own procedures, networks, and priorities on an individual basis. Much of the growth of the governor's immediate and extended office is tied to enhancing the gubernatorial advisory system so that the best possible information is available for gubernatorial actions. How well these individualized systems worked as assessed by the governors themselves can provide further insights into the functioning of the office.

One question in the 1976 survey of former governors asked who they would have been better off listening to as governor, with a list of individuals and roles provided. Three optional responses for each role were specified: listen more, listen less, neither. These responses are presented in Table 15.2.

Taking the former governors' "neither" response level as an indication that they received just about the right amount of advice from a particular individual or role, it is clear that the governors were relatively satisfied with the amount of advice they received from many of these individuals or roles. Rated especially high were their executive assistants, their immediate families, and their budget staffs. Several other roles, their agency heads, legislative leaders from the opposite party, state party leaders, their personal secretaries and legislative liaisons, were also rated highly. It comes closer to a 50/50 ratio when considering the role played in the advisory system by influential citizens, the governors' own party legislative leaders, their press secretaries, close personal friends and especially notable, newspaper editors. With a few exceptions, those close to or within the governor's office were perceived as having provided about the right amount of advice than were those further removed from the office and indeed outside of government itself.

An overall advisory score was derived to see which of these roles in the gubernatorial advisory system the former governors in retrospect felt they needed to have listened to more or which less. The responses were standardized as noted in the table to provide a score ranging from +1.00 (should have listened to them more) to −1.00 (should have listened to them less). While the actual scores ranged on the plus side from 0.01 to 0.85 the former governors obviously wished they had listened to those closest to them even more—their immediate families and their personal secretaries. Many felt that listening to the budget staff and influential citizens more would have been helpful. Also of interest is where the former governors disagreed—they were split in their assessments concerning legislative leaders of both parties, their executive assistants, close personal friends, and newspaper editors. In fact more former governors felt they should have listened to newspaper editors more *or* less, but could not agree which.

What is significant about these assessments is the general sense that the individualized gubernatorial advisory systems do not necessarily fit into the hierarchical, chief of staff model of organization. In fact, one gains a sense of these advisory systems comporting more closely to the political model where the governor sits at the center of "spokes of the wheel." And just what and who the spokes are varies considerably, including those outside the office and official positions. Thus there is a disjuncture between how a governor may organize his office and how his advisory system operates.

Gubernatorial advisory systems like presidential advisory systems vary greatly from administration to administration and depend "much on the style and ideology of the incumbent."[31] Since the question and responses provide no information on the quality and nature of the advice provided we cannot fully assess these advisory systems. One former governor provided his own advice on this score: "In every category you should listen as much as there is time for— but be wary and canny about what you hear."[32]

Assessing Office Performance In Ten States

In the 1970s the governors of the fifty states took steps to enhance their own public interest organization, the National Governors' Association (NGA). Dues were increased, staff added for a more intensive Washington, D.C., lobbying presence, and a Center for Policy Research established to conduct research and service activities for NGA. One part of the center, the Office of State Services, focuses its attention in helping governors perform their responsibilities within their own states.

NGA has used the center and this office to prepare materials for and to conduct the biennial Seminar for New Governors, held in mid-November following elections in the even numbered years.[33] These seminars, for which incumbent governors serve as faculty, bring the newly elected governors together for sessions on various topics of critical interest and importance for their upcoming administrations: organizing and operating a governor's office, management of the executive branch, executive-legislative relations, press and public relations, intergovernmental relations, and ethics.

More recently the center, through the Office of State Services, has provided on-site consultative service to governors at their own request. While some of the requests concern specific activities, policies or problems for which some specialized assistance is needed, there is now a growing tendency to ask for an assessment of how the governor's office is functioning and for recommendations to ameliorate any problems. Between September 1979 and April 1981 NGA staff visited ten states, assessing performance of the governor's office and making suggestions for improvement.

These assessments provide us with two basic bits of information. First they clearly set out the "state-of-the-art" consensus as to how a governor's office should be run as developed by NGA and the governors. Second they may suggest just what problems still are present in the governors' offices at least on recent on-site visits to one-fifth of the offices. Since the assessments were in the form of long letter style reports to the governor (two states), the executive assistant (seven states), and/or another ranking individual in the governor's office (two states), a content analysis of the reports was used to determine the relevant findings and recommendations. Table 15.3 contains the results of this content analysis by the major categories assisting the governor, policy management, and specific office functions.

Clearly the need to assist the governor better was at the top of the list of recommendations both in terms of the role of the executive assistant and having an appropriate decision-making model for the governor. The recommendations as to the executive assistant were to designate one if there were none already, or if there were one to indicate how that role might be strengthened. In discussing just what the executive assistant's role should encompass the reports suggested the following responsibilities:

Table 15.3. Governor's office performance: a ten-state assessment

	Number of states
Assisting the governor	
Executive assistant's role	10
a. Need one, too many report to governor	5
b. Need to strengthen and expand EA's role	5
Appropriate decision-making model for governor	9
a. Need structure and accountability in governor's decision process	9
b. Need "detail" persons to follow up on various matters	1
Policy management	
Coordination of the executive branch	9
a. Establish cabinet subgroups (human resources, natural resources, public protection, economic development, executive management).	7
b. Establish systems of special assistants for agency liaison	4
c. Monitor activities of special assistants better	1
Program/policy issues	3
a. Need coordination of governor's legislative program development	2
b. Establish coherent goals and "policy program" to guide administration	1
c. Establish intergovernmental, federal-state, or state-local liaison	2
Governor's extended office	2
a. Use planning office more, move toward an OMB	2
b. Promote better policy research effort	1
Specific governor's office functions	
Public contacts	8
a. Improve mail operation in office	7
b. Upgrade constituent services operation	5
c. Improve office reception for visitors and telephone systems	1
d. Need to better public relations/press office effort	2
Managing the governor's office	4
a. Need an office manager	3
b. Too many activities in the office, do not make it a line agency	3
c. Need overall coordination of governor's schedule	2

Source: The data presented in this table represent the distillation of 10 separate reports by staff of the Office of State Services of the National Governors' Association after consultative visits in 10 state governors' offices. The reports were in the form of long analytical letters to the governor (2 states), to the executive assistant (7 states), and/or to another ranking individual in the governor's office (2 states). The reports were written during the period September 1979 to April 1981 and represented visits to 4 midwestern states, 4 southern states, and 2 western states. In terms of population size, one was a "mega state," 5 were mid-sized states, and 4 were smaller-sized states based on 1975 population estimates. The governors were all in their first term. Due to promise of confidentiality none of the states can be identified. All site visit/interviews in these governors' offices and follow-up confidential reports were conducted and written by Daniel B. Garry, Director of NGA's Office of State Services.

1. A confidant and trusted advisor of the governor.
2. Facilitate communication within the governor's office and among key administration people including communications from the governor.
3. Work with the governor not only to see that decisions are made but that they are made at the appropriate level of authority.
4. Insure the governor's decisions are carried out.
5. Provide the governor with a manageable span of control.
6. Run the governor's office.

That the governors themselves felt the importance of this role being fulfilled was indicated by the observation made in these reports that at a recent Seminar for New Governors (1980) there was little or no debate relative to using an executive assistant since all the faculty governors agreed it was the proper thing to do. The discussion focused on how such a person can best be used. This contrasted sharply with the 1976 Seminar in which the governors debated the merits and demerits of having an executive assistant, so it is evident this trend toward a strong chief of staff / executive assistant is growing and supported by incumbent governors.

Close in importance was the finding that more effort needed to be taken to insure that an appropriate decisionmaking model was established for the governor. Some structure and accountability needed to be built into the decision-making process as it related to the governor. This translated into seeing, first, that all opposing points of view are brought to his attention prior to making a decision in the form of presenting the governor with "completed staff work," e.g., facts agreed upon, all affected parties polled and implications assessed, and the options formulated. Secondly, it meant someone, ideally the executive assistant, follow up and be certain that decisions were indeed carried out as intended.

The second group of observations has to do with how policy is managed in state government. Here recommendations were made concerning how to provide coordination of the executive branch either through creating cabinet subgroups (human resources, natural resources, public protection, economic development, and executive management), and/or developing a system of special assistants for agency liaison within the office. There were also concerns about how the governor's programs and policies were coordinated and articulated to the administration as well as the need to develop an intergovernmental focus within the office.

The third group of observations and recommendations concerned how specific functions were being performed in the office such as public contacts, be they mail, telephone or visitors, and constituent services (i.e., case work). "With rare exception everyone who walks into the governor's office wants the governor to do something he would not otherwise do."[34] How such requests are handled has much to do with how well the governor's office is perceived to operate. Other areas of concern in the assessment of specific functions were press relations and managing the governor's office, i.e., how support and clerical services are managed.

From an overall perspective the view which these assessments provides is one of an attempt to structure the office around the governor and his basic role as a decision maker. An executive assistant is called for to head the structure and attendant processes, a decision-making model based on "completed staff work" and follow up processes is suggested, and better methods of policy management are set out.

The fear which appears to drive these assessments and proposals is of an office in which there are too many important people and too few carrying out the necessary work, of an office without a clear line of command or manager, and above all an office which hinders rather than helps a governor in fulfilling his various roles ranging from making decisions to coordinating state government activities to meeting with the people.

Conclusion

Governors' offices are obviously not little "Offices of the Presidency." Yet there are similarities in terms of recent growth in staff and budget size, the need for a chief of staff/gatekeeper, the expansion of the "extended office," and most importantly the focus on facilitating the chief executives' decision-making and policy management roles. As the federal system has expanded in scope and responsibilities over the past few decades so have these executive offices expanded. Further it is now the governors themselves and their multi-state organization, the National Governors' Association, that are attempting to develop and implement a model set of roles, responsibilities and processes which will aid them in fulfilling their mandate as chief executives. And this model moves the governorships from the more personal styles of the past to a more institutionalized model.

Some may feel this trend will lead to a similar set of criticisms about an all too powerful gubernatorial establishment in a state where the governor appears to be lodged in "a powerful inner sanctum of government, isolated from tradition, constitutional checks and balances" as Cronin suggested about the presidency. Others, noting the history of weak chief executives in the states, may follow the argument of former North Carolina Governor Terry Sanford that the single key for making state governments effective is to "make the chief executive of the state the chief executive of the state."[25] The first step to do so is within the chief executive's office itself. No doubt the seeds for such a debate are being sown across the states.

One further observation on the comparison of the governor's office and the White House patterns of organization should be made. Our last two presidents have come from governor's chairs and bring with them governor's office models and experience to use in structuring their White House office. The comments of two of President Reagan's top assistants indicate how significant this previous gubernatorial experience has been for organizing the presidency.

Ronald Reagan came to office as president of the United States with considerable experience in the art of making decisions, establishing policy and being sure that policy was implemented. And his training ground, of course, was the eight years that he spent as governor of California. And during that period of time he evolved a system of decision-making, which started from scratch literally, in 1967.[36]

. . . the Carter administration tried a system called. . . . "Spokes of the Wheel" where you had a number of senior assistants to the president who had ready access to the president at any time, random access almost, they could walk into the Oval Office at any time. . . . [This organizational arrangement was abandoned] as being unsatisfactory, as not really protecting the president from being blindsided and as being somewhat disorderly and disorganized. Our system [Reagan's] is a return to the Chief of Staff system . . . where every appointment and every piece of paper comes from one central point or one central funnel before it goes to the president.[37]

The contrast between the less formal "spokes of the wheel" model and the more hierarchical, chief of staff model are clear. Of interest in this chapter is the fact that almost everyone concerned—governors, staff members, the National Governors' Association, and academics—feels the executive assistant/chief of staff model is the way a governor's office should be organized. Yet, when examining just how a governor's office operates in terms of the gubernatorial advisory system, the more personalized, non-institutional approach still seems to be in use by governors. And this may be as it should be.[38]

16. Planning and Budgeting Offices: On Their Relevance to Gubernatorial Decisions

Lynn R. Muchmore

Modernization of state executive branches during the 1960s and 1970s gave new prominence to the managerial role of governors. The organization and procedural changes that accompanied this transition are easily identified and have been discussed elsewhere. To be sure, modification of structure or technique is only a means to an end. The question remains whether new and more sophisticated extensions of central management have had a beneficial effect upon the governors' capacity to make rational, informed and timely public policy decisions. Qualitative issues of that sort seldom yield to direct inquiry. Instead, the answer awaits the gradual accumulation of indirect evidence—an emerging mosaic that will eventually prove or disprove the expectations of reformers.

This analysis probes the relationship between the governor and two of the most important among those central management organizations commonly employed to reinforce his executive leadership—the state budget office and the state planning agency. Budget bureaus, once preoccupied with the custodial functions of auditing and accounting, have begun new and conceptually rich systems of management decision making: zero-base budgeting, PPBS, and management by objective. State planning agencies, once weak and orphaned imitations of city planning nursed along by federal subsidies, have vigorously pursued their own billing as "the best means available to strengthen the management hand of the governor."[1] The governors themselves seem to have adopted the view that planning and budgeting personnel should reside at the very apex of executive management, and that the performance of the planning and budgeting offices is crucial to their effectiveness. Yet it is not clear that this rhetoric is matched by a day-to-day involvement, and it is only presumed that the planning and budgeting organizations have become more useful to the governors as their management responsibilities have been broadened.

The data relied upon here were collected by the National Governors' Association (NGA) during the summer of 1978 through a series of questionnaires to planning offices, budget offices and governors' offices. The survey returned fifty-one responses from budget and planning officials, and thirty responses from governors. As expected the latter were supplied by someone on a governor's staff rather than by the governor himself.[2]

Table 16.1. Percentage of governors' offices receiving selected services from planning and budgeting agencies

	Provided by	
Service	Planning	Budgeting
Develop gubernatorial legislative program	59	66
Lobby for gubernatorial legislative program	41	59
Develop policy options not requiring legislative action	75	81
Develop management options not requiring legislative action	66	84
Develop or monitor gubernatorial management systems such as management by objective	28	68
Perform trouble-shooting activities such as solving problems existing in another agency	63	72
Review federal legislation, rules, regulations, and guidelines	84	66
Respond to gubernatorial correspondence, including information requests	81	84

Services to the Governor's Office

The first of three lines of inquiry pursued through the questionnaire is simply put: What kinds of services do planning and budget agencies provide to the governor? To secure some basis for a services profile, governors' offices were presented a list of eight activities and asked to indicate which of these might be requested of the planning or budget offices by the governor. Table 16.1 displays the percentage of positive responses.

By this measure, governors show a slight preference for budget offices over planning offices as a source of management support: the average of the first column is 62 percent, while the budget offices received an average of 73 percent affirmative replies. Differentiation between the two agencies is strong in four of the eight categories. Planning offices are more likely to be perceived as a source of assistance where federal regulations of guidelines are at issue. This image undoubtedly owes to the association that state planning has had with such funding sources as the Department of Housing and Urban Development, and to the fact that many state planning offices were initially established to meet federal planning requirements. Budget offices are regarded as a stronger base for lobbying gubernatorial programs in the legislature. This response is not surprising, as legislators in many states have voiced doubts whether state planning should even exist, and planners have survived their assaults by seeking additional funds from the federal government—a maneuver that has strained relationships even more.[3] However, with the budget cuts that have been the hallmark of the Reagan Administration, these additional federal government funds are increasingly hard to come by, if not eliminated.

The most striking statistic in Table 16.1 is the difference between planning and budgeting in the two categories explicitly related to "management." Only 23 percent of the governor's offices would confirm state planning as a possible source of support for gubernatorial management systems, while 68 percent said that budget offices would be a likely source. The same distinction occurs in the management options category. It appears that the identification of management processes with budgeting is considerably stronger in the minds of the governor and his immediate staff than is the association between management and planning. Overall, however, the percentages given in Table 16.1 would seem to suggest a healthy level of involvement by both planning and budgeting. In three-fourths of the states, the planning or budgeting office is viewed as a credible source of policy options for the governor. In nearly two-thirds of the states, one or the other would be relied upon to resolve interagency disputes or to perform the critical "trouble-shooting" functions, presumably as a representative of the governor.

Expected Involvement in Decisions

A more discriminating type of analysis can be achieved by graduating from the general and open ended service categories of Table 16.1 to some specific decisions that typically confront governors. Here the data permit a rough comparison among perceptions of planners, budgeters and the governors' office staffs as to the likelihood that the central management agencies will be involved in the resolution of controversial issues. The twenty issues used in the survey are listed in abbreviated form in Table 16.2. Planning directors and budget officers were asked to indicate whether they would expect to have any role in the listed decision were that decision to be made by the governor.

Budget officers anticipate a marginally higher rate of participation than do planning directors; the average of all the decisions is 62 percent for budget and 57 percent for planning. Interestingly, budget officers expect to be involved as frequently as planners, even where the decisions have no explicit connection with fiscal operations. If six items that refer specifically to some funding problem are deleted, the rates of expected involvement are 52 percent for budget and 53 percent for planning. Clearly, budget directors consider their agencies to be influential in gubernatorial deliberations on a broad scale basis—beyond purely budgetary matters. Both agencies expect a rather substantial level of participation in all decisions except the governor's policy on ethics and the filling of a major vacancy.

Although the two lists are not directly comparable, there seems to be no significant conflict between the perceptions of governors' office staff regarding the services shown in Table 16.1 and the perceptions of planning and budgeting heads regarding the decisions shown in Table 16.2. For example, planning directors are optimistic that they will be consulted where a pending decision

Table 16.2. Twenty gubernatorial decisions: perceived involvement of planning and budgeting agencies (in percent)

Decision	Positive perceptions by		Gubernatorial perceptions of		
	Planners	Budgeters	Planning	Budgeting	Other
1. Establish comprehensive policy	96	83	53	47	63
2. Interagency dispute: welfare referrals	37	54	40	47	73
3. Interagency dispute: use of land	63	26	40	30	80
4. Interagency dispute: computer hardware	35	89	17	60	73
5. Interagency dispute: job classification	12	46	20	53	90
6. Location of a major state facility	61	59	50	57	83
7. To build correctional facilities	59	91	47	80	90
8. Total spending: governor's budget	61	100	30	90	30
9. Cost of state pay raise	37	94	23	90	63
10. Change in school aid formula	61	80	23	73	67
11. Content of state park capital budget	49	94	40	77	90
12. Resources to regional planning	86	70	63	43	47
13. Increase aid to local governments	63	78	37	73	53
14. Major citizen participation exercise	69	24	33	10	27
15. To support municipal league proposals	73	65	47	50	70
16. State response to disaster	69	65	13	17	97
17. Fill major line vacancy	22	13	17	20	33
18. Governor's ethics policy	33	20	10	7	30
19. Title V plans and projects	61	24	50	30	57
20. Contest federal decision	92	65	57	37	60
Average	57	62	35	50	64

involves federal policy. Budget directors have a slightly greater expected involvement in the resolution of interagency disputes, although they defer to planners where the dispute involves land use.

It is interesting to speculate whether planning and budgeting agencies have developed influence and expertise in ways that are complementary or whether they perceive their roles as duplicative. Complementarity should be reflected by patterns of expected involvement that dovetail; that is, planners should expect to participate in subject areas where the expertise of the budget office is low, whereas budget directors would expect greater involvement on matters that the planning agency tends to avoid. A duplicative or competitive model would suggest parallel levels of involvement across the decision categories. Surprisingly, the data in Table 16.2 support neither model. The two "perceptions" columns are simply uncorrelated.[4] Statistically, the likelihood that a planning director expects to participate in a decision is independent of the expectation by budget directors regarding that same decision.

Actual Participation in Decisions

The third and fourth columns of Table 16.2 record judgments by governors' office staffs as to likely participation by planning and budgeting offices in the twenty listed decisions. While the information provided by the governor's immediate staff is vulnerable to some challenge, it is assumed here that staff is in a position to give a more accurate indication of the probable participants in a gubernatorial decision than anyone except the governor himself. By this standard, it is clear that both planning directors and budget directors greatly overrate the participation of their own agencies in important gubernatorial decisions. The tendency is more obvious among planners than among budgeters, but is pronounced in both cases.

An extreme example is the state's response to a hypothetical disaster, where gubernatorial leadership is highly visible and often dominant. Two-thirds of the planning directors and budget officers indicated that they would be involved in some way with decisions about state reaction. Governors' office staffs viewed planning and budgeting as likely participants in only about 15 percent of the cases.

Although there is a remarkable difference between the perceived levels of participation, the governors' staffs are in rough agreement with the planning and budgeting directors regarding the types of decisions that the two central management agencies are most likely to be involved in. Thus, the first and third columns are positively correlated, as are the second and fourth columns.[5] The independence of planning and budgeting roles that seems to be reflected in the patterns of involvement expected by the agency heads is also confirmed by responses from the governors' offices.[6] Given a randomly selected decision, it is not possible to predict the involvement of one office based purely upon knowledge about the involvement of the other. High participation by planning means neither that budget participation will be low, nor that it is likely to be high.

"Participation" or "involvement" is a different measure than "influence," and that distinction is important to an interpretation of the data. A budget or planning director may be a participant in some decision without exerting any significant influence over the outcome of the decision, as when he is called upon to provide raw data. The responses in Table 16.2 are only relevant to participation; they do not address the question of influence. For example, the fact that 47 percent of the time planning offices are likely to be participants in a decision whether to build additional corrections facilities does not mean that they will necessarily be influential participants in those deliberations. Regarding the influence on the overall course of gubernatorial management, columns three and four, which already demonstrate that the role of planning and budgeting offices is less prominent than believed by their directors, are even so an inflated statement of their actual importance.

The last column of Table 16.2 is the percentage of responses for governors' offices where other executive branch agencies, such as line departments or advisory commissions, were listed as participants in the decision process. This data provides some added perspective on the participation of the central management agencies relative to other sources of expertise within the executive branch. Obviously, most governors regularly reach beyond planning and budgeting for consultation on important decisions. In only two instances of the twenty do governors rely upon planning agencies more frequently than line or other departments. Budget offices are more competitive, although the several areas in which they achieve greater participation are reflections of their financial duties rather than overall central management responsibilities.

The Effect of Reorganization

A second view of the data that helps to set a perspective on the role of planning and budgeting is the breakdown in Table 16.3. If executive reorganization is a hallmark of modern state government, and modernization has a significant impact upon the level and pattern of involvement by central management agencies in decisions made by governors, then that impact should be reflected in differing participation rates between reorganized and unreorganized states. When the survey responses are disaggregated as in Table 16.3, evidence seems to dispute the conventional wisdom. While the level of participation is roughly the same for budget offices regardless of reorganization status, planning is more likely to be involved in gubernatorial decisions in those states that have not reorganized during the past five years than in those that have made some major change in executive branch structure. The involvement of other departments and agencies seems to rise in those states that have reorganized. This suggests a rather novel hypothesis regarding the relationship between executive reorganization and the

Table 16.3. Rates of participation in twenty gubernatorial decisions, by organization status (in percent)

	Agency		
Status	Planning	Budgeting	Other (executive)
Unreorganized	40.0	48.6	56.4
Reorganized[a]	31.8	50.0	68.2

a. Reorganized states are those states that have had a major reorganization within the past five years.

centralization of authority. A better structured, more streamlined and accountable organization of executive branch agencies leads to a broader circle of involvement in gubernatorial decisions, even though reorganization typically reduces the number of line departments and independent boards and commissions by dramatic proportions. This view is supported by additional data, not reported in Table 16.3, showing that the governor's immediate staff is less likely to participate in important decisions in reorganized states. Whereas that participation rate is over 90 percent in unreorganized states, it falls to less than 75 percent in states that have undergone a major reorganization during the past five years.

This argues for the following interpretation of reorganization impact: (1) line agencies will be more frequent participants in gubernatorial decisions; (2) the rate of participation of staff groups, including the immediate staff within the governor's office, will diminish; and (3) the involvement of the budget office will be little changed. Budget, it appears, is protected by the fact that important decisions frequently have fiscal implications that are unaltered by any change in organizational structure. The advisory services of both planning and the immediate staff are more vulnerable to replacement by high-quality input from the line agencies. Planning seems to preserve its involvement only in those areas that represent key features of their perceived role. Thus, planning has a high level of participation in both reorganized and unreorganized states where the decision involves contesting a federal policy, supporting municipal league proposals, or providing funds or other resources to regional planning units. Over twelve of the remaining seventeen decisions, planning loses involvement as one shifts from unreorganized to reorganized states.

Conclusion

It is always dangerous to burden a small sample such as the one collected here with more rigorous interpretation than it can possibly bear. Before conclusions can be drawn, it will be necessary to apply new and independently constructed data to the several hypotheses that seem to emerge from NGA's initial surveys. Nevertheless, it is apparent that some of the commonly held assumptions about the role of central management agencies in the decisionmaking arena should be treated with skepticism. The importance of their access and advice to the governor is probably not as great as is commonly supposed, and is quite likely to be less than has been assumed by the planning and budget directors themselves. There is no support in this data for the presumption that planning and budgeting gain influence as executive reorganization focuses attention upon the governor's role as manager. On the contrary, it suggests that centralized sources may recede as participants in gubernatorial decisionmaking while line agencies become more deeply involved.

17. Science Advice to Governors: Non-Politics in the Policy Process

Lynn R. Muchmore

In such areas as energy, environment, and health, among others, many issues require an understanding of certain scientific or technological elements; however, it has not been determined (1) the degree to which such knowledge would improve the ability of elected or appointed officials to make public policy, and (2) the extent to which a specific science and technology information mechanism would be a significant addition to the information resources currently available.[1]

During 1978 and 1979, 49 governors and 41 legislatures began exploratory studies to probe the use of scientific knowledge in state policymaking. The occasion for the initiative was the State Science, Engineering, and Technology Program (SSET), funded and administered by the National Science Foundation. This chapter is an interpretation of several of the more significant findings contained in SSET studies conducted within the executive branch.[2] Although the focal issue of the executive SSET program has been how to supply scientific information or advice to the governor, many who have tried to define that issue observe that the fundamental question is a much broader one: what is the proper blend of political intuition and rational knowledge in deliberations on the public interest? Those who believe that the capacity for wise policy decisions can be "built" and institutionalized argue that the structures and procedures within which a governor functions have a significant effect upon the quality of his decisions. As they begin their search for a "mechanism" that would guarantee consideration for the scientific and technical aspects of any major gubernatorial decision, SSET studies suggest relationships between current patterns of organization and the relative paucity of scientific input. These invite a somewhat unconventional interpretation of the governorship, and a different perspective on the choice between political and non-political sources of advice.

The Governor's Office as a Policy Center

The popular notion that the governor resides at the apex of an organization pyramid, with a commanding view of the domain below, is discounted as unrealistic by both practitioners and theorists. Nevertheless, the classical model continues to be used as a point of departure, and the non-conforming realities of gubernatorial behavior are explained as violations of the public administration rules. This habit, the SSET studies say, does not really help understand how state governments create a policy response to complex issues. A more productive approach is to visualize the governor's office as *a separate organization that is distinct from the bulk of the executive branch*. Intra-organizational behavior, the mainstay of public administration theory, is not nearly so descriptive of gubernatorial management as inter-organizational behavior. The typical governor's office is small and non-bureaucratic (although this has been changing considerably in recent years), whereas many of the organizations to which it must relate are large and mature bureaucracies. These relationships are disjointed, and they account both for charges that the bureaucracy is unresponsive and for frequent mutterings that "the governor's office doesn't know what it's doing."

Because governors must face a spectrum of issues that extends far beyond their personal expertise, their performance is limited by the quality of advice and information they receive. Governors endure a continual barrage of fact, speculation, and rumor, much of it unsolicited and most of it tarnished by special interest. Evidence taken from interviews with former governors, and reinforced by the SSET studies, indicates that most governors come to rely heavily upon the judgements of their personal staff.[3] These are people with whom the governor has frequent and direct contact, and who by providing operational support gradually become trusted extensions of his own personality. Often they are not employed as advisors, but assume that status in fact. Speech writers, press secretaries, and appointment secretaries are examples. Together they constitute the governor's office. Typically, the group is small and its internal operations informal. Position titles are only marginally descriptive, and duties are interchangeable. The staff avoids rigid rules and procedures. Its goals are shared and understood, but never formally expressed. It is, in short, a prototype of the non-bureaucratic organization.

It is the personal staff that many SSET studies identify as the conduit for policy-related information and advice of all types. It can also be a bottleneck to non-political expertise, and it is a major source of frustration for those convinced that policy should proceed from an open and free environment, replete with rational dialogue and full use of scientific knowledge where it is applicable.

The governor's staff rarely have training or experience in science. As a result, they may be unable either to communicate an information need with precision to the most appropriate source or to evaluate the quality of the response. Moreover, they may be at a distinct disadvantage in dealing with scientists or with engineers who can overwhelm them with technical jargon or professional status. This handicap can lead to excessive delay or to information and advice that is biased, inadequate or off the mark.[4]

This conclusion raises one of the most perplexing problems identified in the SSET studies—credentialling. Those who condemn governors for failing to heed the experts usually neglect to specify *which* experts. Experts do not always speak with unanimity. It is easy to recite examples of equally noted scientists drawing contradictory conclusions from the same set of scientific facts, and with equal sincerity and confidence. The absence of training upon which to base even elementary judgements about the relative worth of expert opinions, coupled with the importance given non-professional credentials, provoked this statement in one of the studies:

> [Science and technology] advice to the governor flows through a number of competing channels. Some material moves through a line department to the governor; other material moves through a staff agency such as State Planning Office; still other material is developed for the Governor in the private sector and moves to him from that source. This unevenness seems to create problems in the balance of technical and political discussion that is contained in particular S&T materials forwarded to the governor.[5]

Thus scientific and technical information, in this particular view, goes to the governor only through a "filter" that is more sensitive to political implications than to substantive content.

Even the filtering effect would be accepted and understood, if it operated in a systematic and predictable manner. One SSET principal is fond of observing, "Governors do not exactly deal in world-class information," by way of the point that much of the input to policy decisions is collected in an ad hoc erratic way. The point is reinforced in the Oregon SSET study by reference to an episode wherein the U.S. Department of Labor, because of a mistaken notion about the toxicity of selected pesticides, banned the use of child labor in the strawberry harvest. The economic impact would have been disastrous had the prohibition been sustained. Scientific staff from the Oregon Office of Science and Technology (OST), by consulting experts and reviewing research findings, was able to muster enough scientific evidence to secure a reversal. The author notes that the only reason OST scientists got involved at all was because the science coordinator happened to be talking to the governor's aide when a call came from the Department of Labor. Otherwise, he surmises, OST would have been ignored as a potential resource because it was not "a legitimate part of the policy process."[6] He further observes: "There is generally great reluctance to involve 'outsiders' in policy matters."[7]

Governors must rely upon staff as a buffer against the undisciplined stream of entreaties they would face in the absence of any control. Among several apologies for the "closed door" image that sometimes discourages legitimate scientific or technical advice, two seem noteworthy. The first is that additional information is frequently a political nuisance because it makes decisions more difficult rather than less difficult. Choices that seemed simple can become extremely complicated when all of the alternatives are considered in detail. By dint of the heavy volume of business most governors become "satisficers;" that is, they will expend the time and effort to find an *acceptable* decision, but having done so will not commit additional resources to find an optimal decision. No staffer dcsires to make the governor's life more difficult, so he may summarily reject policy input, whatever its extraordinary qualities, when he knows that a decision has already been made or will be made on other grounds.[8]

A second, more subtle consideration is that a governor's search for more information from "outsiders" can provoke an unpredictable reaction. "In terms of both the long and short-term information requirements, the political setting of the governor's office may condition even a simple request for information so as to produce an erroneous signal of gubernatorial intent. Targeted information needs are, therefore, sometimes not pursued in preference to more general unspecific information."[9] Thus an innocent request for the latest scientific evidence on the health effect of certain effluents may be translated as an indication that the governor is about to change his position on environmental standards.

This explanation helps to clarify the pessimistic returns from a survey of SSET project managers. Of fifteen willing to respond to the question, only two said that "unlimited access to scientific and technical resources" would have made any significant difference in decisions reached by the governor and his advisors during the past four years.[10]

Reluctance to seek scientific knowledge and expertise, it should be clear, is neither a "siege mentality" nor some malevolent insulation. The symptoms described here are quite explainable as a consequence of organizational separation. For a gubernatorial staffer, the "we" of state government refers to the governor's office, *not* to the executive branch. While the assorted bureaucracies of the executive branch may be equipped with the specialists needed to sort out the credentials of experts, these bureaucracies fall into the "they" category. The governor's office relies upon informal and highly personal means of deciding who will be listened to. Frequently this is described as "political influence." Put in a more positive light, it is simply non-bureaucratic behavior.

The symptoms of organizational separation are scattered throughout the SSET studies. Authors of one study note the "nagging problem" of never really being able to identify the "appropriate range of issues" or analyze the "true needs" of the governor's office. While there was a sincere recognition of the need for scientific and technical input to the policy process, efforts to translate that general concern into specific action in order to experiment with alternative response mechanisms failed: "During the study period, we were not successful in getting any issues designated by the governor's office for science and technology analysis."[11] Similar experience was reported in another state where the governor created a Science Advisory Council in part to "respond to the requests of the Governor with objective scientific or technological advice."[12] Despite a commitment from the scientific community to supply information and analysis when called upon, when the SSET study was completed some twenty-two months later only one inquiry had been received.[13] A slightly better record was compiled in a third state, where three requests for information were received from the governor or his office during a five-month experiment with a state science advisor.[14]

The Use of Expertise in the Line Agencies

There are some striking differences between patterns of consultation and specialized advice in the operating departments and those of the typical governor's office. A portion of the SSET studies is given to determining where information used for line agency decisions originates. Skepticism about the quality of professionals employed by state government appears to be unwarranted. In no study was the conclusion reached that levels of competence were so deficient as to jeopardize state performance. "The professional staff in state departments, agencies, boards, and commissions, for the most part, are well trained, competent and highly motivated."[15]

It is useful to distinguish between the caliber of personnel that might be deemed adequate for research endeavor at an academic institution and the level of sophistication needed to apply existing knowledge to problem solutions in a mission-oriented environment. Basic research is outside the mandate of most executive departments, and the tendency to judge state-employed scientific or technical personnel by standards ordinarily applied within the university research setting is one of the explanations for the frequent but apparently incorrect assumption that state governments cannot attract high-quality talent.[16]

Line agency experts are deployed under a pattern of extreme specialization. A consequence disturbing to authors of the SSET studies concerned about policy management is the restricted view of the public interest that results: ". . . a relatively narrow perspective, a bias reflecting the perceived mission of their agency, and/or a tendency to perceive problems from the standpoint of the constituency they represent."[17] The lack of cross-disciplinary interest became obvious during extensive interviews with state administrators in Virginia: "Agency knowledge of resources available within the individual disciplines central to their work is extensive. There is little knowledge of disciplines germane to, but not directly bearing on their operational responsibilities."[18] A similar survey prompted the Florida study team, which apparently began with the impression that state government could not muster the scientific expertise to address modern problems, to exclaim: "Within Florida, scientific, engineering, and technological information abounds." The difficulty at the policy level is not a failure of quality or quantity, but the fact that "the degree of specialization in state government is not an environment conducive to the effective flow of information between and among its agencies."[19]

Unlike the typical governor's office, the line agencies are most often self-supporting; that is, they develop an in-house staff with sufficient training to cope with the bulk of the specialized issues in their functional area. When new or unusual problems demand additional expertise, their resort is to the federal government. "The principle external sources of S&T information in most state agencies are the federal and regional agencies specializing in the same function or technical field. These can be queried readily by telephone or letter, and the responses are almost always prompt and satisfactory."[20] The second option is the private consultant, for despite the difficulties some administrators seem to have with contract management, the consultant is a source of immediate and often highly trained expertise that is sensitive to the political dimension of government issues. University institutions provide a third type of resource, though less often through formal agreements with departments or colleges than through informal ties with individual faculty. These informal ties are extensive in some states, although the relationship between executive branch agencies and the university qua university is poorly developed. While many SSET studies refer to the "under-utilization" of the universities as potential sources of help on specialized questions, none supplies any but shop-worn explanations for the persistence of the problem.

Thus evidence collected from the operating agencies for the excecutive branch will support two arguments: Department administrators are confident that technical expertise secured via existing channels is adequate. Most have faith in the competence of in-house staff. Secondly, the strata of science professionals is distributed across line agencies in specialized clusters. Each of these is isolated from others, but maintains a variety of professional contact within its own specialty, including ties with university faculty and counterpart federal personnel.

Ironically, the extreme specialization that frustrates observers preoccupied with broad-scale policy is but a manifestation of the scientific method applied to organizational form. The product is bureaucracy.

Complex organizations are constantly confronted with complex problems which require complex solutions . . . these solutions can only be found if the problems are successively subdivided into a series of related simple problems. A bureaucratic organization satisfies this requirement by segmenting the overall organization into a set of highly specialized subunits, each assigned responsibility for a single phase of the overall operation. . . . By subdividing a complex problem into simple manageable proportions, ideally a set of simplified solutions will emerge that can be unified into a complex solution to the previously unmanageable complex problem.[21]

The Governor's Office and the Executive Branch

While the generalization that technical staff in the operating agencies of state government is competent and qualified may be a surprise, the finding that these personnel function as specialists with a narrow perspective is a predictable attribute of large organizations. The heart of the "problem" is not ineptitude in the executive branch, but the effective use of its expert resources at the central policymaking level. To use Gawthrop's framework, state government has been more successful at "subdividing complex problems into simple and manageable proportions" then at unifying the individual solutions into a policy that addresses a "previously unmanageable complex problem." Hierarchical structure is supposed to foster synthesis; that is, information and feedback produced at the base of the bureaucratic pyramid is supposed to converge through successive levels of consolidation until those who occupy top-level policy positions can act through a composite knowledge that is uniquely comprehensive. The performance of this structure depends heavily upon vertical lines of communication. Horizontal communication is not essential so long as vertical channels function well, because coordination is inherent to the system.

The hierarchical model loses its effectiveness whenever vertical communications are interrupted, and the SSET reports suggest that a discontinuity persists at the highest level of the executive branch. Governors' offices are unable to exploit expertise that resides within the operating agencies because governors' offices are not integrated into bureaucracy. Alternatively, they are separate organizations, sustained outside the bureaucracy and disconnected from it.

The consequences of this discontinuity have been recognized before, although within a different frame of reference. Executive reorganization, popular among reformers during the past two decades, is but an effort to perfect vertical communications by introducing a new layer of intermediaries to unify previously fragmented bureaus and agencies. Campaigns to gain the acceptance of reorganization usually stress the need to "make agencies more accountable" or to "get the bureaucracy under control." But they could equally well be presented as measures to integrate the governor's office with the executive branch—to establish its role in a bureaucratic model and diminish its identity as a separate non-bureaucratic organization.

Strategies for Change

If this analysis is correct, then those who believe that governors must respond to the increasing complexity of state policy problems by increasing their reliance upon specialized knowledge at the expense of political intuition would seem to have available two broad strategies.

The first respects the governor's office as a separate non-bureaucratic organization and harmonizes with that model. Among the SSET studies, the most prevalent of these recommendations is the "science advisor" approach. The science advisor has no institutional identity apart from the governor's office, but is a member of the personal staff. He does not operate as a specialist, but his training and background give him a sensitivity to the scientific and technical aspects of pending issues. Typically, he is depicted as a point of contact between the governor's office and other organizations with scientific and technical resources, such as the universities, the line agencies, the federal government or private research institutions. Thus one report summarized the characteristics of the science advisor under three major points: (1) he is a member of the personal staff, preferably a designated member of *existing* staff; (2) he serves as a broker, soliciting expert input as needed; and (3) he maintains personal contact with a wide variety of resource institutions, including the universities and the private sector.[22]

This version of the science advisor has several advantages; not least being the fact that it has proved workable in practice. It also suffers some critical problems, most due to the failure to change the fundamental operating mode of the governor's office. It is rarely possible for a third party to "establish" a gubernatorial advisor. The advisor emerges out of a personal chemistry whose course can neither be controlled nor predicted. For the same reason, continuity from administration to administration can never be assured. Even personnel turnover within a single administration can be the undoing of the whole approach. Success requires a happy accident; namely, that someone who gains sufficient confidence from the governor to acquire an influential position on the personal staff also happens to have the training and experience needed to interact effectively with the scientific community.

One countermeasure that has virtually always failed has been the creation of the Science Advisor (note the capitalization) as a formal position with duties prescribed in statute or executive order.[23] The expectation that the science advisor will have credibility *because he is science advisor* is never fulfilled. The reverse proposition; namely, that someone may become science advisor because he has the confidence of the governor, is plausible. Hence the several states where the formal science advisor approach has proved effective are simply cases where someone who the governor relied upon and who would have been supplying advice of a scientific and technical nature in any event has assumed the title pro forma.

The second workable strategy requires that the governor's office be converted from the non-bureaucratic to the bureaucratic model. The need for specialization and the movement toward greater management capacity in the governors' offices has already proceeded in some states, and the trend toward "bureaucratization of the governor's office" is maturing. Consider this description:

Policy analysts in the governor's office are assigned to issue areas and are responsible for keeping track of current activities within those areas. For issues where the state has not yet developed policy guidelines, the analysts are charged with identifying all aspects of the issue, finding the best possible information on those sub-topics, and suggesting ways in which the state might best address the issue. In addition the analysts work on: the development of legislation after the adoption of a policy direction, the guidance of that legislation through the Legislative process, the continued awareness of state agency activities that have direct relevance to the executive office activities, and the coordination of related programs being carried out by multiple agencies.[23]

Specialization by policy area affords gubernatorial staff the time to develop substantive knowledge and, perhaps more important, to learn how the related sections of the executive bureaucracy work. This satisfies some prerequisites for effective communication with the line agencies, and opens at least indirect access to their scientific and technical capacities. Further, staff organized like that in Rhode Island tend toward formal procedures, stabilized roles, and systematic treatment of policy input. To outsiders, these make the governor's office more predictable and more objective—attributes that, according to SSET studies, have a positive effect upon interaction with experts. It is not incidental that such staffs also rely more heavily upon written communication than their non-bureaucratic counterparts. Hence policy directives, policy guidelines, decision memoranda, issue papers and similar devices are more frequently encountered. This also creates an environment in which scientific and technical products, nearly always embodied in written material, assume more importance.

But integrating the governor's office into the bureaucracy also poses some hazards. Specialization breeds further specialization and an appetite for an even larger staff. The temptation to graduate from staff functions into program administration is ever-present, a temptation fired both by the political need to control politically sensitive programs and by the unfortunate habit among federal agencies to seek status for new federal-state programs by encouraging their location in the governor's office.

It should be noted that the role of the Governor's advisory staff has dramatically increased in importance during the past gubernatorial administrations. As recently as fifteen years ago, there were as few as a half dozen advisors whose specialties dealt primarily with legal and press matters. By the early 1970s, however, the number of governor's advisors had nearly tripled and had assumed responsibilities for more than twenty functional and substantive areas. This growth continues today and is expected to increase because of increased demands upon the office of the Governor and other executive branch policymakers.[25]

Liaisons who are supposed to create a more productive interface between the operating departments and the governor's office can, if not diplomatic, become a resented obstacle in that relationship. Perhaps the worst case occurs when a governor retreats from his now enlarged and specialized personal staff into a more restricted circle of advisors, so that a non-bureaucratic suborganization appears within the bureaucratic office. This is a sure recipe for conflict. It defeats the advantages that a bureaucratically organized staff group can provide but leaves a demoralized support team that chafes at its lack of involvement and may play out that resentment through arrogance toward the line departments.

Conclusions

While the management activism that has spread among the governors' offices creates some new problems, it also meets many of the complaints raised by critics who believe that the public interest requires a greater emphasis upon scientific knowledge as a foundation for policy. The staff machinery that the governors have traditionally relied upon to gather and evaluate political information and advice has been pressed to find a different set of sources in order to satisfy the managerial image. Programs like SSET that hasten this transition assume a gradual and harmonious convergence of scientific and non-scientific information in the policymaking process. "Ideally," one state report notes, "scientific information would be treated no differently than any other kind of information."[26] But in this statement of the ideal the fundamental questions remain. Can scientific information or expertise be absorbed without being politicized? Is scientific knowledge a superior knowledge that will, if given an audience, displace a value judgment and the compromises of politics? Or is this conflict more imaginary than real? These can only be answered, it appears, through experience. And the governors who have begun to turn to the scientific community for cooperation and support will add to that experience during the next several years.

18. Governors and Intergovernmental Relations: Middlemen in the Federal System

Thad L. Beyle and Lynn R. Muchmore

Taken in its broadest meaning, "intergovernmental relations" includes some of the most important dynamics of American political development. The Constitution replaced the Articles of Confederation because of a crisis in intergovernmental relations; the Civil War was an intergovernmental breakdown; and the Great Depression, although commonly regarded as a purely economic disaster, was also a period of severe intergovernmental stress. More recent history has seen remarkable alterations of conflict and cooperation between the national government and its constituent states, and the growth of a new jargon to describe the complicated and sometimes erratic course of federalism.

Various analogies have been drawn to furnish the imagery of this ever-changing system. The "layer cake" model pictured the three levels of government as distinct, one lying atop another, with the national government at the apex. This was supplanted by another culinary model, the "marble cake" of shared functions and responsibilities where the three layers lost their distinctiveness as govenmental services were performed. The "picket fence" model saw the three levels of government as the connecting cross slats which merely hold the various intergovernmental programs in line, never bringing them together. In this latter model the power lies in the vertical pickets or programs of our governmental system—the various service bureaucracies.

But while intergovernmental relations has taken firm shape as an object of analysis and study only during the past decades, it should be clear that the raison d'être—the coexistence of multiple governments obligated to provide identical clients with overlapping services under authority not clearly distinguishable—is indigenous to the American system.

For American governors during the 1970s, however, the idea that intergovernmental relations is a continuing intrigue with ponderous historical consequences was remote. Their perspective was a much narrower and more practical one. Any newly elected governor of that decade, fresh from a victorious campaign in which the term was probably never mentioned, quickly learned that intergovernmental affairs are a vital dimension of administrative reality. In 1970, for example, federal agencies were providing $24 billion to state and local governments, which increased to $49.8 billion in mid-decade and nearly $91.5 billion by 1980, for an increase of 380 percent between 1970 and 1980. In the late 1970s, national fiscal programs were providing nearly 57 percent of the funding for all social welfare programs, ranging from a low of over 9 percent in education, to over two-thirds of all health and medical care, to a high of over 93 percent in housing.[1]

No governor could afford to maintain an insular attitude. The consequences of revised distribution formulas, changes in the conditions under which federal grants could be received, and reductions in congressional appropriations or authorization levels could be direct and immediate, and politically catastrophic. The antecedents upon which intergovernmental relations in the 1970s were based do not, however, reach to the Civil War, nor even to the 1930s. The decade of the 1970s is more accurately described as a denouement of the 1960s. Thus the 1970s produced very little that was genuinely new. The 1960s had been confused and frenetic, and the governors of the 1970s occupied themselves with the task of sorting out the aftermath. Reorganization and management reform were major parts of this sorting out process.

The Programmatic Muddle

The determination to convert governance at the state level into a more orderly, rational, and systematic process made the tattered boundaries between state and federal governments an inviting target for management reform. State activities could be grouped neatly into programs; the programs and their costs could be counted; and the numbers could be used to measure changes and to issue management directives. But governors soon found that no one really knew how many federal programs the state was participating in, how much money was involved, how much discretion was available to the state administration of grants-in-aid, or the extent to which joint federal-state commitments would encumber state funds in the indefinite future. A cursory survey of nine federal agencies conducted by the Bureau of the Budget in 1969 furnished the kind of language that governors viewed as the core of the intergovernmental relations problem:

> . . . there are over 70 administering organizations at headquarters managing over 500 federal programs. The nine agencies also reported over 100 separate structures reaching from Washington to the field containing over 20,000 separate field units. . . . The picture is quite heterogeneous; one agency uses two field structures to administer over 70 federal programs while another agency has over 60 identifiable field structures administering about 150 Federal programs.[2]

The lack of elementary information about federal involvement in state programs was alarming to many governors; they became convinced that it simply reflected a failure by the national government to apply any consistent theory of federalism. Absent any conceptual framework, narrow interest groups, aligned with congressional committees and myopic federal bureaus (the so called iron triangle of policy making)[3] were free to proceed with individually tailored programs to satisfy immediate political demands, disregarding their relationship with other programs and ignoring completely the cumulative effect upon state governments. For some governors, the chaos had a sinister design. Thus Governor Robert Bennett of Kansas, instructing his agencies and departments to cooperate in a state study of intergovernmental impacts, wrote:

> I am increasingly convinced that our participation in federal programs is contributing to an erosion of state sovereignty. Public decisions properly within the sphere of state and local officials are being dominated by bureaucratic fiefdoms at the federal level, a maze of rapidly expanding federal regulations, and self-interest associations of professional bureaucrats and narrow clientele groups.[4]

By 1976, complaints from the governors about the incompatibility of state management reform and continued disorder in the grant-in-aid system had become more than vague rhetoric of discontent. When the Office of Management and Budget Director James Lynn requested that the governors be specific about their grievances, they quickly responded with two monographs under the significant title, *Federal Roadblocks to Efficient State Government*.[5] The reports contain examples of problems the governors thought most serious, along with recommendations for change. They were grouped under six general issues which represent the intergovernmental agenda from the state level:

1. Lack of coordination among federal agencies;
2. Federal encroachment upon matters under the jurisdiction of states;
3. Regulations oriented toward administrative methodology rather than program results;
4. Excessive paperwork and reporting requirements;
5. Administrative breakdowns within federal agencies, with funding delays, and the failure to produce guidelines in a timely manner; and
6. Uncoordinated and inconsistent procedures for indirect cost determination.

In the introduction to the report, the governors expressed their overall concern with "roadblocks to efficient state government": ". . . the report illustrates a lack of sensitivity to the impact of management decisions on states and a lack of commitment to resolve questions raised by those responsible for implementing federal programs. The result is the creation of purposeless burdens which strain federal-state relations and impair the efficiency and effectiveness of both levels of government."[6] The reference to "efficiency and effectiveness" should be underscored, for it was the principal motif of intergovernmental relations in the mid-1970s.

Despite the references to eroding state sovereignty illustrated in the memorandum of Governor Bennett and the allusion to state jurisdiction in the "*Roadblocks Report*," discussion seldom centered on such great and weighty issues as the appropriate responsibility of government in general and the proper distribution of that responsibility between the state and federal levels. Instead it focused upon the pragmatics of administration and management.

The expansion of federal influence that occurred during the heyday of the "Great Society" continued at a diminished rate throughout the 1970s, but if the governors did not accept it, they at least perceived that it was propelled by forces beyond their control, and they addressed themselves to the question of how to cope with the interweaving of state and federal interests at a practical level.

The Washington Presence

The predominance of administrative issues in the intergovernmental discussion of the 1970s caused many governors to question whether congressional delegations, the traditional conduit through which state interests are voiced in Washington, were actually adequate spokesman for the state interests:

> The central federal relations problem for states is the fact that when members of the congressional delegation say they represent a state, they mean the mix of constituencies, interests, issues and individuals which combine to elect them to office. Generally, they do not include the policy and operational concerns of the state government in the list of interests they represent. The differentiation between the state and the state government is not intentional; rather, it is a natural consequence of the members' national or local perspective.[6]

Many of the details of program management and administration that governors found to be "roadblocks to efficient state government" were outside the purview of Congress; instead, they were found within the rule-making and standard-setting domain of the federal mission agencies. Communications from state government through the congressional office to obscure sections of the federal bureaucracy are not particularly effective, both because the bureaucracy is insulated from congressional entreaties and because the Congressmen and their staffs tend to be remote from state government operations. This, of course, was not a new discovery; most state agency directors corresponded regularly with their federal counterparts, and some enjoyed longstanding relationships.

What was new was the rapidly developing role of the governors as executives, and their determination to shift the overall responsibility for intergovernmental discourse out of the "picket fence" mode and consolidate it under their central supervision. Thus governors began to equip themselves for a role as chief lobbyist for state government—on Capitol Hill, but more importantly, within the federal executive agencies.

The first phase of this consolidation was underway as the 1970s began. Several governors had hired an intergovernmental relations coordinator, a federal-state relations person in their office. Some other governors created an "Office of Federal-State Relations" or some equivalent unit, often attached directly to the governor's office. Duties performed by these federal-state relations personnel varied from state to state. Some asserted the governor's interest in the myriad of federal grant programs by vigorously exercising OMB Circular No. A-95 review power over proposed federally funded projects in order to enhance their own coordination and control of what federally funded activities might be proposed in their state; others attempted an "early warning" function by advising the governor in advance of pending rules, regulations, or congressional action that had a potential impact on state government and the state; yet others tried to maximize the flow of federal funds into the state by offering technical assistance to grant applicants. Generally, however, the federal-state relations offices served three purposes: (1) they assembled and interpreted for the governor a base of information that had not been available before; (2) they provided a central coordinating point for a miscellany of intergovernmental activity in which the governor and his cabinet agencies would otherwise be involved on a haphazard basis; and (3) they introduced a gubernatorial perspective into negotiations and discussions between federal agencies and various parts of the state executive branch. The National Governors' Association (NGA) surveyed the governors' offices in 1976 to obtain a better understanding of the functions of those persons concerned with federal-state relations in the governor's office. These results are presented in Table 18.1.

In dealing with the federal executive branch—its departments and agencies— the former governors' interviews indicated a mixed picture of success. In terms of the mechanics of penetrating federal agencies, the governors operated on a division of labor concept. If the matter was important enough for the governor's attention, then generally he would deal directly with a federal cabinet secretary, agency head, or someone at the White House, including the president. This was to be expected, of course, by the status of a governor's position. Matters of lesser import were delegated to a governor's cabinet secretary or other subordinate and usually handled through a federal regional office or at least through lower levels of the federal bureaucracy in Washington.

Beyond the federal-state relations offices created as a part of central management in the state capitols, governors began opening new "Washington offices" as early as the 1960s, especially those from several larger states including California and New York. The rationale behind this was the interests of state government could be advanced more aggressively through an "outpost" of state personnel who could maintain a presence with the federal agencies and who would develop a working liaison with congressional staffs. By 1976, about half the states had Washington offices. At last count, the number was thirty.[8] The case for a Washington office was put this way by one former governor:

> So many federal programs, both ongoing and incipient, have a direct bearing on the operations of states that it behooves governors and their staffs to pay constant attention to maintaining a high degree of liaison with various elements of the federal government—the state's congressional delegation and the national administration and its various agencies. For a state like [mine] ... with its impoverished urban masses and highly industrialized work force, the establishment of a governor's staff office in Washington is more than justified

Table 18.1. Functions of the federal-state liaison in the governor's office (N=29)

	Performed (in percent)		
	Always or very frequently	Sometimes	Never or rarely
1. Letter writing to members of state's congressional delegation	48	41	10
2. Sign-offs under OMB Circular A-95	48	10	41
3. Serving as point of liaison with the NGA on federal-state questions	45	45	10
4. Studies of the amount of federal aid received in your state	41	41	17
5. Meetings with counterparts from other states	38	52	10
6. Serving as staff for the governor's regional governors' conference responsibilities	34	38	28
7. Review of proposed federal legislation	31	66	3
8. Serving as state contact point for general revenue sharing	31	17	52
9. Staffing governor's role as a member of an NGA standing committee	29	43	29
10. Assistance to local programs in dealing with federal program	28	48	26
11. Letter writing to other states' members of Congress	24	59	17
12. Review of proposed federal regulations	24	52	24
13. Locating additional sources of federal dollars not currently utilized by the state	21	59	21
14. Follow-through on state agency requests for federal grants or loans	21	45	34
15. Writing proposals for federal assistance on projects of special interest to the governor	3	52	45
16. Case work referred to you by a member of your state's delegation to Congress as involving state rather than federal matters	3	38	59
17. Case work (individual problems such as benefit claims) for individuals with federal problems	3	21	76

Source: Thad L. Beyle, Harold A. Hovey, and Kenneth C. Olson, "Intergovernmental Relations in the Governor's Office," State Government 50 (Spring 1977):93. The original figures reported in that publication have changed slightly due to later arriving responses and the deletion of territorial responses.

in terms of the federal help needed and the federal dollars which are sometimes only available if a state administration is fully alert to and industrious in obtaining all possible federal grants and assistance.[9]

An obvious advantage of the Washington office approach is geography: "... people in the Washington offices are usually in a stronger position to understand the nuances of actions by the administration and Congress and to assess the state-federal implications of positions being urged by the Governor. Washington also is a much better location for working out compromises that are acceptable to a variety of states and other interests."[10] Most of the Washington offices are co-located in the Hall of the States, an office building occupied by the National Governors' Association (NGA) in 1977 that also houses several national associations of state officials. The Hall of the States is itself a symbol of some importance, for it reflects the sentiment among the governors collectively that led to management reform in the individual states: the consolidation of otherwise scattered and sometimes weak lobbying efforts into a centralized and coordinated machinery for exerting state interests.

The increased stature and presence of the NGA in Washington is further indication of the governors' collective interests in intergovernmental relations. Created in 1908 as an annual meeting and continued in that manner for sixty years, the NGA has now become one of the major public interest associations on Capitol Hill with a lobbying, research, and state service staff of over fifty persons, an increase from a staff of four in the late 1960s. Meeting several times a year, governors themselves are also more active in national issues, as they provide analyses or testimony and seek to bring or hold senatorial and congressional votes in the states' interest. In fact to dramatize the changing role the governors envisioned, the name of their organization was changed from the National Governors' Conference with its meeting connotation to the National Governors' Association—a more ongoing organization in name.

Governors and Congress

The governors relate to the Congress, one former chief executive has observed, on two levels. The first involves issues that are particular to a state, and require some interaction between a governor and his own congressional delegation. The second involves issues that are of general importance to the states in general or to state government, issues that may precipitate a common concern among all of the governors or at least the governors of a particular region.

It is not clear that significant changes occurred in either of these relationships during the 1970s, although governors have been hyperactive on the regional front. The end of the decade saw organizations of the western governors, the northwestern governors, and the southern governors that were either completely new or greatly strengthened as compared with earlier versions.

In fact by the late 1970s a whole new type of intergovernmental politics had evolved, centered on the so-called "snowbelt-sunbelt" conflict. As more federal grant programs became driven by formula rather than active grantsmanship or other factors, fights emerged over what variables to include in the formulas and with what weightings. While the game appeared to be played by statisticians and computers, the real world stakes of large shifts of money either north and midwest or south and west were unmistakable. The governors took leading roles in these conflicts, establishing research and lobbying groups (e.g., North-east-Midwest Coalition) groups or changing the direction of activities of established organizations (Southern Growth Policies Board). While they had as their basic goal the protection of the federal funds they felt due them in their state and region, not the least of the reasons they had to organize was to alert their own congressmen and senators to their own state and regional needs and responsibilities.[11]

Despite sincere overtures toward collective action as guardians of the states as a level of government, the governors remain understandably preoccupied with the individual problems of their own particular constituencies. Their relationships with their own delegations are a more vital interest, therefore, than their ability to levy influence upon the Congress in general. As might be expected, the degree of cooperation between governors and their congressional delegation varies greatly. A few governors seem to find their delegation remote, inaccessible, and suspicious of any kind of joint venture, while others report a personal camaraderie with senators or congressmen, even those from the opposing political party. However, there is no institutional structure currently available or working to enhance these relationships. It must be based on personal friendship and interaction.

There is a greater consistency among the governors' perceptions of their own status vis-à-vis the Congress as an institution. Several governors have used the term "toleration" to describe the indifferent response they receive when attempting to persuade congressional committees or to influence action on a major piece of national legislation. Though opinion was mixed in the series of former governor interviews, most of them thought testifying before Congress was not particularly helpful, nor were resolutions or petitions passed by the governors in their various assemblies. A majority did believe that governors as a group were more influential on and more respected by Congress than in the 1960s. But even so, there was near universal doubt that governors could or did have much impact on national policy, except as it particularly affected a specific state.

The most frequently cited exception to this is the feeling that governors did have a significant effect upon revenue-sharing enactment in 1972 and its subsequent renewal in 1976. But there are some disquieting signs as we move into the difficult budgetary politics of the 1980's. As U.S. Senator James Exon, a former governor of Nebraska for eight years, noted:

> But I will say that there is consternation here in the Senate today regarding actions of some of the governors on several matters. To bring it right down to a case in point, I told many of my colleagues when they were here in February for the winter meeting that those of us who are up here in the United States Senate developing budgets and setting tax rates are becoming somewhat critical of actions of some governors who say, "Yes sir, balance the federal budget, but don't bother to cut any federal revenue sharing; don't bother to

cut any of our goodies." . . . I am not accusing anybody of bad faith, but the actions of some states and governors are causing the states difficulties here in congress.[12]

In fact, however, the intergovernmental techniques put to use in the 1970s, including the Washington offices and the more elaborate management mechanisms in state government, were only incidentally supportive of collective action. Their primary objective, which they achieved in some proportion, was to give the governor a stronger base for dealing with federal executive agencies and to enrich the gubernatorial dialogue with the state's own congressional delegation. How they will work in contracting budgetary politics of the 1980s with cutbacks rather than expansions the rule is an open question. Can the governors maintain their collective identity during such difficult times or will they return to more individualized "protect their own particular interests and constituencies" politics of the past? In fact, with decreasing national level emphasis on intergovernmental programs and grant-in-aid funds, will there be as great a need for a governor to maintain a Washington office?

In closing this discussion on the Washington presence of the governors, it is instructive to look briefly at the perceptions of the federal system held by governors and some of their state-federal relations coordinators in the mid 1970s. As indicated in Table 18.2, the state-federal relations coordinators had very strong feelings that the federal system had swung toward federal dominance, and that the Washington decision makers did not understand the state and local government impact of the programs they implement. But note that they also feel low level federal bureaucrats often take the position they can tell the governor what to do in programs within his or her state and that too many federal programs develop direct federal-local links without providing an appropriate role for the states. Thus the states and the governors are seen as very junior partners in the federal system and in any federal programs, often caught in the middle between the federal top down programs and the local bottom up needs.

How about the states' relations with Congress? They do not see Congress as a whole as being more responsive to state rather than local positions, although members of the state's own congressional delegation, and especially their U.S. senators, are much more responsive than Congress as a whole. Of interest is the fact that the U.S. senators, the other state-wide elected officials in major policy making positions, are perceived as being most responsive to the state officials. Electoral constituency obviously plays a part in these findings. However, this all suggests that on broad policy issues concerning the federal system, the states were at a disadvantage vis-à-vis Congress, *except* as such policies might affect a particular state.

Turning now to the responses of sixteen incumbent governors (Table 18.3), we find an interesting contrast in their views toward the federal and local governments. While the comparison is not direct and uses the state legislature as the base point, we see a virtual reversal of their views toward the other two levels of

Table 18.2. Perceptions of the federal system by state-federal relations coordinator in the governor's office, 1976 ($N=29$)

Propositions	State responses		
	Agree	Not sure or no opinion	Disagree
The decision makers in Washington do not understand well the impact on state and local governments of the programs they implement.	97%	0%	4%
The balance in the American federal system has swung too strongly toward federal dominance.	90	0	10
Low level bureaucrats in federal agencies often take the position that they can tell the governor what to do in the operation of federal programs.	79	7	14
Too many federal programs have direct federal/local ties that deny the states an appropriate role.	76	14	10
Congress seems to be more responsive to the positions of local officials than to those of state officials.	28	28	45
Our state's congressional delegation seems to be more responsive to the positions of local officials than to those of state officials.	17	28	55
Our state's U.S. senators are more responsive to the positions of local officials than to those of state officials.	14	17	69

Source: Center for Policy Research, *Governor's Office Series (10): State-Federal Relations in the Governor's Office* (Washington, D.C.: National Governors' Association, 1976), p. 11. The original figures reported in that publication have changed slightly due to later arriving responses and the deletion of territorial responses.

Table 18.3. Incumbent governors' views on federal-state-local relations, 1976

	Agree	Not sure	Disagree
Relations with the federal government are almost as important as with the state legislature.	11	1	4
Relations with the local government of this state are more important than those with the state legislature.	2	2	12

Source: Center for Policy Research, National Governors' Association, 1976 Survey, unpublished data.

government. It might be inferred from these responses that there is more concern on their part about state-federal government relations than there is about state-local government relations. Of course, they may feel that working with the legislature and its local representatives fulfills part of that state-local role of the governor. Whatever the situation, we now turn to the relationship to local governments.

The States' Children

To complete the intergovernmental circle, we must note the concern of the former governors and others over the growth of direct linkages between the federal government and the local units of government. This has occurred particularly in recent years as more and more grants from Washington have bypassed the states and flowed directly to the cities and counties. For example, between 1972 and 1977, direct federal aid to local governments grew by 147.9 percent, and federal money passed through states to local governments increased by 68.3 percent.[13] In 1967 slightly over half the municipalities over 25,000 in population participated in a federal assistance program, by 1972 nearly 63 percent did, and with General Revenue Sharing and the Comprehensive Employment and Training Act and Community Development Block Grants, all municipalities did.[14]

This specific development causes serious concern among the former governors, for it threatens the states' role in the federal system. The governors do not generally oppose grant money to the cities, but they do prefer, by and large, that at least the governor's office play a coordinating role for these programs which have statewide coverage. Former Utah Governor Rampton was not too bothered if grant money allocated only to major cities went to Salt Lake City, Provo, or Odgen, but those dollars that were to go to cities of all sizes, he preferred to be channelled though state government to insure fair distribution and adequate coordination.[15] Former South Dakota Governor Wollman argues: "But this is a sovereign nation with many sovereign states, not a sovereign nation with many sovereign cities."[16] Former governors Edwards (South Carolina) and Schrieber (Wisconsin) had even more sharply diverging views. The former: "As a person who believes in strong state government and the federal system of government, this is offensive to me." The latter, noting the object of government was to serve the citizens, indicated if cities could get federal funds to help them, "God bless their souls and more power to them."[17]

On dealing with the federal-local governmental link, these former governors were near unanimous on at least one solution, called "an emerging federalism" by former Massachusetts Governor Dukakis. This model of federalism would have the federal government setting broad program guidelines and then turn block grants and major administrative responsibility over to the states.[18]This model's theme of block grants and delegated authority and responsibility to the states was consistent among the governors, without regard to party affiliation or overall political philosophy. Some suggested a further federal role in a post-audit or performance audit function to insure that block grant money was spent within the guidelines. The initial proposals of the Reagan administration on how federal domestic programs and intergovernmental relations should work seem to fit well with the prescriptions of these former governors.

Conclusion

The governors feel they sit in the middle of the federal system with its problems flowing from below and solutions from above. They exert their own views and priorities into this intergovernmental system through their performance of an intergovernmental role. This role is less structured or understood than others they perform, and in many ways they are constrained in the impact they might have and seek. Yet with the federal dollar making up 23.6 percent of the states' budgets in 1980,[19] if governors neglect this role, it is at their own peril.

Conclusion

Conclusion

Thad L. Beyle, Lynn R. Muchmore, and Robert Dalton

This book has presented part of the picture of what being governor is about in the mid-1970s to the early 1980s. We have attempted to use the words, opinions, and views of governors, former governors, and their closest aides in developing this book.

It is clear that gubernatorial roles and responsibilities have changed from what they were in the past; and it is equally clear they are going to continue changing in the future. The responsibilities of the states and their elected officials are increasing, not decreasing, and the demands on the fifty states are growing, especially in the face of the shifting of the priorities now in process at the national level.

The governors of the fifty states sit in the middle of a governmental and policy environment. As governors they must make the decisions, set the priorities, and see that the programs are implemented. Yet the milieu in which they must carry out these responsibilities is difficult at best. Within state government they face resurgent legislatures seeking at a minimum a sense of parity with the executive branch in general and the governor in particular, and they often find key parts of the executive branch in the control of separately elected officials or policy boards which they have varying abilities to influence. They are part of a federal system in which the partner at the top is cutting back not only in programs and grant-in-aid funds, but also reducing its responsibilities to answer to the needs of our states and local communities. And now finding themselves faced with a tighter revenue situation than at any time in the recent past, governors must decide whether to raise taxes or cut back on the programs and activities of their state governments. Neither choice is attractive to governors or the people they serve.

The final chapter on governors and their administration should include an assessment of gubernatorial performance. How well do they perform as key actors in our state governments? To date that is a relatively unresearched and analyzed question, yet it is the basic question to be answered when an incumbent governor seeks to succeed him- or herself. Governors themselves, although obviously biased, certainly have a view on how successful their tenure was. Reflecting on their experiences as state chief executives, the fifteen former governors, whose interviews are presented in *Reflections on Being Governor*,[1] were nearly unanimous in their opinion of how successful they had been. In general, they expressed a fairly high level of satisfaction with their accomplishments and with their ability to steer the ship of state government.

This feeling of satisfaction extended across a number of dividing lines: Democrats and Republicans; those who won the governorship in their own right and those lieutenant governors who succeeded to the office, those who won reelection and those who lost—all felt themselves reasonably successful as governors. As to whether he had a great impact on the state of Kansas, Governor Exon replied, "Yes, I did."[2] Governor Rampton of Utah asserted "I felt like I was in charge."[3] Governor Bennett of Kansas, who lost his bid for re-election, still took a fairly philosophical view, "It's been an enjoyable four years, a very educational four years. I think I've learned a lot, and I think we've done a lot."[4]

What does it take to be an outstanding governor? Former Governor Tom McCall of Oregon suggested that "a good governor's got to throw himself under the train now and then."[5] Former Governor Terry Sanford of North Carolina argued that such a governor is "one who tried to make state government work for the benefit of the people."[6] George Weeks, who has spent many years working with Governor William Milliken of Michigan, selected ten outstanding governors over the twentieth century by looking for those who "made a difference not only in their states but also on behalf of the states in the federal system . . . either by example or endeavor."[7] Larry Sabato, using ability, competence, hard work, dedication, and meeting the needs of the people as his criteria, rated three out of every eight governors who have served in the fifty states since 1950 as outstanding.[8] Duane Lockard in his study of New Jersey governors sought "men of firmness, ability, and principle."[9]

But what is it that we want of a governor? A charismatic leader? A super competent manager? An intergovernmental leader? An innovator? One who maintains the status-quo? As Martha Weinberg suggests, governors "all fall victim to the often conflicting criteria for performance that the public has for them."[10]

Of these fifteen governors interviewed for *Reflections on Being Governor*, none felt 100 percent in control or completely satisfied with their performance as governor. All mentioned some failure or inability, and they recognized that no one governor can completely or singly control events or state government. As for how events can shape an administration, listen to former Pennsylvania Governor Milton Shapp:

> You would never know on any one day what was going to come out of left field. That includes emergencies. Governor [Dick] Thornburgh, as you probably noticed, has had his hands full in the last few days with the radiation leak at Three Mile Island. I would say that during my administration a major part of the problem we had was the number of emergencies. Starting in 1971, I had to come back from the National Governors' Conference in Puerto Rico because there was a flood in eastern Pennsylvania; then [Hurricane] Agnes in 1972. In 1973, we had minor emergencies, but nothing like Agnes. In 1974, there was a national truckers' strike in which I became heavily involved. In 1975, there was [Hurricane] Eloise, which was followed by a very severe winter. In 1976, we had very severe weather again; and in 1977, we had the

Johnstown flood. In the spring of 1978, we had high snow drifts again. Between that and 1974, we had major ice storms in the western part of the state. We also had fires, and both the West and the East had a drought one year. The gypsy moth came to visit us for about four years running. When you look at the Constitution of Pennsylvania, you don't see any mention of those being part of the administrative functions of the governor, but they do play a major role in what you are doing. And then you have the man-made disasters, such as dealing with the Legislature.[11]

Former Governor Dan Walker of Illinois noted that one thing he did not perceive early enough was to pick out a manageable number of issues on which to concentrate.[12] Further, he indicated that "it was in large part the inability to solve problems and the increasing difficulties in spending my time where I wanted to spend my time that caused me halfway through my administration to decide I would not run again. I changed my mind, obviously" (as he did seek re-election but lost).[13]

Yet, despite these problems, and the fact that the voters often turn them out of office by not re-electing them, most governors would probably agree with former Massachusetts Governor Michael Dukakis when he summed up his experience: ". . . greatest job in the world, as most governors, I suspect, tell you."[14]

Appendix A. Selected Bibliography on the Governorship

Books and Articles

Backman, Ada E. "The Item Veto Power of the Executive." *Temple Law Quarterly*, 31 (Fall 1957): 27–34.

Bernick, E. Lee. "Gubernatorial Tools: Formal vs. Informal." *Journal of Politics*, 41 (May 1979): 656–64.

_____ . "The Impact of U.S. Governors on Party Voting in One-Party Dominated Legislatures." *Legislative Studies Quarterly*, 3 (1978): 431–44.

Beyle, Thad L., "The Governor's Formal Powers: A View from the Governor's Chair," *Public Administration Review*, 28 (1968): 540–45.

_____ , and Williams, J. Oliver. *The American Governor in Behavioral Perspective.* New York: Harper and Row, 1972.

Black, Earl. *Southern Governors and Civil Rights: Racial Segregation as a Campaign Issue in the Second Reconstruction.* Cambridge: Harvard University Press, 1976.

Brooks, Glenn. *When Governors Convene: The Governors' Conferences and National Politics.* Baltimore: Johns Hopkins Press, 1961.

Bryan, Frank. "The New England Governorship: People, Position and Power." In Josephine F. Milburn and Victoria Schuck, eds. *New England Politics.* Cambridge, Massachusetts: Schenkman Publishing Co., 1981, pp. 75–105.

Center for Policy Research. *Governing the American States: A Handbook for New Governors.* Washington, D.C.: National Governors' Association, 1978.

_____ . *The Governor's Office.* Washington, D.C.: National Governors' Association, 1976.

_____ . "The Governors: Strengthening the American Federal System," Special Issue, *State Government*, 52 (Summer 1979).

_____ . "Politics and The American Governors." Special Issues, *State Government* 53 (Summer 1980).

_____ . *Reflections on Being Governor.* Washington, D.C.: National Governors' Association, 1981.

Crain, W. Mark, and Tollison, Robert D. "The Executive Branch in the Interest-Group Theory of Government ." *Journal of Legal Studies*, 8 (1979): 555–67.

Dometrius, Nelson C. "Measuring Gubernatorial Power." *Journal of Politics*, 41 (1979): 589–610.

Dye, Thomas R. "Executive Power and Public Policy in the States." *Western Political Quarterly*, 27 (1969): 926–39.

Education Commission of the States. *The Role of the Governor in Education.* Denver: Education Commission of the States, 1979.

Ewing, Cortez A.M. "Southern Governors," *Journal of Politics*, 10 (1948): 385–409.

Gove, Samuel K. "Why Strong Governors?" *National Civic Review*, 53 (1964): 131–36.

Haider, Donald. *When Governments Come to Washington: Governors, Mayors, and Intergovernmental Lobbying.* New York: Free Press, 1974.

Jewell, Malcolm E. "Voting Turnout in State Gubernatorial Primaries." *Western Political Quarterly,* 30 (1977): 236–55.

Kallenbach, Joseph E. *The American Chief Executive: The Presidency and the Governorship.* New York: Harper and Row, 1966.

Lipson, Leslie. *The American Governor: From Figurehead to Leader.* New York: Greenwood Press, 1968.

Lockard, Duane, ed. "A Mini-Symposium—The Strong Governorship: Status and Problems." *Public Administration Review,* 36(1976): 90–98.

Long, Norton E. "After the Voting is Over." *Midwest Journal of Political Science,* 6 (1962): 183–200.

McCally, Sarah P. "The Governor and his Legislative Party." *American Political Science Review,* 60 (1966): 923–42.

Miller, Edward J. "The Governor and Legislation: The Initiation of Central Clearance in Maryland." *State Government,* 47 (1974): 94–95.

Moncrief, Gary A., and Thompson, Joel A. "Partisanship and Purse-Strings: A Research Note on Sharkansky." *Western Political Quarterly,* 33 (1980): 336–40.

Morehouse, Sarah McCally. "The Governor as Political Leader." In Herbert Jacob and Kenneth Vines, eds., *Politics in the American States: A Comparative Analysis,* 3rd ed. (Boston: Little, Brown and Co., 1976), pp. 196–241.

———. "The State Political Party and the Policy Making Process." *American Political Science Review,* 67 (1973): 55–72.

Morgan, David. *The Capitol Press Corps: Newsmen and the Governing of New York State.* Westport: Conn.: Greenwood Press, 1978.

Olson, Kenneth C. "The States, Governors and Policy Management: Changing the Equilibrium of the Federal System." *Public Administration Review,* 35 (1975): 764–70.

Pomper, Gerald M. "Governors, Money and Votes." In Pomper, *Elections in America* (New York: Dodd, Mead & Co., 1968), pp. 126–48, 270–73.

Prescott, Frank W. "The Executive Veto Power in American States," *Western Political Quarterly,* 3 (1950): 98–112.

———. "The Item Veto of the Governors." *Georgia Historical Quarterly,* 42 (1958): 1–25.

Ransone, Coleman B., Jr., ed. "Symposium on the American Governor in the 1970s." *Public Administration Review,* 30 (1970): 1–44.

———. *The Office of the Governor in the South.* University, Alabama: University of Alabama Press, 1951.

———. *The Office of the Governor in the United States.* University, Alabama: University of Alabama Press, 1956.

Sabato, Larry. *Goodbye to Good-time Charlie: The American Governor Transformed, 1950-1975.* Lexington, MA: Lexington Books, 1978.

———. "The Governorship as Pathway to the Presidency." *National Civic Review,* 67 (1978): 512–18.

Schlesinger, Joseph A. *Ambition and Politics: Political Careers in the U.S.* Chicago: Rand McNally, 1966.

———. *How They Became Governor: A Study of Comparative State Politics, 1870–1950.* East Lansing: Michigan State University Press, 1957.

———. "The Politics of the Executive." In Herbert Jacob and Kenneth Vines, eds., *Politics in the American States: A Comparative Analysis,* 2nd ed., (Boston: Little, Brown and Co., 1971), pp. 210–37.

Sharkansky, Ira. "Agency Requests, Gubernatorial Support and Budget Success in State Legislatures." *American Political Science Review*, 62 (1968): 1220–31.

_____ , and Hofferbert, Richard I. "Dimensions of State Politics, Economics, and Public Policy." *American Political Science Review*, 63 (1969): 867–79.

Sigelman, Lee, and Smith, Roland. "Personal, Office, and State Characteristics as Predictors of Gubernatorial Performance." *Journal of Politics*, 43 (1981): 169–80.

Skok, James E. "Federal Funds and State Legislatures: Executive-Legislative Conflict in State Government." *Public Administration Review*, 40 (1980): 561–67.

Solomon, Samuel R. "The Governor as Legislator." *National Municipal Review*, 40 (1951): 515–20.

_____ . "Master of the House: Recent Efforts Toward State Governmental Reform Give Promise of New Balance in Legislative-Executive Relations." *National Civic Review*, 57 (1968): 68–74.

Sprengel, Donald P. *Gubernatorial Staffs: Functional and Political Profiles.* Iowa City: Institute of Public Affairs, University of Iowa, 1969.

Swinerton, E. Nelson. "Ambition and American State Executives." *Midwest Journal of Political Science*, 12 (1968): 538–49.

Tropp, Peter. "Governors' and Mayors' Offices: The Role of the Staff." *National Civic Review*, 63 (1974): 242–49.

Wiggins, Charles W. "Executive Vetoes and Legislative Overrides in the American States." *Journal of Politics*, 42 (1980): 1110–17.

Williams, Charles H. "The 'Gatekeeper' Function on the Governor's Staff." *Western Political Quarterly*, 33 (1980): 87–93.

Wright, Deil S. "Executive Leadership in State Administration: Interplay of Gubernatorial, Legislative, and Administrative Power." *Midwest Journal of Political Science,* 11 (1967): 1–26.

_____ . "The States and Intergovernmental Relations." *Publius*, 1 (1972): 7–68.

Wyner, Alan J. "Gubernatorial Relations with Legislators and Administrators." *State Government*, 41 (1968); 199–203.

Reference Sources

Barone, Michael et. al. *The Almanac of American Politics.* New York: E.P. Dutton. Published biennially.

Council of State Governments. *Book of the States.* Lexington, KY: Published biennially.

_____ . *The American Governors: Their Backgrounds, Occupations and Governmental Experience.* Lexington, KY. Published periodically.

Appendix B. Selected Data on Governors and State Executive Systems

Table B.1. The governorship—tenure, election, succession, compensation, and qualifications for the office

	Tenure			Lieutenant governor		Compensation		Qualifications for the office			
State	Length of regular term	Election year	Maximum consecutive terms allowed by constitution	Joint election of gov. and lt. gov.	Official who succeeds gov.	Governor's salary	Official residence	Age	U.S. citizen (years)	State citizen (years)	Other
Alabama	4	1982	2	No	LG	$50,000	Yes[h]	30	10	7	7 —
Alaska	4	1982	2	Yes[a]	LG	74,196	Yes	30	7	7	7
Arizona	4	1982	—		SS	50,000	No	25	10	5	
Arkansas	2	1882	—	No	LG	35,000	Yes	30	j	7	
California	4	1982	—	No	LG	49,100	Yes[h]	18	5	5	—
Colorado	4	1982	—	Yes	LG	50,000	Yes	30	j	2	
Connecticut	4	1982	—	Yes	LG	42,000	Yes	30	30	—	—
Delaware	4	1984	2[b]	No	LG	35,000	Yes	30	12	6	
Florida	4	1982	2	Yes	LG	65,000	Yes	30	—	7	—
Georgia	4	1982	2	No	LG	65,934	Yes	30	15	6	

State		Year				$					
Hawaii	4	1982	2	Yes	LG	50,000	Yes	30	—	5	i
Idaho	4	1982	—	No	LG	40,000	Yes	30	—	2	—
Illinois	4	1982	—	Yes	LG	58,000	Yes	25	5	3	—
Indiana	4	1984	2	Yes	LG	48,000[f]	Yes	30	—	5	—
Iowa	4	1982	—	No	LG	60,000	Yes	30	—	2	—
Kansas	4	1982	2	Yes	LG	45,000	Yes	[p]	—	—	—
Kentucky	4	1983	0	No	LG	50,000	Yes[h]	30	—	6[k]	k
Louisiana	4	1983	2	No	LG	73,400	Yes	25	5	5	—
Maine	4	1982	2	[a]	PS	35,000	Yes	30	15	5	—
Maryland	4	1982	2	Yes	LG	60,000	Yes	30	—	5	i, m
Massachusetts	4	1982	—	Yes	LG	60,000[g]	No	—	—	7	—
Michigan	4	1982	—	Yes	LG	70,000	Yes	30	—	—	—
Minnesota	4	1982	—	Yes	LG	66,500[g]	Yes	25	—	1	—
Mississippi	4	1983	0	No	LG	53,000	Yes	30	20	5	—
Missouri	4	1984	2[b]	No	LG	55,000	Yes	30	15	10	—
Montana	4	1984	—	Yes	LG	43,360	Yes	25	—	2	—
Nebraska	4	1982	2	Yes	LG	40,000	Yes	30	5	5	—
Nevada	4	1982	2	No	LG	50,000	Yes	25	—	2	—
New Hampshire	2	1982	—	[a]	PS	51,830[g]	Yes	30	—	7	—
New Jersey	4	1985	2	[a]	PS	85,000[g]	Yes	30	20	7	—
New Mexico	4	1982	0	Yes	LG	60,000	Yes	30	—	5	—
New York	4	1984	—	Yes	LG	85,000	Yes	30	—	5	—
North Carolina	4	1984	2[b]	No	LG	57,864	Yes	30	5	2	—
North Dakota	4	1984	—	Yes	LG	47,000[g]	Yes[h]	30	—	5	—
Ohio	4	1982	2	Yes	LG	50,000[g]	Yes[h]	18[p]	—	—	i, n
Oklahoma	4	1982	2	No	LG	48,000	Yes	31	—	—	—
Oregon	4	1982	2	[a]	SS	55,423	Yes	30	—	3	—
Pennsylvania	4	1982	2	Yes	LG	66,000	Yes	30	—	7	—
Rhode Island	2	1982	—	No	LG	49,500	No	18	1 mo.	1 mo.	i, o
South Carolina	4	1982	2	No	LG	60,000	Yes	30	5	5[k]	—
South Dakota	4	1982	2	Yes	LG	46,750	Yes	—	—	2	—
Tennessee	4	1982	2	No	SpS[d]	68,226	Yes	30	—	7	—
Texas	4	1982	—	No	LG	78,700	Yes[h]	30	—	5	—
Utah	4	1984	—	Yes[e]	LG	48,000	Yes[h]	30	—	5[k]	—
Vermont	2	1982	—	No	LG	44,850	No	—	—	4	—

Table B.1. The governorship—tenure, election, succession, compensation, and qualifications for the office

State	Tenure			Lieutenant governor		Compensation		Qualifications for the office			
	Length of regular term	Election year	Maximum consecutive terms allowed by constitution	Joint election of gov. and lt. gov.	Official who succeeds gov.	Governor's salary	Official residence	Age	U.S. citizen (years)	State citizen (years)	Other
Virginia	4	1985	0	No	LG	75,000	Yes	30	—	5	—
Washington	4	1984	—	No	LG	63,000	Yes	18	—	—	—
West Virginia	4	1984	2	a	PS	60,000	Yes	30	—	5	—
Wisconsin	4	1982	—	Yes	LG	65,801	Yes	18	—	—	—
Wyoming	4	1982	—	a	SS	55,000	Yes	30	—	5	—

Source: The Council of State Governments, *The Book of the States, 1982–83* (Lexington, Ky.: 1982), pp. 151–152, 172–73.

Key: LG—Lieutenant Governor; SS—Secretary of State; PS—President of the Senate; SpS—Speaker of the Senate.

a. No Lieutenant Governor.
b. Absolute two-term limitation, but not necessarily consecutive.
c. After two consecutive terms must wait four years before being eligible again.
d. This official bears the additional statutory title "Lieutenant Governor."
e. Effective with 1984 election. Till then Lieutenant Governor and Secretary are the same.
f. In Indiana, governor receives an additional $12,000 for expenses; in North Dakota, governor receives a $17,250 supplement.
g. In Massachusetts, current governor accepted a salary of $40,000 and donated $20,000 to charity; in Minnesota, current governor accepted a salary of $58,000; in New Hampshire current governor accepted a salary of $44,520; in New Jersey the governor receives an additional $55,000 for expenses; in North Dakota the governor receives an $11,608 supplement; in Ohio governor turned down a salary increase of $5,000.
h. Governor does not occupy residence.
i. Must be a qualified voter, Maryland—5 years; Michigan—4 years; Oklahoma—6 months; Virginia—5 years.
j. Number of years not specified.
k. Resident and citizen.
l. Governor must be resident of the state during the term for which he is elected.
m. No person convicted of a felony shall be eligible to hold office until his final discharge from state supervision; no person of unsound mind, as determined by a court, is qualified and hence eligible to hold office.
n. No person convicted of embezzlement of public funds shall hold any office.
o. No bribery convictions.
p. Kansas and Ohio have no constitutional qualifications for the office of governor. Ohio provides that no member of Congress or other person holding a state or federal office should be governor.

Table B.2. The state cabinet

State	Authorization for cabinet system	Criteria for membership	Number of members in cabinet (inc. gov.)	Frequency of cabinet meetings	Open cabinet meetings
Alabama	T	R	25	D	Yes
Alaska	G	A	16	D	No
Arizona	—	—	—	—	—
Arkansas	S	A	15	D	No
California	G	A,R	9	D	No

Table B.2. (continued)

State	Authorization for cabinet system	Criteria for membership	Number of members in cabinet (inc. gov.)	Frequency of cabinet meetings	Open cabinet meetings
Colorado	C	A	19	OM	No
Connecticut	S	A	15	D	Yes[d]
Delaware	S	R[b]	16	D	Yes
Florida	C	E	6	OW	Yes
Georgia	—	—	—	—	—
Hawaii	S	A	18	D	No
Idaho	G	R	29	D	Yes
Illinois	T	A	21	D	Yes
Indiana	—	—	—	—	—
Iowa	S	E	5	W	Yes[d]
Kansas	G	R	15	M[c]	Yes[e]
Kentucky	S	A	11	OM	Yes[d]
Louisiana	—	—	—	—	—
Maine	T	R[b]	22	M	Yes[e]
Maryland	S	A[b]	22	D	No
Massachusetts	S	A,R	11	D	No
Michigan	G	—	—	D	—
Minnesota	—	—	—	—	—
Mississippi	G	R	6	D	No
Missouri	—	—	—	—	—
Montana	G	A	17	Q	Yes
Nebraska	—	—	—	—	—
Nevada	—	—	—	—	—
New Hampshire	—	—	—	—	—
New Jersey	C	A	19	D(OW)	No
New Mexico	S	A	12	D	Yes
New York	T	A	22	D	Yes[d]
North Carolina[a]	G	R	10	W	No

State	Authorization	Criteria		Frequency	
North Dakota	—	—	—	—	—
Ohio	S	A,R	23	D	Yes[e]
Oklahoma	G	R	9[f]	M	Yes
Oregon	G	A	—	W	No
Pennsylvania	S	A	19	D	Yes[d]
Rhode Island	G	A	17	M	No
South Carolina	—	—	—	—	—
South Dakota	G	A,F	23	D	No
Tennessee	T	A	21	D	Yes
Texas	—	—	—	—	—
Utah	—	—	—	—	—
Vermont	G	R	17	D	No
Virginia	S	R	7	M	No
Washington	G	R	—	D	No
West Virginia	—	—	—	—	—
Wisconsin	—	—	—	—	—
Wyoming	—	—	—	—	—

Source: The Council of State Governments, *The Book of the States, 1982-83* (Lexington, KY: 1982), p. 162.

Key:

Authorization
C—Constitution
G—Governor
S—Statute
T—Tradition

Criteria
A—Appointed to specified office
E—Elected to specified office
R—Gubernatorial appointment regardless of office

Frequency
D—Governor's discretion
M—Monthly
W—Weekly
OM—Every other month
OW—Every other week
Q—Three-four times a year

a. Constitution provides for a Council of State made up of the state elective administrative officials. This body makes policy decisions for the state while the cabinet acts more in an advisory function.
b. With consent of Senate.
c. Weekly during legislative session.
d. Some exceptions, i.e. executive sessions, unless closed session mandated by law, policy sessions.
e. Not formally designated closed but in practice the media and others do not attend.
f. Governor meets with all department heads once a week.

Notes

Introduction

1. Larry Sabato, *Goodbye to Goodtime Charlie: The American Governor Transformed, 1950–1975* (Lexington, MA: Lexington Books, 1978).

1. Governors in the American Federal System

1. Terry Sanford, *Storm Over the States* (New York: McGraw-Hill Book Co., 1967), p. 184.
2. *Ibid*, pp. 188–206.
3. Larry Sabato, *Goodbye to Goodtime Charlie: The American Governor Transformed, 1950–1975* (Lexington, MA: Lexington Books, 1978), p. 63.
4. Advisory Commission on Intergovernmental Relations (ACIR), "The States in 1977," *Intergovernmental Perspective* 4 (Winter 1978):15.
5. Mavis Mann Reeves, "The State Role and State Capability," Advisory Commission on Intergovernmental Relations, *State and Local Roles in the Federal System* (Washington, D.C.: ACIR, 1981), p. 67.
6. Thad L. Beyle and Edward W. Crowe, *State Government Reorganization: A Bibliography* (Lexington, KY: The Council of State Governments, 1979), p. vii.
7. ACIR, "The States in 1977," p. 16.
8. Beyle and Crowe, *State Government Reorganization*, pp. vii, ix–x; and George R. Bell, "State Administrative Activities, 1972–1973," *The Book of the States, 1974–1975* (Lexington, KY: The Council of State Governments, 1974), pp. 138–39.
9. Judith Nicholson, "State Administrative Organization Activities, 1976–1977," *Book of the States, 1978–1979* (Lexington, KY: The Council of State Governments, 1978), p. 107.
10. Jack L. Walker, "The Diffusion of Innovations among the American States," *American Political Science Review* 62 (September 1969):887–98.
11. Nicholson, p. 109.
12. Thad L. Beyle, Thomas E. Peddicord, and Francis H. Parker, *Integration of State Environmental Programs* (Lexington, KY: The Council of State Governments, 1975), pp. 19–33.
13. Nicholson, "State Administrative Organization Activities," p. 110.
14. Ibid., p. 108.
15. Sabato, *Goodtime Charlie*, p. 1.
16. Ibid., p. 57.
17. Ibid., p. 91.
18. Reeves, "State Role," pp. 106.
19. Ibid.
20. Council of State Governments, *Book of the States, 1982–83* (Lexington, KY: The Council of State Governments, 1982), p. 151.
21. Reeves, "State Role," p. 129.
22. Kenneth Howard, *Changing State Budgeting* (Lexington, KY: The Council of State Governments, 1973), p. 269.
23. Center for Policy Research, *Reflections on Being Governor* (Washington, D.C.: National Governors' Association, 1981).
24. The Council of State Governments, *Book of the States, 1982–1983*, pp. 168–69.
25. See Ross Clayton, Patrick Conklin, and Raymond Shapek, eds., "Policy Management Assistance—A Developing Dialogue," *Public Administration Review*, special issue, 35 (December 1975): 764–85.
26. Center for Policy Research, *Governing the American States: A Handbook for New Governors* (Washington, D.C.: National Governors' Association, 1978), pp. 85–118, 151–74.

2. Governors' Views on Being Governor

This chapter appeared in *State Government* 52 (Summer 1979): 103–109.

1. Coleman B. Ransone, Jr., *The Office of the Governor of the United States* (University, AL: University of Alabama Press, 1956), p. 115.

2. Larry Sabato, *Goodbye to Goodtime Charlie: The American Governor Transformed, 1950–1975* (Lexington, MA: Lexington Books, 1978), p. 13.

3. Center for Policy Research, *Governing the American States: A Handbook for New Governors* (Washington, DC: National Governors' Association, 1978) p. 3.

4. Thad L. Beyle, Harold A. Hovey, and Kenneth C. Olson, "Intergovernmental Relations in the Governor's Office," *State Government*, 50 (Spring 1977):89–95.

5. Kenneth C. Olson, "The States, Governors and Policy Management: Changing the Equilibrium of the Federal System," *Public Administration Review*, 35, special issue on policy management (December 1975):764–70; Lynn Muchmore, "Policy Management as an Approach to Gubernatorial Decision-Making," paper presented at the 1979 Midwest Political Science Association Annual Meeting, Chicago, IL, April 20, 1979.

6. For example, the National Governors' Association had developed several papers on the governors and their international role, and held a joint Woodrow Wilson Center (Smithsonian Institution) seminar in April 1979 on the international role of states and governors. The seminar led off with a background paper by Richard Huszagh of the University of Georgia.

7. Sabato, *Goodtime Charlie*.

8. Joseph A Schlesinger, "The Politics of the Executive," in Herbert Jacob and Kenneth N. Vines (eds.), *Politics in the American States*, 2nd ed. (Boston, MA: Little, Brown and Company, 1971), p. 232.

9. See, for example, Ransone, *Office of the Governor*, pp. 146 ff., and Malcom E. Jewell and Samuel C. Patterson, *The Legislative Process in the United States*, 2nd ed. (New York, NY: Random House, 1973), pp. 300 ff.

10. See, V. O. Key, Jr., *American State Politics: An Introduction* (New York, NY: Alfred A. Knopf, 1956), pp. 52 ff., and Austin Ranney, "Parties in State Politics," in Jacob and Vines, *Politics in the American States*, pp. 107–17.

11. The Council of State Governments, *The Book of the States: 1968–1969*, pp. 42, 64–65, and *1978–1979*, pp. 5, 36–37 (Lexington, KY: 1968 and 1978).

12. Center for Policy Research, *Governing the American States*, pp. 3–4.

13. Alan J. Wyner, "Governor-Salesman," *National Civic Review*, 56 (February 1967):86.

14. Based on returns from the 1976 survey of governor's office managers from thirty-four states, NGA concluded that "the size of governors' offices tends to vary directly with the population of the state being served. However, in proportion to population, staffs tend to be larger in the least populated states" due to a certain minimum level needed to run a governor's office. They estimated the "normal" size to approximate a base of twelve staff members plus four more for each million people in the state population. National Governors' Association, "Managing the Governor's Office," *The Governor's Office*, vol. 8 (Washington, DC: 1976), pp. 9–10.

15. Sabato, *Goodtime Charlie*, p. 43.

16. National Governor's Association, "On Being Governor," *The Governor's Office*, vol. 1, pp. 24–34.

17. Lynn Muchmore, *Evaluation of State Planning*, State Planning Series No. 3 (Washington, DC: Council of State Planning Agencies, 1978), p. 3.

18. Personal letter, April 2, 1979.

3. A Day in the Life of a Governor

1. Center for Policy Research, *Governing the American States—A Handbook for New Governors* (Washington, DC: National Governors' Association, 1978), pp. 10–20. This also appeared in *State Government*, 52 (Summer 1979): 110–16.

4. The Governor as Party Leader

This chapter appeared in *State Government* 53 (Summer 1980): 121–24.

1. Charles Adrian, *State and Local Governments* (New York: McGraw-Hill Book Co., 1960), p. 255.

2. Center for Policy Research, *Governing the American States: A Handbook for New Governors* (Washington, DC: National Governors' Association, 1978), p. 3.

3. Terry Sanford, *Storm Over the States* (New York: McGraw-Hill Book Co., 1967), p. 185.

4. Center for Policy Research, *Reflections On Being Governor* (Washington, DC: National Governors' Association, 1981).

5. Ibid., p. 167.

6. Ibid., p. 208.

7. Ibid., p. 63–64.

8. Ibid., p. 14.

9. Ibid., p. 44.

10. Ibid., pp. 65, 108–9.

11. Ibid., p. 232.

12. Ibid., pp. 87–88.

13. Ibid., p. 250.

14. Ibid., p. 134.

15. Ibid., p 190.

16. Ibid., p. 154.

17. Ibid., p. 44.

18. Ibid., pp. 108–9.

19. Ibid., p. 118.

20. Ibid., p. 109.

21. See, for example, David Broder, *The Party's Over* (New York: Harper and Row, 1972); Austin Ranney, "Parties in State Politics" and Joseph A. Schlesinger, "The Politics of the Executive," in Herbert Jacob and Kenneth N. Vines, eds., *Politics in the American States: A Comparative Analysis* (Boston, MA: Little, Brown & Co., 1965 and 1971); and Larry Sabato, *Goodbye to Goodtime Charlie: The American Governor Transformed, 1950–1975* (Lexington, MA: Lexington Books, 1978).

22. See Sarah McCally Morehouse, "The State Political Party and the Policymaking Process," *American Political Science Review*, 6 (March 1973):55–72.

23. Center for Policy Research, *Reflections On Being Governor*, pp. 209, 109, 45.

24. Ibid., p. 31.

25. Ibid., p. 89.

26. Ibid., p. 155.

27. Remarks by Daniel Garry, former executive assistant to Governor Richard Kneip (South Dakota) to a political science seminar at Chapel Hill, North Carolina, February 7, 1980.

28. Suggested by Robert Dalton, a graduate student in political science, University of North Carolina at Chapel Hill, in an unpublished paper, February 1980.

5. The Governor and the Public

Portions of this chapter appeared in *State Government* 51 (Summer 1978):180–86.

1. Terry Sanford, *Storm Over the States* (New York: McGraw-Hill Book Co., 1967), pp. 184–85.

2. Center for Policy Research, *The Governor's Office Series: 1, On Being Governor* (Washington, D.C.: National Governors' Association, 1976).

3. See Center for Policy research, *The Governor's Office Series: 5, The Governor's Press Relations* (Washington, D.C.: National Governors' Association, 1976) for a report on the 1976 survey results.

4. See chapter 13 in this book.

5. Alan J. Wyner, "Governor-Salesman," *National Civic Review* 56, 2 (February 1967):86.

6. Center for Policy Research, *Governing the American States*, (Washington, D.C.: National Governors' Association, 1978), p. 131.

7. For purposes of this analysis, the states were divided into population quintiles based on the 1970 census. The power of the governor was determined by using an updated version of Joseph A. Schlesinger's index of formal gubernatorial powers. Formal gubernatorial powers were defined as the appointment power, budget power, tenure, and veto power. Joseph A. Schlesinger, "The Politics of the Executive" in Herbert Jacob and Kenneth N. Vines, eds., *Politics in the American States* (Boston, MA: Little, Brown and Company, 1971), p. 232.

8. It is clear that the size of governors' office staffs varies almost directly with the size of the state, with the exception that the very smallest states have larger than proportionate staffs due to every office having certain basic tasks which must be performed by a minimum number of people. As of 1976 estimates, "the normal Governor's staff size is 12 persons plus 4 more for each million persons population . . . the cost of the Governor's office depends primarily on the size of the staff . . . the cost was about $22,000 per employee." See Center for Policy Research, *The Governor's Office Series: 8, Managing the Governor's Office*, (Washington, D.C.: National Governors' Association, 1976) pp. 10,12.

9. Comment of a former governor in Center for Policy Research, *The Governor's Office Series: 6, Relating the Governor's Office to the Public*, (Washington, D.C.: National Governors' Association, 1976), p. 6.

10. *The Governor's Press Relations*, p. 8.

11. Ibid., p. 6.

12. Ibid.

13. Joseph P. McLaughlin, Jr., "The Public Information Office and Public Policy," *State Government* 50, 1 (Winter 1977):22.

14. Dierdre Carmondy, "Carey's Relations with Reporters are Characterized as Impromptu, The Opposite of Usual Managed News," *The New York Times*, June 5, 1976.

15. *The Governor's Press Relations*, p. 9.

16. Ibid., p. 11.

17. McLaughlin, "Public Information Office," p. 23.

18. *The Governor's Press Relations*, p. 6.

19. *On Being Governor*, pp. 28–30.

20. Sanford, *Storm Over the States*, p. 48.

21. Tom Littlewood, "What's Wrong with Statehouse Coverage?" *Columbia Journalism Review* 10 (March/April 1972):40, 42.

22. Sanford, *Storm Over the States*, p. 48.

23. Center for Policy research, *Reflections on Being Governor* (Washington, D.C.: National Governors' Association, 1981), p. 219.

24. Littlewood, "What's Wrong with Statehouse Coverage?" p. 45, 40.

25. *Reflections on Being Governor*, p. 60.

26. Ibid., p. 37.

27. Ibid., p. 240.

28. William T. Gromley, Jr., "Coverage of State Government in the Mass Media," *State Government* 52 (Spring 1979):47.

29. Ibid., pp. 46–57 and "Television Coverage of State Government," *Public Opinion Quarterly* 42 (Fall 1978):354–60.

30. David Morgan, *The Capitol Press Corps: Newsmen and the Governing of New York State* (Westport, CN: Greenwood Press, 1978), p. xiii.

31. See, for example, Donald L. Shaw and Maxwell E. McCombs, *The Emergence of American Political Issues; The Agenda-Setting Function of the Press* (St. Paul: West Publishing Company, 1977).

32. William T. Gormley, Jr., "Newspaper Agendas and Political Elites," *Journalism Quarterly* 52 (Summer 1975):304–8.

33. William T. Gormley, Jr., "Political Controversies in North Carolina: A Study in Newspaper Agendas," in Thad L. Beyle and Merle Black, *Politics and Policy in North Carolina* (New York: MSS Information Corporation, 1975), pp. 54–68.

6. Governors and Ethics

1. For an historical overview of the situation, see George C. S. Benson, *Political Corruption in America* (Lexington, MA: Lexington Books, 1978).

2. Ibid., pp. 119–36. See also *U.S. News and World Report* 82, 8 (Feb. 28, 1977): 36–38 and 86, 2 (June 4, 1979):40–41.

3. The interviews were conducted under the auspices of the National Governors' Association by Lynn Muchmore and Thad Beyle in 1978 and 1979 and are reported in: Center for Policy Research, *Reflections on Being Governor* (Washington, D.C.: National Governors' Association, 1981).

Because their terms ended in 1976 or after, these men served in the early and middle 1970s, making the time factor equivalent if not exactly equal. Twelve completed one or more full terms, usually of four years each, so they have significant experience on which to reflect. Eleven are Democrats and four are Republicans. Though this may seem unbalanced, during most of the 1970s, the Democrats did control the majority of the governorships. Furthermore, from responses to questions regarding the role of partisanship in the conduct of their offices, the former governors indicate its relative unimportance. Regionally, five are from the Southern/Border states, two from the Northeast, five from the Midwest/Central region, and two from the West. Thus, the list is overly representative of the South and Midwest, though whether this seriously affects my analysis is doubtful.

The interview schedule was consistent across the former governors, and the questions were open-ended, thus allowing the governors to construct their answers freely. Although this does mean answers to the same questions are sometimes difficult to compare directly, this is not a major obstacle.

There are several other research sources: (1) the transcripts of the annual National Governors Conferences, 1973–77, and (2) a policy statement adopted by the 1972 meeting, and (3) a summary of 1976 gubernatorial state of the state addresses, subtitled "towards a restoration of trust in government." These sources reflect the same period as the terms of the governors interviewed, and though they do not include exactly the same people, they should overlap partially in personnel. Moreover, these sources provide the opinions of a broader range of governors, though perhaps with less focused attention to the ethical and moral questions of government service.

4. Edward E. Banfield, "Corruption as a Feature of Governmental Organization," *Journal of Law and Economics* 18 (1975):587.

5. Benson, *Political Corruption*, p. xiii.

6. Center for Policy Research, *Reflections On Being Governor*, p. 34.

7. Ibid.

8. Ibid., p. 96.

9. Ibid., p. 197.

10. Ibid., p. 96.

11. Ibid., p. 257.

12. Ibid., p. 19.

13. Ibid., p. 143.

14. Ibid., p. 219–20.

15. James Q. Wilson, "Corruption: the Shame of the States," *The Public Interest* 2 (1965–66):31. See also Banfield, "Corruption," pp. 587–605, who argues that the very institutional form of American government lends itself to at least official corruption, if not personal corruption, though the latter too may be encouraged.

16. National Governors' Conference (NGC), *Proceedings of the National Governors' Conference, 1974* (Washington, D.C., and Lexington, KY: National Governors' Conference, 1974), p. 94.

17. Center for Policy Research, *Reflections On Being Governor*, p. 173.

18. Ibid., p. 160.

19. Ibid., p. 199.

20. Ibid., p. 129–36.

21. Ibid., pp. 19, 50–51, 96, 143.

22. Melvin G. Cooper, "Administering Ethics Laws: The Alabama Experience," *National Civic Review* 68 (1979):80.

23. Richard G. Terapak, "Administering Ethics Laws: The Ohio Experience," *National Civic Review* 68 (1979):82–83.

24. NGC, *Proceedings, 1974*, pp. 95, 97.

25. Ibid., p. 101.

26. Ibid., pp. 96, 104, 106, 107.

27. Center for Policy research, *Reflections On Being Governor*, p. 125.

28. Ibid., p. 34.

29. Ibid., p. 143.

30. NGC, *Proceedings, 1974*, pp. 96, 106.

31. National Governors' Conference (NGC), *Proceedings of the National Governors' Conference, 1975* (Washington, D.C.: National Governors' Conference, 1975), p. 384.

32. Center for Policy Research, *Reflections On Being Governor*, p. 220.

33. Ibid., p. 239.

34. Ibid., p. 74.

35. Ibid., p. 35.

36. Ibid., p. 97.

37. Ibid., p. 160.

38. Ibid., p. 259.

39. Ibid., pp. 144, 239.

40. J. R. Shakleton, "Corruption: An Essay in Economic Analysis," *Political Quarterly* 49 (1978): 25–37.

41. National Governors' Conference (NGC), *Constraints and Concern: Toward the Restoration of Trust in Government* (Washington, D.C.: National Governors' Conference, 1976).

42. NGC, *Constraints and Concern*, pp. 1–2.

43. Ibid., pp. 7–8.

44. Center for Policy Research, *Reflections On Being Governor*, pp. 19, 36, 97, 126, 144, 259.

45. Ibid., pp. 51, 75, 159, 183, 239.

46. Ibid., p. 51.

47. Ibid., p. 51.

48. Ibid., p. 76.

49. Ibid., p. 126.

50. Ibid., p. 159.

51. Ibid., p. 34.

52. Ibid., p. 143.

53. Ibid., p. 196.

54. Cooper, "Administering Ethics Laws," 80.

55. National Governors' Conference (NGC), *Proceedings of the National Governors' Conference, 1973* (Lexington, KY: National Governors' Conference, 1973), pp. 5, 10–12, 20, 33–34.

56. Ibid., p. xii. At several recent "New Governors Seminars," the participants (incumbent governors as faculty and newly elected governors as students) held closed door sessions on ethics, from which all but the governors were excluded.

57. NGC, *Proceedings, 1974*, pp. 84–107.

58. Ibid., p. 221.

59. NGC, *Proceedings, 1975*, p. 304; *1976*, pp. 107–08; *1977*, p. 136.

7. The Governor as Manager

This article appeared in *State Government* 54, 3 (1981):71–75.

1. Leslie Lipson, *The American Governor: From Figurehead to Leader* (Chicago: University of Chicago Press, 1939).

2. Center for Policy Research, *Reflections On Being Governor* (Washington, D.C.: National Governors' Association, 1981), p. 34.

3. Ibid., p. 203.

4. Ibid., pp. 266–67.

5. Larry Sabato, *Goodbye to Goodtime Charlie* (Lexington, MA: Lexington Books, 1978), p. 56.

6. *Reflections*, p. 104.

8. The Political Nature of the Governor as Manager

This chapter appeared in *State Government* 54, 3 (1981):76–81.

1. Larry Sabato, *Goodbye to Goodtime Charlie* (Lexington, MA: Lexington Books, 1978), pp. 89, 90–91, 207–208.

2. Lynn Muchmore, "Introduction" in Center for Policy Research, *Reflections on Being Governor* (Washington, D.C.: National Governors' Association, 1981), p. 5.

3. *Reflections on Being Governor*, pp. 104, 128, 184, 243–44, 266.

4. *Governing the American States: A Handbook for New Governors* (Washington, D.C.: Center for Policy Research, National Governors' Association, 1978).

5. Ibid., p. 204.

6. See chapter 10 in this book.

7. *Reflections on Being Governor*, p. 231.

8. Ibid., p. 242.

9. H. Edward Flentje, ed., *Selected Papers of Governor Robert F. Bennett: A Study in Good Government and "Civics Book" Politics* (Wichita, KS: Center for Urban Studies, Wichita State University, 1979), p. 259.

10. Martha Wagner Weinberg, *Managing the State* (Cambridge, MA: The MIT Press, 1977), pp. 174, 202.

11. For further elaboration in reference to the national arena, see H. Edward Flentje, "Shaping the Administrative Powers of the President," paper presented to the Midwest Political Science Association, Chicago, Illinois, April 24, 1980, pp. 4–10.

12. Robert H. Connery and Gerald Benjamin, *Rockefeller of New York: Executive Power in the Statehouse* (Ithaca, NY: Cornell University Press, 1979), p. 153.

13. York Wilbern, "The States as Components in an Areal Division of Powers" in Arthur Maas, ed., *Area and Powers* (Glencoe, IL: The Free Press, 1959), pp. 74, 77–81.

14. *Reflections on Being Governor*, p. 67.

15. Ibid., p. 234.

16. Sources of information for parenthetical references to governors in this paragraph are as follows: for Bennett, Dukakis, and Rampton, see *Reflections on Being Governor*, pp. 45–46, 65, 74–75, and 178, respectively; and for Sargent, see Weinberg, pp. 37, 87–88.

17. *Reflections on Being Governor*, p. 169.

18. Sources of information for parenthetical references to governors in this paragraph are as follows: for Bennett, see *Reflections on Being Governor*, pp. 54–55; for Rockefeller, see Connery and Benjamin, *Rockefeller, Managing the State*, pp. 157–58; for Sargent, see Weinberg, pp. 50, 66, 136, 168–71, 216; and for Shapp, see *Reflections on Being Governor*, pp. 206–7.

19. Sources of information for parenthetical references to governors in this paragraph are as follows: for Apodaca, Bennett, Edwards, and Pryor, see *Reflections on Being Governor*, pp. 20, 58, 105, and 166, respectively; and for Rockefeller, see Connery and Benjamin, *Managing the State*, pp. 160–62, 167–71.

20. James L. Garnett, *Reorganizing State Government: The Executive Branch* (Boulder, Colorado: Westview Press, 1980), p. 145.

21. Flentje, ed., *Papers of Governor Robert F. Bennett*, p. 264.

22. Sabato, *Goodtime Charlie*, pp. 107–18.

23. See for example: Thomas J. Anton, *The Politics of State Expenditures in Illinois* (Urbana: University of Illinois Press, 1966); Allen Schick, *Budget Innovation in the States* (Washington, D.C.: The Brookings Institution, 1971), pp. 164–218; and Neil Snortland, *The Budget Process in Kansas* (Lawrence: Institute for Social and Environmental Studies, University of Kansas, 1973).

24. Sources of information for parenthetical references to governors in this paragraph are as follows: for Bennett, see Flentje, pp. 125–26; for Dukakis and Edwards, see *Reflections on Being Governor*, pp. 69 and 84, respectively; and for Ogilvie, see *Papers in Public Finance: The Ogilvie Years* (Springfield: Illinois Bureau of the Budget, 1973), p. 363.

25. *Reflections on Being Governor*, p. 109.

26. See Ibid., 242–43; and Weinberg, p. 45.

27. Connery and Benjamin, *Rockefeller*, pp. 171–74, 430.

28. Muchmore, "Introduction," p. 2.

29. Joseph A. Schlesinger, "The Politics of the Executive" in Herbert Jacob and Kenneth N. Vines, eds., *Politics in the American States* (Boston: Little, Brown and Company, 1965), p. 211.

30. Phillip Selznick, *Leadership in Administration* (New York: Harper & Row, 1957).

31. This paragraph is my own brief translation of Neustadt's thesis on presidential power; see Richard E. Neustadt, *Presidential Power: The Politics of Leadership from FDR to Carter* (New York: John Wiley and Sons, Inc., 1980).

9. Governor's Views on Management

This chapter appeared in *State Government* 54 (1981):3, 66–70.

1. Center for Policy Research, *Reflections on Being Governor* (Washington, D.C.: National Governor's Association, 1981).

2. Ibid., pp. 13, 46, 57, 128, 191, 234.

3. Ibid., pp. 211–12.

4. Ibid., pp. 67, 185.

5. Ibid., 162, 189–90.

6. Ibid., pp. 166–67.

7. Ibid., pp. 84–86.

8. Ibid., pp. 83, 87–88.

9. Ibid., 13, 40, 206–7.

10. Ibid., pp. 230, 267.

11. Ibid., p. 238.

12. Ibid., pp. 226–27.

10. Appointment Power: Does It Belong to the Governor?

This chapter appeared in *State Government* 54 (1981): 2–13.

1. H. Edward Fletje, "Shaping the Administrative Powers of the Presidency," (Paper presented at the Annual Meeting of the Midwest Political Science Association, Chicago, Illinois, April 24, 1980), p. 11.

2. See, for example, Leslie Lipson, *The American Governor: From Figurehead to Leader* (Chicago, IL: University of Chicago Press, 1939); Coleman B. Ransone Jr., *The Office of Governor in the United States* (University, AL: University of Alabama Press, 1956); and Larry Sabato, *Goodbye to Goodtime Charlie: The American Governor Transformed, 1950-1975* (Lexington, MA: Lexington Books, 1978).

3. See for example, Joseph A. Schlesinger, "The Politics of the Executive," in Herbert Jacob and Kenneth N. Vines (eds.), *Politics in the American States* (Boston, MA: Little, Brown & Co., 1965), pp. 222–25; Deil S. Wright, "Executive Leadership in State Administration," *Midwest Journal of Political Science* 11 (February 1967):15-17; Thad L. Beyle, "The Governor's Formal Powers: A View from the Governor's Chair," *Public Administration Review* 28 (November-December 1980): 540-45; Nelson Dometrius, "Measuring Gubernatorial Power," *Journal of Politics* 41 (May 1979):589-610; Dometrius, "The Efficacy of a Governor's Formal Powers," *State Government* 52 (Summer 1979):121-25; and E. Lee Bernick, "Gubernatorial Tools: Formal vs. Informal," *Journal of Politics* 41 (May 1979):656-64.

4. Duane Lockard (ed.), "A Mini-Symposium: The Strong Governorship: Status and Problems," *Public Administration Review* 36 (January-February 1976):90-98.

5. Terry Sanford, *Storm Over the States* (New York, N.Y.: McGraw-Hill, 1967), p. 187.

6. Those interviewed were: Jerry Apodaca (N.M.); Reubin O'D. Askew (Fla.); Robert F. Bennett (Kan.); Michael Dukakis (Mass.); James B. Edwards (S.C.); Daniel J. Evans (Wash.); James Exon (Neb.); James E. Holshouser Jr. (N.C.); Blair Lee III (Md.); David H. Pryor (Ark.); Calvin H. Rampton (Utah); Martin J. Schreiber (Wis.); Milton Shapp (Pa.); Dan Walker (Ill.); and Harvey Wollman (S.D.). The interviews were conducted between Nov. 1978 and Oct. 1979, under the auspices of the Center for Policy Research of the National Governors' Association.

7. James L. Garnett, *Reorganizing State Government: The Executive Branch* (Boulder, CO: Westview Press, 1980), pp. 1, 5; and David B. Walker, "The States and the System: Changes and Choices," *Intergovernmental Perspective* 6 (Fall 1980):7. Those states having major reorganizations between 1965 and 1980 are Michigan (1965); Wisconsin (1967); Colorado (1968); California (1968); Arkansas (1968); Florida (1969); Massachusetts (1969); Delaware (1969); Maryland (1969); Maine (1970); Montana (1971); North Carolina (1971); Georgia (1972); Virginia (1972); Kentucky (1972); South Dakota (1973); Idaho (1974); Missouri (1974); Louisiana (1975); Connecticut (1977); and, New Mexico (1977).

8. Advisory Commission on Intergovernmental Relations, "The States in 1977: Executive Reorganization," *Intergovernmental Perspective* 4 (Winter 1978):16.

9. Sabato, *Goodtime Charlie*, p. 67.

10. Ibid., p. 75.

11. National Conference of State Legislatures, *State of the Legislatures* (Denver, Colo.: NCSL, 1978), p. 7.

12. The assignment of particular agencies and departments to broader functional categories flows from experience the senior author has had in the recent reorganization efforts in two states, Connecticut and Illinois. These groupings seem to "hang together" in a real world sense to those concerned with how to organize state government for economy, efficiency, manageability and accountability reasons. They also seem to have some rather solid conceptual differentiation. We were limited in the selection of agencies and departments to those contained in *The Book of the States* at both points in time.

13. To determine which appointment scores were significantly different than others, we used an arbitrary minimum differential of ± .5, which is 10 percent of the total possible difference in scores (0.0 to 5.0).

14. For the classic presentation of this argument see Robert Highsaw, "The Southern Governor—Challenge to the Strong Executive Theme," *Public Administration Review* 19 (Winter 1959):7–11.

15. Lipson, *American Governor*, pp. 200–203; Ransone, *Office of Governor*, p. 338; and Sabato, *Goodtime Charlie*, pp. 71–72. However, Sabato has begun to question this gubernatorial view as either a rationalization or an attempt to put the best face on a disappointing trend. He now advocates some politization of the state bureaucracy (Letter to authors, Nov. 21, 1980).

16. See chapter 4, this volume.

17. Daniel P. Moynihan and James Q. Wilson, "Patronage in New York State, 1955–59," *American Political Science Review* 58 (June 1964):300.

18. In *Elrod v. Burns*, 96 S. Ct. 2673 (1976), the court's decision in effect banned many firings of patronage employees, and in *Branti V. Finkel* (1980) forbade firing of subordinates from patronage jobs solely on the basis of their political beliefs.

19. William Ecenbarger of *The Philadelphia Inquirer* reported in *The Washington Monthly* 12 (September 1980):10.

20. See chapter 4, this volume.

21. See for example, Clark D. Ahlberg and Daniel P. Moynihan, "Changing Governors—and Policies," *Public Administration Review* 20 (Autumn 1960):195–205; Thad L. Beyle and John E. Wickman, "Gubernatorial Transition in a One Party Setting," *Public Administration Review* 30 (January/February 1970):10–17; Norton E. Long, "After the Voting is Over," *Midwest Journal of Political Science* 6 (May 1962): 183–200; Wayne F. McGown, "Gubernatorial Transition in Wisconsin," *State Government* 44 (Spring 1971):103–06; and Kenneth Warner, "Planning for Transition," *State Government* 34 (Spring 1961):102–03.

22. Center for Policy Research, *Governing the American States: A Handbook for New Governors* (Washington, D.C.: National Governors' Association, 1978), pp. 33–69, 71–84.

11. The Gubernatorial Appointment Power: Too Much of a Good Thing?

This chapter appeared in *State Government* 55 (1982):88–92.

1. See chapter 10 in this book.

2. Governors' comments drawn from interviews with fifteen former governors published in Center for Policy Research, *Reflections on Being Governor* (Washington, D.C.: National Governors' Association, 1981), and from the author's personal interviews with Arkansas Governors Dale Bumpers, David Pryor, and Bill Clinton.

3. Aides' views and comments based on the author's personal interviews with the Appointment, Legislative, and Executive Secretaries to Arkansas Governors Winthrop Rockefeller, Dale Bumpers, David Pryor, and Bill Clinton.

4. Governor James E. Holshouser, Jr., in *Reflections on Being Governor*, p. 138.

5. Governor Robert F. Bennett, in ibid., p. 44.

6. Governor Milton J. Shapp, in ibid., p. 210.

7. Governor Blair Lee III, in ibid., p. 156.

8. Governor Dan Walker, in ibid., p. 235.

9. Holshouser, in ibid., p. 138.

10. Governor Jerry Apodoca, in ibid., p. 16.

11. Governor David H. Pryor, in ibid., p. 166.

12. Walker, in ibid., p. 234.

13. Shapp, in ibid., p. 210.

14. Pryor, personal interview, January 3, 1977.

15. Governor Reubin O'D. Askew, in *Reflections on Being Governor*, p. 28.

16. Governor Bill Clinton, personal interview, June 19, 1981.

17. Apodoca, in *Reflections on Being Governor*, p. 16.

18. Walker, in ibid., p. 236.

19. Governor Dale Bumpers, personal interview, December 30, 1976.

20. Governor Michael Dukakis, in *Reflections on Being Governor*, p. 67.

21. Walker, in ibid., p. 234.

22. Aides to Governors Bumpers, Pryor, Clinton, personal interviews, 1976 to 1981.

23. Beyle and Dalton, "Appointment Power," p. 3.

24. Alan J. Wyner, "Gubernatorial Relations with Legislators and Administrators," *State Government* 41 (Summer 1968):200.

25. Larry Sabato, *Goodbye to Goodtime Charlie: the American Governor Transformed 1950–1975* (Lexington, MA: Lexington Books, 1978), p. 71. See also Center for Policy Research, *Governing the American States* (Washington, D.C.: National Governors' Association, 1978), pp. 71–72.

26. Charles Bell and Charles Price, *California Government Today: Politics of Reform* (Homewood, IL: Dorsey Press, 1980), pp. 218–22.

27. See *Reflections on Being Governor* pp. 157, 210.

28. For example, see Joseph A. Schlesinger, "The Politics of the Executive," in Herbert Jacob and Kenneth N. Vines, eds., *Politics in the American States*, 2nd. ed. (Boston: Little Brown and Co., 1971), p. 226. Also see Nelson C. Dometrius, "The Efficacy of a Governor's Formal Powers," *State Government* 52, 3 (Summer 1979):122–23. Similarly, interviewers for *Reflections on Being Governor* asked the governors about criteria for "major personnel choices," or "key personnel in major administrative positions."

29. See, for example, Governor Calvin L. Rampton's comments in *Reflections on Being Governor*, pp. 179–80.

30. Sabato, *Goodtime Charlie*, pp. 71–74, 89. See also Lynn Muchmore and Thad L. Beyle, "The Governor as Party Leader," chapter 4 in this book.

12. The Governor and the State Legislature

1. Charles Adrian, *State and Local Governments*, (New York: McGraw-Hill Book Company, 1960), p. 255.

2. Center for Policy Research, *Governing the American States: A Handbook for New Governors* (Washington, D.C.: National Governors' Association, 1978), p. 3.

3. Jane F. Roberts, "States Respond to Tough Fiscal Challenges," Advisory Commission on Intergovernmental Relations, *Intergovernmental Perspective* 6 (Spring 1980): 22.

4. Center for Policy Research, *Reflections On Being Governor* (Washington, D.C.: National Governors' Association, 1981), p. 203.

5. Ibid., p. 231.

6. Ibid., p. 21.

7. Seven agreed strongly, nine mildly. Data provided by the Center for Policy Research, National Governors' Association, Washington, D.C., 1976.

8. *Reflections On Being Governor*, p. 189.

9. Ibid., p. 189.

10. National Conference of State Legislatures, *State of the Legislatures: A Summary of Legislative Improvement and Policy Initiatives*, (Denver: NCSL, 1978), p. 1.

11. William Pound, "The State Legislatures," *Book of the States, 1980–81* (Lexington, KY: The Council of State Governments, 1980), p. 77.

12. Edgar G. Crane, "Legislatures as a Force for Government Accountability: The Organizational Challenge of New Tools of Program Review," Abdo I. Baaklini and James J. Heaphey, eds., *Comparative Legislative Reforms and Innovations* (Albany: State University of New York at Albany, 1977), pp. 115–53.

13. Malcolm E. Jewell and Samuel C. Patterson, *The Legislative Process in the United States*, 3rd ed. (New York: Random House, 1977), pp. 445–50, 458, 466–67.

14. George Bunn and Jeff Gallagher, "Legislative Committee Review of Administrative Rules in Wisconsin," *Wisconsin Law Review* (1977):935–88; "Legislative Review of Administrative Action: Is the Cure Worse than the Illness?" *Southern Illinois University Law Journal* (December 1979):579–97; Daniel A. Taylor, "Legislative Vetoes and the Massachusetts Separation of Powers Doctrine," *Suffolk University Law Review* 13 (Winter 1979):1–13; and "Wyoming's Administrative Regulations Review Act," *Land and Water Law Review* (1979):189–206.

15. *Reflections On Being Governor*, p. 33.

16. Ibid., p. 232.

17. Pound, "State Legislatures," p. 77.

18. Advisory Commission on Intergovernmental Relations, "The States in 1977," *Intergovernmental Perspective* 4 (Winter 1978): pp. 17–18.

19. *Reflections On Being Governor*, p. 33.

20. See, Sarah P. McCally [Morehouse], "The Governor and His Legislative Party," *American Political Science Review* 60 (December 1966):923–42; Sarah McCally Morehouse, "The State Political Party and the Policy-Making Process," *American Political Sceince Review* 67 (March 1973):59–72; and Sarah McCally Morehouse, "The Governor as Political Leader," in Herbert Jacob and Kenneth N. Vines, eds., *Politics in the American States*, 3rd ed. (Boston, Toronto: Little, Brown and Company, 1976), pp. 196–241.

21. See for example, Thomas R. Dye, "State Legislative Politics," in Jacob and Vines, *Politics*, 2nd ed. pp. 205–6; Samuel A. Kirkpatrick, *The Legislative Process in Oklahoma: Policy-Making, People and Politics* (Norman: University of Oklahoma Press, 1978), pp. 150–51; Richard C. Elling, "State Party Platforms and State Legislative Performance: A Comparative Analysis," *American Journal of Political Science* 23 (May 1979):383–405; and E. Lee Bernick, "Gubernatorial Tools: Formal vs. Informal," *Journal of Politics* 41 (May 1979):660.

13. The Governor as Chief Legislator

Portions of this chapter appeared in *State Government* 51 (Winter 1978):2–10.

1. These percentages total more than 100 percent as several had served in more than one of these capacities.

2. Formal gubernatorial powers are defined as the appointment power, budget power, tenure, and veto power. See Joseph A. Schlesinger, "The Politics of the Executive," in Herbert Jacob and Kenneth N. Vines, eds., *Politics in the American States* (Boston, MA: Little, Brown & Co., 1971), pp. 210–37.

3. Center for Policy Research, *The Governor's Office, 3: The Governor's Legislative Relations* (Washington, D.C.: National Governors' Association, 1976) p. 6.

4. Ibid, p. 11.

5. Council of State Governments, *The Book of the States, 1980–81* (Lexington, KY: 1980), pp. 104–5.

6. Charles W. Wiggins, "Executive Vetoes and Legislative Overrides in the American States," *Journal of Politics*, 42 (November 1980):110–17.

7. *The Governor's Legislative Relations*, p. 14.

8. Ibid., p. 16.

14. Governors and Lieutenant Governors

Portions of this chapter appeared in *State Government* 52 (Autumn 1979):187–95.

1. The National Conference of Lieutenant Governors, *The Lieutenant Governor: The Office and Its Powers* (Lexington, KY: The Council of State Governments, 1976), pp. 9–10.

2. Warren R. Isom, "The Office of the Lieutenant Governor in the States," *American Political Science Review* 31, 5 (October 1938):923, 926.

3. These questionnaires were part of a National Governors' Association project to prepare a series of handbooks for newly elected governors and their staffs which would be based on information and ideas provided by governors, former governors, and selected staff members of governors' offices. A broad range of questions on gubernatorial activities, relationships, and staff responsibilities was explored in these questionnaires. Portions of this research were financed by the U.S. Civil Service commission through an Intergovernmental Personnel Act grant to the National Governors' Association. A grant from the University of North Carolina Research Council also aided in preparation of this chapter. Because of restrictions on obtaining and using the data, no state, governor, or individual respondent can be identified.

4. While responses rely to a large extent on recall data, the problems with this are not as serious as with other uses of recall data. There is a big difference between asking a voter to remember a minor matter like a vote four or eight years ago, and asking a governor about an important facet of his administration during what must be a highly salient and memorable part of his or her life.

5. Eugene Declercq and John Kaminski, "A New Look at the Office of Lieutenant Governor," *Public Administration Review* 38, 3 (May/June 1978):258.

6. This actually overstates the situation in the sample, as seven of the fifteen respondents had lieutenant governors of both their party and the opposite party during their multiple terms as governor. For our purposes, they have been classified as being of the opposite party.

7. The sample includes only one case where the governor and lieutenant governor are required to run as a team in the primary election, and two cases where both are nominated by a convention. With so few cases, these factors could not be used as independent variables in the analysis.

8. However, one current observer of the governorship indicated legislative skills were important to recent successful governorships. See Larry Sabato, *Goodbye to Goodtime Charlie: The American Governor Transformed, 1950-1975* (Lexington, MA: Lexington Books, 1978), p. 55.

9. Ibid., p. 75.

10. See footnote *a*, Table 14.5 for definition of these types.

11. Personal letter, August 28, 1979.

12. The definitions of the four models are: (1) *Traditional Plan*—Lieutenant governor presides over the state senate and has "some responsibilities within the executive branch, and generally serves as 'combination' officers with both executive and legislative duties." (2) *Executive Plan*—Lieutenant governor is "an exclusively executive officer with no legislative responsibilities." (3) *Legislative Plan*—Lieutenant governor "may perform some executive branch duties but has primarily legislative responsibilities. . . . [is] presiding officer of a legislative house and [has] significant legislative powers." (4) *Administrative Plan*—Lieutenant governor totally performs the functions traditionally assigned to the secretary of state, or the secretary of state is first in line of succession. The National conference of Lieutenant Governors, *The Lieutenant Governor*, pp. 5–8 and 22–30.

13. Council of State Government, *State Headlines*, July 27, 1981, p. 3.

14. Letter from Allen Pease, University of Southern Maine, July 22, 1981.

15. Governors' Offices

Portions of this research were funded by a grant from the Earhart Foundation. The author wishes to thank Robert Dalton for his research assistance.

1. Thomas E. Cronin, *The State of the Presidency*, 2nd. ed. (Boston: Little, Brown & Company, 1980), p. 243.

2. Ibid., and Hugh Heclo, *Studying the Presidency: A Report to the Ford Foundation* (New York: The Ford Foundation, 1977), p. 21.

3. Cronin, *State of the Presidency*, pp. 244–46.

4. Leslie Lipson, *The American Governor: From Figurehead to Leader* (Chicago: University of Chicago Press, 1939), pp. 128–30.

5. Homer E. Scace, "The Governor Needs Staff," *National Municipal Review* 40 (October 1951): 462–67, 479.

6. Leslie D. Howe, "Pennsylvania's Governor's Office Revamped," *National Municipal Review* 44 (July 1955):366–67.

7. Coleman B. Ransone, Jr., *The Office of the Governor in the United States* (University, AL: University of Alabama Press, 1956):302–62.

8. Elmer E. Cornwell, Jr., et al. "Professional Staff for Governors' Office Subject of Questionnaires," *Bureau of Government Research Newsletter* (Kingston, RI: University of Rhode Island, 1968), p. 1.

9. Donald P. Sprengel, *Gubernatorial Staffs: Functional and Political Profiles* (Iowa City, IA: Institute of Public Affairs, University of Iowa, 1969), pp. 51–52.

10. Center for Policy Research, *Governor's Office Series: 2, The Governor's Executive Assistant* (Washington, D.C.: National Governors' Association, 1976), 2:6.

11. Peter Tropp, "Governor's and Mayor's Offices: The Role of the Staff," *National Civic Review* 63 (May 1974):242–49.

12. Sprengel, *Gubernatorial Staffs*, p. 4, and personal letter, May 20, 1981.

13. Unpublished data from 1976 and 1979 NGA surveys of former governors and governors' offices. Due to promises of confidentiality, the following quotations from former governors cannot be attributed to any individual former governors.

14. Center for Policy Research, *Governing the American States* (Washington, D.C.: National Governors' Association, 1978), p. 39.

15. Charles H. Williams, "The 'Gatekeeper' Function on the Governor's Staff," *Western Political Quarterly* 33 (March 1980):87–93.

16. Ransone, *Office of the Governor*, p. 44.

17. Center for Policy Research, National Governors' Association unpublished data from 1976 and 1979 surveys of governors' offices. Forty and forty-one states responded to each survey respectively. The adjusted averages exclude the one or two very largest states as their size would skew the overall averages to thirty-eight and forty-one respectively.

18. Larry Sabato, *Goodbye to Goodtime Charlie: The American Governor Transformed, 1950–1975* (Lexington, MA: Lexington Books, 1978), p. 87.

19. Center for Policy Research, *Governor's Office Series: 8, Managing the Governor's Office*, pp. 9–10.

20. Data from NGA surveys conducted in 1976 and reported in part in Center for Policy Research, *Governor's Office Series: 1, On Being Governor* (Washington, D.C.: National Governors' Association, 1976), pp. 12–13.

21. Thad L. Beyle, "The Governor and the Public," chapter 5 in this book.

22. Advisory Commission on Intergovernmental Relations, *State and Local Roles in The Federal System* (Washington, D.C.: ACIR, 1981), pp. 52.

23. Ibid., pp. 113, 117.

24. Unpublished data from a 1979 survey conducted by the Center for Policy Research of the National Governors' Association. One state indicated that the fifty-four people in the planning office performed federal-state duties in the governor's office. This response was excluded to calculate the average.

25. Lynn Muchmore, "Planning and Budgeting Offices: On Their Relevance to Gubernatorial Decisions," *State Government* 52 (Summer 1979): 126.

26. Bob Dozier, "At the Top of the Heap: How the Governor Organizes His Power," *NC Insight* 1 (Summer 1978): 13.

27. H. Edward Flentje, "Knowledge and Gubernatorial Policy Making: Policy and Management Context," Office of State Services, *State Science, Engineering and Technology: Gubernatorial Policy Making Through Science Advice* (Washington, D.C.: National Governors' Association, 1982), p. 28.

28. Robert N. Wise, "State Planning," *Book of the States, 1980–81* (Lexington, KY: Council of State Government, 1980), p. 234.

29. Flentje, "Knowledge and Gubernatorial Policy Making," p. 28.

30. Personal letter, May 19, 1981.

31. Thomas E. Cronin and Sanford D. Greenberg, *The Presidential Advisory System* (New York: Harper and Row, 1969), p. 326.

32. Center for Policy Research, *Governor's Office Series: 1, On Being Governor* (Washington, D.C.: National Governors' Association, 1976), p. 20.

33. These materials, all published by the National Governors' Association, were *The Critical Hundred Days: A Handbook for the New Governor* (1974); *The Governor's Office Series* (1976); *Gubernatorial Transition: A Guide* (1976); and *Governing the American States* (1978).

34. Flentje, "Knowledge and Gubernatorial Policy Making," p. 20.

35. Terry Sanford, *Storm Over the States* (New York: McGraw-Hill, 1967), p. 188.

36. Edwin Meese, III, counselor to the president in speech to the American Society of Newspaper Editors, Washington, D.C., April 23, 1981. CQ, *Congressional Quarterly Weekly Report* 39 (May 9, 1981): 827.

37. James A. Baker, III, White House Chief of Staff in speech to American Society of Newspaper Editors, Washington, D.C., April 23, 1981, ibid., p. 828.

38. H. Edward Flentje, personal letter, May 27, 1981.

16. Planning and Budgeting Offices

This chapter appeared in *State Government* 52 (Summer 1979):126–30.

1. National Governors' Conference on State Planning, *A Strategy for Planning* (Lexington, KY: The Council of State Governments, 1967), p. 5.

2. In only a few cases were the questionnaires to the governors' offices completed by budget or planning personnel. Thus, the responses from planning or budgeting sources can be presumed independent of those from governors' offices.

3. See Norman F. Kron, Jr., "Planectomy—The Surgical Removal of State Planning Agencies," *State Planning Issues* 2 (Summer 1977):6–12.

4. Thus, $r^2 = 0.062$, where r is the Pearson product-moment coefficient of correlation.

5. Thus, r^2 measuring the correlation of columns one and three is 0.515, while r^2 between columns of two and four is 0.846.

6. Thus, r^2 measuring the correlation of columns three and four is 0.120; statistically insignificant.

17. Science Advice to Governors

1. State of Connecticut, *Final Report of the Steering Committee on the Establishment of a State Science, Engineering, and Technology Program for Connecticut* (Hartford: Office of Policy and Management, 1979), p. 6.

2. While the author was privileged to examine draft reports from almost all of the states participating in the SSET program, the formal references here are only to those reports that have been submitted to the National Science Foundation as final completions.

3. This point is particularly clear in interviews with former Governors Reuben Askew of Florida and Dan Walker of Illinois in Center for Policy Research, *Reflections on Being Governor* (Washington, D.C.: National Governors' Association, 1981), pp. 24, 230.

4. State of Oregon, *Science and Technology Information and Advice: A Policy Management Instrument for the Governor of Oregon* (Salem: Executive Department, 1979), pp. 3–4.

5. State of Maine, *Science in the Statehouse* (Augusta, GA: State Planning Office, 1979), p. 16.

6. Oregon, *Science and Technology Information and Advice,* p. 6.

7. Ibid.

8. This hypothesis owes to observations by Gary Passmore, executive aide to former Governor Joseph P. Teasdale of Missouri, October 10, 1979.

9. State of Rhode Island, *Rhode Island SSET Report* (Providence: Office of the Governor, 1979), p. 18.

10. The survey was administered by the author to participants at a national conference held in Menlo Park, California on May 7–8, 1979.

11. State of Arizona, *Recommendations for Applying Science, Engineering, and Technology Re-*

sources to the Needs of the Governor's Office (Phoenix: Office of the Economic Planning and Development, 1979), p. 29.

12. Iowa Executive Order Number 23, Item (2), July 28, 1978.

13. State of Iowa, *The Iowa Science, Engineering, and Technology Project* (Des Moines: Office for Planning and Programming, 1979), p. 35.

14. State of Nevada, *The State Science, Engineering, and Technology Study of the Nevada Executive Branch* (Carson City: Office of Planning Coordination, 1979), Appendix I, p. 15.

15. Oregon, *Science and Technology Information and Advice*, p. 4.

16. An excellent survey that bears indirectly on this question is Deil S. Wright, Mary Wagner, and Richard McAnaw, "State Administrators, Their Changing Characteristics," *State Government* 50, 3 (Summer 1977): 152–59.

17. Oregon, *Science and Technology Information and Advice*, p. 4.

18. State of Virginia, *A State Science, Engineering and Technology Capacity in Virginia State Government* (Richmond, VA: Department of Intergovernmental Affairs, 1978), p. 12.

19. State of Florida, *Science, Engineering, Technology, and Florida's Government* (Tallahassee, FL: Division of State Planning, 1979), p. 30.

20. Connecticut, *Final Report*, p. 15.

21. Louis Gawthrop, *Bureaucratic Behavior in the Executive Branch* (New York: Macmillan Publishing Co., 1969), p. 8.

22. Nevada, *State Science*, p. iii.

23. See Lynn Muchmore, "Science, Technology and Gubernatorial Policy-Making: A Survey of State Experience," *SSET Workshop Papers* (Washington: National Governors' Association, 1977), pp. 9–20.

24. Rhode Island, *SSET Report*, p. 3.

25. State of Oklahoma, *Oklahoma State of Science, Engineering and Technology Program* (Oklahoma: Department of Economic and Community Affairs, 1979), Vol. II, p. 10.

26. Connecticut, *Final Report*, p. 7.

18. Intergovernmental Relations

1. Advisory Commission on Intergovernmental Relations, *Significant Features of Fiscal Federalism, 1980–81* (Washington, D.C.: ACIR, 1981), pp. 58, 18.

2. U.S. Bureau of the Budget, *Simplifying Federal Assistance to States and Communities* (Washington, D.C.: 1969), p. 8.

3. Louis C. Gawthrop, *Bureaucratic Politics in the Executive Branch* (New York: The Free Press, 1969).

4. Governor Robert Bennett, memo to state agency heads, September 26, 1975, reported in H. Edward Flentje, ed., *Selected Papers of Governor Robert F. Bennett: A Study in Good Government and 'Civic Book' Politics* (Wichita: Center for Urban Studies, Wichita State University, 1979), pp. 303–4.

5. National Governors' Association, Washingtion, D.C., 1976, 1977.

6. National Governors' Association, *Federal Roadblocks to Efficient State Government* (Washington, D.C.: NGA, 1976), p. viii.

7. Center for Policy Research, *Governing the American States* (Washington: National Governors' Association, 1978), p. 179.

8. Advisory Commission on Intergovernmental Relations, *State-Local Relations Bodies: State ACIRs and Other Approaches* (Washington, D.C.: ACIR, 1981), pp. 2–3.

9. Center for Policy Research, *Governor's Office Series: 10, State-Federal Relations in the Governor's Office* (Washington, D.C.: National Governors' Association, 1976), p. 10.

10. Center for Policy Research, *Governing the American States*, p. 196.

11. See Deil S. Wright, *Understanding Intergovernmental Relations* (Scituate, MA: Duxbury Press, 1978).

12. Center for Policy Research, *Reflections On Being Governor* (Washington, D.C.: National Governors' Association, 1981), pp. 122–23.

13. Mavis Mann Reeves, "Galloping Intergovernmentalization as a Factor in State Management," *State Government* 54, 3 (1981):104.

14. Robert M. Stein, "The Impact of Federal Grant Programs on Municipal Functions: Empirical

Analysis," ACIR, *The State and Local Roles in The Federal System* (Washington, D.C.: ACIR, forthcoming), noted in Reeves, "Intergovernmentalization," p. 104.

15. Center for Policy Research, *Reflections,* p. 182.

16. Ibid., p. 257.

17. Ibid., pp. 95–96, 195.

18. Ibid., p. 73.

19. ACIR, *A Crisis of Confidence and Competence Report,* A-77 (Washington: ACIR, July 1981), p. 120.

Conclusion

1. Center for Policy Research, *Reflections on Being Governor* (Washingtion, D.C.: National Governors' Association, 1981).

2. Ibid., p. 128.

3. Ibid., p. 184.

4. Ibid., p. 58.

5. Quoted in Larry Sabato, *Goodbye to Goodtime Charlie: The American Governor Transformed, 1950–1975* (Lexington, MA: Lexington Books, 1978), p. 51.

6. Ibid.

7. George Weeks, "Statehouse Hall of Fame: Ten Outstanding Governors of the 20th Century," paper presented at the annual meeting of the Southern Political Science Association, Memphis, Tennessee, November 1981.

8. Sabato, *Goodtime Charlie,* pp. 50–56.

9. Duane Lockhard, *The New Jersey Governor: A Study in Political Power* (Princeton, NJ: D. Van Nostrand, 1965), p. 1.

10. Martha Wagner Weinberg, *Managing the State* (Cambridge, MA: The MIT Press, 1977), p. 230.

11. *Reflections on Being Governor,* p. 203.

12. Ibid., p. 230.

13. Ibid., p. 245.

14. Ibid., p. 81.

Index

Contributors

Thad L. Beyle is Professor of Political Science, University of North Carolina at Chapel Hill.

Diane Kincaid Blair is Assistant Professor of Political Science, University of Arkansas, Fayetteville.

Robert Dalton is a doctoral candidate in Political Science, University of North Carolina at Chapel Hill.

Nelson C. Dometrius is Assistant Professor and Acting Director of the Center for Public Service, Texas Tech University.

H. Edward Flentje is Associate Professor and Associate Director of The Center for Urban Studies, Wichita State University.

Lynn Muchmore is Director of The Division of The Budget, State of Kansas.

Of related interest

Duke Press Policy Studies

What Role for Government?
Lessons from Policy Research
Edited by Richard J. Zeckhauser *and* Derek Leebaert

Rebuilding the American Infrastructure
An Agenda for the 1980s
Edited by Michael Barker

State Employment Policy in Hard Times
Edited by Michael Barker

Financing State and Local Economic Development
Edited by Michael Barker

State Taxation Policy
Edited by Michael Barker

Duke Press Paperbacks

America in Ruins
The Decaying Infrastructure
Pat Choate *and* Susan Walter